Mr. and
Mrs. Dunbar

Mr. and Mrs. Dunbar

Poems, Plays and Prose

Paul Laurence Dunbar
and Alice Dunbar Nelson

MINT EDITIONS

Mr. and Mrs. Dunbar: Poems, Plays and Prose contains work first published between 1892–1918.

This edition published by Mint Editions 2022.

ISBN 9781513211114 | E-ISBN 9781513209913

Published by Mint Editions®

MINT
EDITIONS

minteditionbooks.com

Publishing Director: Jennifer Newens
Design & Production: Rachel Lopez Metzger
Project Manager: Micaela Clark
Typesetting: Westchester Publishing Services

Contents

PAUL

An Introduction from the Publisher

This book does not exist to romanticize the turbulent marriage of Paul Laurence and Alice Dunbar; rather, it was conceived under the premise of highlighting the talent of one of, if not *the most* prolific poets of African descent in the late 19th century and one of the most outspoken activists for Black women's rights during the time of absolute artistic expression that was the Harlem Renaissance.

In a perfect world, Paul wouldn't have died at the hands of tuberculosis at the age of thirty-three; and Alice wouldn't have suffered abuse brought on by the alcohol he used to treat it—but given that this is not the case; that Paul died and Alice suffered—we are only left with the work they have given us and the questions of what might have been.

We will never know what two masters of the pen could've gone on to create together; whether Paul could've produced more novels or if Alice could've enjoyed a greater sense of celebrity—but it is in this collection that we have decided to highlight the best of what they both offered to the world; one legacy intertwined with the other.

M.Clark
Mint Editions
Berkeley, CA

POEMS

ALICE

Amid the Roses

There is tropical warmth and languorous life
    Where the roses lie
    In a tempting drift
Of pink and red and golden light
Untouched as yet by the pruning knife.
And the still, warm life of the roses fair
    That whisper "Come,"
    With promises
Of sweet caresses, close and pure
Has a thorny whiff in the perfumed air.
There are thorns and love in the roses' bed,
    And Satan too
    Must linger there;
So Satan's wiles and the conscience stings,
Must now abide—the roses are *dead*.

April is on the Way!

April is on the way!
I saw the scarlet flash of a blackbird's wing
As he sang in the cold, brown February trees;
And children said that they caught a glimpse of the sky on a bird's
    wing from the far South.
(Dear God, was that a stark figure outstretched in the bare branches
    Etched brown against the amethyst sky?)

April is on the way!
The ice crashed in the brown mud-pool under my tread,
The warning earth clutched my bloody feet with great fecund fingers,
I aw a boy rolling a hoop up the road,
His little bare hands were red with cold,
But his brown hair blew backward in the southwest wind.
(Dear God! He screamed when he say my awful woe-spent eyes)

April is on the way!
I met a women in the lane;
Her burden was heavy as it is always, but today her step was light,
And a smile drenched the tired look away from her eyes.
(Dear God, she had dreams of vengeance for her slain mate,
Perhaps, the west wind has blown the mist of hate from her heart,
The dead man was cruel to her, you know that, God)

April is on the way!
My feet spurn the ground now, instead of dragging on the bitter
    road.
I laugh in my throat as I see the grass greening beside the patches of
    snow.
(Dear God, those were wild fears. Can there be hate when the
    Southwest wind is blowing?)

April is on the way!
The crisp brown hedges stir with the bustle of bird wings.
There is business of building, and songs from brown thrush throats
As the bird-carpenters make homes against Valentine Day.

(Dear God, could they build me a shelter in the hedge from the icy
     winds that will come with the dark?)

April is on the way!
I sped through the town this morning. The florist shops have put
     yellow flowers in the windows,
Daffodils and tulips and primroses, pale yellow flowers
Like the tips of her fingers when she waved me that frightened
     farewell.
And the women in the market have stuck pussy willows in long
     necked bottles on their stands.
(Willow trees are kind, Dear God. They will not bear a body on their
     limbs)

April is on the way!
The soul within me cried that all the husk of indifference to sorrow
     was but the crust of ice with which winter disguises life:
It will melt, and reality will burgeon forth like the crocuses in the glen.
(Dear God! Those thoughts were from long ago. When we read poetry
     after the day's toil and got religion together at the revival meeting)

April is on the way!
The infinite miracle of unfolding life in the brown February fields.
(Dear God, the hounds are baying!)
Murder and wasted love, lust and weariness, deceit and vainglory—
     what are they but the spent breath of the runner?
(God, you know he laid hairy red hands on the golden loveliness of
     her little daffodil body)
Hate may destroy me, but from my brown limbs will bloom the
     golden buds with which we once spelled love.
(Dear God! How their light eyes glow into black pin points of hate!)

April is on the way!
Wars are made in April, and they sing at Easter time of the
     Resurrection.
Therefore I laugh in their faces.
(Dear God, give her strength to join me before her golden petals are
     fouled in the slime!)
April is on the way!

Chalmetle

Wreaths of lilies and immortelles,
Scattered upon each silent mound,
Voices in loving remembrance swell,
Chanting to heaven the solemn sound.
Glad skies above, and glad earth beneath;
And grateful hearts who silently
Gather earth's flowers, and tenderly wreath
Woman's sweet token of fragility.

Ah, the noble forms who fought so well
Lie, some unnamed, 'neath the grassy mound;
Heroes, brave heroes, the stories tell,
Silently too, the unmarked mounds,
Tenderly wreath them about with flowers,
Joyously pour out your praises loud;
For every joy beat in these hearts of ours
Is only a drawing us nearer to God.

Little enough is the song we sing,
Little enough is the tale we tell,
When we think of the voices who erst did ring
Ere their owners in smoke of battle fell.
Little enough are the flowers we cull
To scatter afar on the grass-grown graves,
When we think of bright eyes, now dimmed and dull
For the cause they loyally strove to save.

And they fought right well, did these brave men,
For their banner still floats unto the breeze,
And the pæans of ages forever shall tell
Their glorious tale beyond the seas.
Ring out your voices in praises loud,
Sing sweet your notes of music gay,
Tell me in all you loyal crowd
Throbs there a heart unmoved today?

Meeting together again this year,
As met we in fealty and love before;
Men, maids, and matrons to reverently hear
Praises of brave men who fought of yore.
Tell to the little ones with wondering eyes,
The tale of the flag that floats so free;
Till their tiny voices shall merrily rise
In hymns of rejoicing and praises to Thee.

Many a pure and noble heart
Lies under the sod, all covered with green;
Many a soul that had felt the smart
Of life's sad torture, or mayhap had seen
The faint hope of love pass afar from the sight,
Like swift flight of bird to a rarer clime
Many a youth whose death caused the blight
Of tender hearts in that long, sad time.

Nay, but this is no hour for sorrow;
They died at their duty, shall we repine?
Let us gaze hopefully on to the morrow
Praying that our lives thus shall shine.
Ring out your bugles, sound out your cheers!
Man has been God-like so may we be.
Give cheering thanks, there dry up those tears,
Widowed and orphaned, the country is free!

Wreathes of lillies and immortelles,
Scattered upon each silent mound,
Voices in loving remembrance swell,
Chanting to heaven the solemn sound,
Glad skies above, and glad earth beneath,
And grateful hearts who silently
Gather earth's flowers, and tenderly wreath
Woman's sweet token of fragility.

Farewell

Farewell, sweetheart, and again farewell;
Today we part, and who can tell
    If we shall e'er again
Meet, and with clasped hands
Renew our vows of love, and forget
    The sad, dull pain.

    Dear heart, 'tis bitter thus to lose thee
And think mayhap, you will forget me;
    And yet, I thrill
As I remember long and happy days
Fraught with sweet love and pleasant memories
    That linger still.

    You go to loved ones who will smile
And clasp you in their arms, and all the while
    I stay and moan
For you, my love, my heart and strive
To gather up life's dull, gray thread
    And walk alone.

    Aye, with you love the red and gold
Goes from my life, and leaves it cold
    And dull and bare,
Why should I strive to live and learn
And smile and jest, and daily try
    You from my heart to tare?

    Nay, sweetheart, rather would I lie
Me down, and sleep for aye; or fly
    To regions far
Where cruel Fate is not and lovers live
Nor feel the grim, cold hand of Destiny
    Their way to bar.

PAUL LAURENCE DUNBAR AND ALICE DUNBAR NELSON

I murmur not, dear love, I only say
Again farewell. God bless the day
    On which we met,
And bless you too, my love, and be with you
In sorrow or in happiness, nor let you
    E'er me forget.

I Sit and Sew

I sit and sew—a useless task it seems,
My hands grown tired, my head weighed down with dreams—
The panoply of war, the martial tred of men,
Grim-faced, stern-eyed, gazing beyond the ken
Of lesser souls, whose eyes have not seen Death,
Nor learned to hold their lives but as a breath—
But—I must sit and sew.

I sit and sew—my heart aches with desire—
That pageant terrible, that fiercely pouring fire
On wasted fields, and writhing grotesque things
Once men. My soul in pity flings
Appealing cries, yearning only to go
There in that holocaust of hell, those fields of woe—
But—I must sit and sew.

The little useless seam, the idle patch;
Why dream I here beneath my homely thatch,
When there they lie in sodden mud and rain,
Pitifully calling me, the quick ones and the slain?
You need me, Christ! It is no roseate dream
That beckons me—this pretty futile seam,
It stifles me—God, must I sit and sew?

If I had Known

If I had known
Two years ago how drear this life should be,
And crowd upon itself allstrangely sad,
Mayhap another song would burst from out my lips,
Overflowing with the happiness of future hopes;
Mayhap another throb than that of joy.
Have stirred my soul into its inmost depths,
                    If I had known.

If I had known,
Two years ago the impotence of love,
The vainness of a kiss, how barren a caress,
Mayhap my soul to higher things have soarn,
Nor clung to earthly loves and tender dreams,
But ever up aloft into the blue empyrean,
And there to master all the world of mind,
                    If I had known.

Impressions

Thought

A swift, successive chain of things,
  That flash, kaleidoscope-like, now in, now out,
Now straight, now eddying in wild rings,
    No order, neither law, compels their moves,
    But endless, constant, always swiftly roves.

Hope

Wild seas of tossing, writhing waves,
A wreck half-sinking in the tortuous gloom;
One man clings desperately, while Boreas raves,
    And helps to blot the rays of moon and star,
    Then comes a sudden flash of light, which gleams on shores afar.

Love

A bed of roses, pleasing to the eye,
Flowers of heaven, passionate and pure,
Upon this bed the youthful often lie,
    And pressing hard upon its sweet delight,
    The cruel thorns pierce soul and heart, and cause a woeful blight.

Death

A traveller who has always heard
That on this journey he some day must go,
    Yet shudders now, when at the fatal word
    He starts upon the lonesome, dreary way.
    The past, a page of joy and woe,—the future, none can say.

Faith

Blind clinging to a stern, stone cross,
    Or it may be of frailer make;
Eyes shut, ears closed to earth's drear dross,
    Immovable, serene, the world away
    From thoughts—the mind uncaring for another day.

Legend of the Newspaper

Poets sing and fables tell us,
Or old folk lore whispers low,
Of the origin of all things,
Of the spring from whence they came,
Kalevala, old and hoary,
Æneid, Iliad, Æsop, too,
All are filled with strange quaint legends,
All replete with ancient tales,—

How love came, and how old earth,
Freed from chaos, grew for us,
To a green and wondrous spheroid,
To a home for things alive;
How fierce fire and iron cold,
How the snow and how the frost,—
All these things the old rhymes ring,
All these things the old tales tell.

Yet they ne'er sang of the beginning,
Of that great unbreathing angel,
Of that soul without a haven,
Of that gracious Lady Bountiful,
Yet they ne'er told how it came here;
Ne'er said why we read it daily,
Nor did they even let us guess why
We were left to tell the tale.

Came one day into the wood-land,
Muckintosh, the great and mighty,
Muckintosh, the famous thinker,
He whose brain was all his weapons,
As against his rival's soarings,
High unto the vaulted heavens,
Low adown the swarded earth,
Rolled he round his gaze all steely,
And his voice like music prayed:

"Oh, Creator, wondrous Spirit,
Thou who hast for us descended
In the guise of knowledge mighty,
And our brains with truth o'er-flooded;
In the greatness of thy wisdom,
Knowest not our limitations?
Wondrous thoughts have we, thy servants,
Wondrous things we see each day,
Yet we cannot tell our brethren,
Yet we cannot let them know,
Of our doings and our happenings,
Should they parted be from us?
Help us, oh, Thou Wise Creator,
From the fulness of thy wisdom,
Show us how to spread our knowledge,
And disseminate our actions,
Such as we find worthy, truly."

Quick the answer came from heaven;
Muckintosh, the famous thinker,
Muckintosh, the great and mighty,
Felt a trembling, felt a quaking,
Saw the earth about him open,
Saw the iron from the mountains
Form a quaint and queer machine,
Saw the lead from out the lead mines
Roll into small lettered forms,
Saw the fibres from the flax-plant,
Spread into great sheets of paper,
Saw the ink galls from the green trees
Crushed upon the leaden forms;
Muckintosh, the famous thinker,
Muckintosh, the great and mighty,
Felt a trembling, felt a quaking,
Saw the earth about him open,
Saw the flame and sulphur smoking,
Came the printer's little devil,
Far from distant lands the printer,
Man of unions, man of cuss-words,

From the depths of sooty blackness;
Came the towel of the printer;
Many things that Muckintosh saw,—
Galleys, type, and leads and rules,
Presses, press-men, quoins and spaces,
Quads and caps and lower cases.

But to Muckintosh bewildered,
All this passed as in a dream,
Till within his nervous hand,
Hand with joy and fear a-quaking,
Muckintosh, the great and mighty,
Muckintosh, the famous thinker,
Held the first of our newspapers.

LOVE AND THE BUTTERFLY

I heard a merry voice one day
And glancing at my side,
Fair Love, all breathless, flushed with play,
A butterfly did ride.
"Whither away, oh sportive boy?"
I asked, he tossed his head;
Laughing aloud for purest joy,
And past me swiftly sped.

Next day I heard a plaintive cry
And Love crept in my arms;
Weeping he held the butterfly,
Devoid of all its charms.
Sweet words of comfort, whispered I
Into his dainty ears,
But Love still hugged the butterfly,
And bathed its wounds with tears.

New Year's Day

The poor old year died hard; for all the earth lay cold
    And bare beneath the wintry sky;
While grey clouds scurried madly to the west,
    And hid the chill young moon from mortal sight.
Deep, dying groans the aged year breathed forth,
    In soughing winds that wailed a requiem sad
In dull crescendo through the mournful air.

The new year now is welcomed noisily
    With din and song and shout and clanging bell,
And all the glare and blare of fiery fun.
Sing high the welcome to the New Year's morn!
    Le roi est mort. Vive, vive le roi! cry out,
And hail the new-born king of coming days.

Alas! the day is spent and eve draws nigh;
The king's first subject dies—for naught,
And wasted moments by the hundred score
    Of past years rise like spectres grim
To warn, that these days may not idly glide away.
Oh, New Year, youth of promise fair!
    What dost thou hold for me? An aching heart?
Or eyes burnt blind by unshed tears? Or stabs,
    More keen because unseen?
Nay, nay, dear youth, I've had surfeit
    Of sorrow's feast. The monarch dead
Did rule me with an iron hand. Be thou a friend,
    A tender, loving king—and let me know
The ripe, full sweetness of a happy year.

Sonnet

I had no thought of violets of late,
The wild, shy kind that spring beneath your feet
In wistful April days, when lovers mate
And wander through the fields in raptures sweet;
The thought of violets meant florists' shops,
And bows and pins, and perfumed papers fine;
And garish lights, and mincing little fops
And cabarets and songs, and deadening wine.
So far from sweet real things my thoughts had strayed,
I had forgot wide fields, and clear brown streams
The perfect loveliness that God has made,—
Wild violets shy and Heaven-mounting dreams.
And now—unwittingly, you've made me dream
Of violets, and my soul's forgotten gleam.

Three Thoughts

First

How few of us
In all the world's great, ceaseless struggling strife,
Go to our work with gladsome, buoyant step,
And love it for its sake, whate'er it be.
Because it is a labor, or, mayhap,
Some sweet, peculiar art of God's own gift;
And not the promise of the world's slow smile
of recognition, or of mammon's gilded grasp.
Alas, how few, in inspiration's dazzling flash,
Or spiritual sense of world's beyond the dome
Of circling blue around this weary earth,
Can bask, and know the God-given grace
Of genius' fire that flows and permeates
The virgin mind alone; the soul in which
The love of earth hath tainted not.
The love of art and art alone.

Second

"Who dares stand forth?" the monarch cried,
    "Amid the throng, and dare to give
    Their aid, and bid this wretch to live?
I pledge my faith and crown beside,
A woeful plight, a sorry sight,
    This outcast from all God-given grace.

    What, ho! in all, no friendly face,
No helping hand to stay his plight?
St. Peter's name be pledged for aye,
    The man's accursed, that is true;
    But ho, he suffers. None of you
Will mercy show, or pity sigh?"

Strong men drew back, and lordly train
    Did slowly file from monarch's look,
    Whose lips curled scorn. But from a nook
A voice cried out, "Though he has slain
That which I loved the best on earth,
    Yet will I tend him till he dies,
    I can be brave." A woman's eyes
Gazed fearlessly into his own.

Third

When all the world has grown full cold to thee,
And man—proud pygmy—shrugs all scornfully,
And bitter, blinding tears flow gushing forth,
Because of thine own sorrows and poor plight,
Then turn ye swift to nature's page,
And read there passions, immeasurably far
Greater than thine own in all their littleness.
For nature has her sorrows and her joys,
As all the piled-up mountains and low vales
Will silently attest—and hang thy head
In dire confusion, for having dared
To moan at thine own miseries
When God and nature suffer silently.

You! Inez!

Orange gleams athwart a crimson soul
Lambent flames; purple passion lurks
In your dusk eyes.
Red mouth; flower soft,
Your soul leaps up—and flashes
Star-like, white, flame-hot.
Curving arms, encircling a world of love,
You! Stirring the depths of passionate desire!

PAUL

A Letter

Dear Miss Lucy:
    I been t'inkin' dat I'd write you long fo' dis,
But dis writin''s mighty tejous, an' you know jes' how it is.
But I's got a little lesure, so I teks my pen in han'
Fu' to let you know my feelin's since I retched dis furrin' lan'.
I's right well, I's glad to tell you (dough dis climate ain't to blame),
An' I hopes w'en dese lines reach you, dat dey'll fin' yo' se'f de same.
Cose I 'se feelin' kin' o' homesick—dat 's ez nachul ez kin be,
Wen a feller's mo'n th'ee thousand miles across dat awful sea.
(Don't you let nobidy fool you 'bout de ocean bein' gran';
If you want to see de billers, you jes' view dem f'om de lan')
'Bout de people? We been t'inkin' dat all white folks was alak;
But dese Englishmen is diffunt, an' dey's curus fu' a fac'.
Fust, dey's heavier an' redder in dey make-up an' dey looks,
An' dey don't put salt nor pepper in a blessed t'ing dey cooks!
Wen dey gin you good ol' tu'nips, ca'ots, pa'snips, beets, an' sich,
Ef dey ain't someone to tell you, you cain't 'stinguish which is which.
Wen I t'ought I's eatin' chicken—you may b'lieve dis hyeah 's a lie—
But de waiter beat me down dat I was eatin' rabbit pie.
An' dey 'd t'ink dat you was crazy—jes' a reg'lar ravin' loon,
Ef you'd speak erbout a 'possum or a piece o' good ol' coon.
O, hit's mighty nice, dis trav'lin', an' I's kin' o' glad I come.
But, I reckon, now I's willin' fu' to tek my way back home.
I done see de Crystal Palace, an' I's hyeahd dey string-band play,
But I has n't seen no banjos layin' nowhahs roun' dis way.
Jes' gin ol' Jim Bowles a banjo, an' he'd not go very fu',
'Fo' he'd outplayed all dese fiddlers, wif dey flourish and dey stir.
Evahbiddy dat I's met wif has been monst'ous kin an' good;
But I t'ink I'd lak it better to be down in Jones's wood,
Where we ust to have sich frolics, Lucy, you an' me an' Nelse,
Dough my appetite 'ud call me, ef dey was n't nuffin else.
I'd jes' lak to have some sweet-pertaters roasted in de skin;
I's a-longin' fu' my chittlin's an' my mustard greens ergin;
I's a-wishin' fu' some buttermilk, an' co'n braid, good an' brown,
An' a drap o' good ol' bourbon fu' to wash my feelin's down!
An' I's comin' back to see you jes' as ehly as I kin,

So you better not go spa'kin' wif dat wuffless scoun'el Quin!
Well, I reckon, I mus' close now; write ez soon's dis reaches you;
Gi' my love to Sister Mandy an' to Uncle Isham, too.
Tell de folks I sen' 'em howdy; gin a kiss to pap an' mam;
Closin' I is, deah Miss Lucy, Still Yo' Own True-Lovin' Sam.

P. S. Ef you cain't mek out dis letter, lay it by erpon de she'f,
    An' when I git home, I'll read it, darlin', to you my own se'f.

A Lost Dream

Ah, I have changed, I do not know
Why lonely hours affect me so.
In days of yore, this were not wont,
No loneliness my soul could daunt.

For me too serious for my age,
The weighty tome of hoary sage,
Until with puzzled heart astir,
One God-giv'n night, I dreamed of her.

I loved no woman, hardly knew
More of the sex that strong men woo
Than cloistered monk within his cell;
But now the dream is lost, and hell.

Holds me her captive tight and fast
Who prays and struggles for the past.
No living maid has charmed my eyes,
But now, my soul is wonder-wise.

For I have dreamed of her and seen
Her red-brown tresses' ruddy sheen,
Have known her sweetness, lip to lip,
The joy of her companionship.

When days were bleak and winds were rude,
She shared my smiling solitude,
And all the bare hills walked with me
To hearken winter's melody.

And when the spring came o'er the land
We fared together hand in hand
Beneath the linden's leafy screen
That waved above us faintly green.

In summer, by the river-side,
Our souls were kindred with the tide
That floated onward to the sea
As we swept toward Eternity.

The bird's call and the water's drone
Were all for us and us alone.
The water-fall that sang all night
Was her companion, my delight,

And e'en the squirrel, as he sped
Along the branches overhead,
Half kindly and half envious,
Would chatter at the joy of us.

'Twas but a dream, her face, her hair,
The spring-time sweet, the winter bare,
The summer when the woods we ranged,—
'Twas but a dream, but all is changed.

Yes, all is changed and all has fled,
The dream is broken, shattered, dead.
And yet, sometimes, I pray to know
How just a dream could hold me so.

A Lyric

My lady love lives far away,
And oh my heart is sad by day,
And ah my tears fall fast by night,
What may I do in such a plight.

Why, miles grow few when love is fleet,
And love, you know, hath flying feet;
Break off thy sighs and witness this,
How poor a thing mere distance is.

My love knows not I love her so,
And would she scorn me, did she know?
How may the tale I would impart
Attract her ear and storm her heart?

Calm thou the tempest in my breast,
Who loves in silence loves the best,
But bide thy time, she will awake,
No night so dark but morn will break.

But though my heart so strongly yearn,
My lady loves me not in turn,
How may I win the blest reply
That my void heart shall satisfy.

Love breedeth love, be thou but true,
And soon thy love shall love thee, too;
If Fate hath meant you heart for heart,
There's naught may keep you twain apart.

An Old Memory

How sweet the music sounded
 That summer long ago,
When you were by my side, love,
 To list its gentle flow.

I saw your eyes a-shining,
 I felt your rippling hair,
I kissed your pearly cheek, love,
 And had no thought of care.

And gay or sad the music,
 With subtle charm replete;
I found in after years, love
 'Twas you that made it sweet.

For standing where we heard it,
 I hear again the strain;
It wakes my heart, but thrills it
 With sad, mysterious pain.

It pulses not so joyous
 As when you stood with me,
And hand in hand we listened
 To that low melody.

Oh, could the years turn back, love!
 Oh, could events be changed
To what they were that time, love,
 Before we were estranged;

Wert thou once more a maiden
 Whose smile was gold to me;
Were I once more the lover
 Whose word was life to thee,—

O God! could all be altered,
    The pain, the grief, the strife,
And wert thou—as thou shouldst be—
    My true and loyal wife!

But all my tears are idle,
    And all my wishes vain.
What once you were to me, love,
    You may not be again.

For I, alas! like others,
    Have missed my dearest aim.
I asked for love. Oh, mockery!
    Fate comes to me with fame!

Booker T. Washington

The word is writ that he who runs may read.
What is the passing breath of earthly fame?
But to snatch glory from the hands of blame—
That is to be, to live, to strive indeed.
A poor Virginia cabin gave the seed,
And from its dark and lowly door there came
A peer of princes in the world's acclaim,
A master spirit for the nation's need.
Strong, silent, purposeful beyond his kind,
    The mark of rugged force on brow and lip,
Straight on he goes, nor turns to look behind
    Where hot the hounds come baying at his hip;
With one idea foremost in his mind,
    Like the keen prow of some on-forging ship.

De Critters' Dance

Ain't nobody nevah tol' you not a wo'd a-tall,
'Bout de time dat all de critters gin dey fancy ball?
Some folks tell it in a sto'y, some folks sing de rhyme,
'Peahs to me you ought to hyeahed it, case hit's ol' ez time.

Well, de critters all was p'osp'ous, now would be de chance
Fu' to tease ol' Pa'son Hedgehog, givin' of a dance;
Case, you know, de critters' preachah was de stric'est kin',
An' he nevah made no 'lowance fu' de frisky min'.

So dey sont dey inbitations, Raccoon writ 'em all,
"Dis hyeah note is to inbite you to de Fancy Ball;
Come erlong an' bring yo' ladies, bring yo' chillun too,
Put on all yo' bibs an' tuckahs, show whut you kin do."

W'en de night come, dey all gathahed in a place dey knowed,
Fu' enough erway f'om people, nigh enough de road,
All de critters had ersponded, Hop-Toad up to Baih,
An' I's hyeah to tell you, Pa'son Hedgehog too, was daih.

Well, dey talked an' made dey 'bejunce, des lak critters do,
An' dey walked an' p'omenaded 'roun' an' thoo an' thoo;
Jealous ol' Mis' Fox, she whispah, "See Mis' Wildcat daih,
Ain't hit scan'lous, huh a-comin' wid huh shouldahs baih?"

Ol' man T'utle was n't honin' fu' no dancin' tricks,
So he stayed by ol' Mis' Tu'tle, talkin' politics;
Den de ban' hit 'mence a-playin' critters all to place,
Fou' ercross an' fou' stan' sideways, smilin' face to face.

'Fessah Frog, he play de co'net, Cricket play de fife,
Slews o' Grasshoppahs a-fiddlin' lak to save dey life;
Mistah Crow, 'he call de figgers, settin' in a tree,
Huh, uh! how dose critters sasshayed was a sight to see.

Mistah Possom swing Mis' Rabbit up an' down de flo',
Ol' man Baih, he ain't so nimble, an' it mek him blow;
Raccoon dancin' wid Mis' Squ'il squeeze huh little han',
She say, "Oh, now ain't you awful, quit it, goodness lan'!"

Pa'son Hedgehog groanin' awful at his converts' shines,
'Dough he peepin' thoo his fingahs at dem movin' lines,
'Twell he cain't set still no longah w'en de fiddles sing,
Up he jump, an' bless you, honey, cut de pigeon-wing.

Well, de critters lak to fainted jes' wid dey su'prise.
Sistah Fox, she vowed she was n't gwine to b'lieve huh eyes;
But dey could n't be no 'sputin' 'bout it any mo':
Pa'son Hedgehog was a-cape'in' all erroun' de flo'.

Den dey all jes' capahed scan'lous case dey did n't doubt,
Dat dey still could go to meetin'; who could tu'n 'em out?
So wid dancin' an' uligion, dey was in de fol',
Fu' a-dancin' wid de Pa'son couldn't hu't de soul.

Frederick Douglass

A hush is over all the teeming lists,
    And there is pause, a breath-space in the strife;
A spirit brave has passed beyond the mists
    And vapors that obscure the sun of life.
And Ethiopia, with bosom torn,
Laments the passing of her noblest born.

She weeps for him a mother's burning tears—
    She loved him with a mother's deepest love.
He was her champion thro' direful years,
    And held her weal all other ends above.
When Bondage held her bleeding in the dust,
He raised her up and whispered, "Hope and Trust."

For her his voice, a fearless clarion, rung
    That broke in warning on the ears of men;
For her the strong bow of his power he strung,
    And sent his arrows to the very den
Where grim Oppression held his bloody place
And gloated o'er the mis'ries of a race.

And he was no soft-tongued apologist;
    He spoke straightforward, fearlessly uncowed;
The sunlight of his truth dispelled the mist,
    And set in bold relief each dark hued cloud;
To sin and crime he gave their proper hue,
And hurled at evil what was evil's due.

Through good and ill report he cleaved his way.
    Right onward, with his face set toward the heights,
Nor feared to face the foeman's dread array,—
    The lash of scorn, the sting of petty spites.
He dared the lightning in the lightning's track,
And answered thunder with his thunder back.

When men maligned him, and their torrent wrath
    In furious imprecations o'er him broke,
He kept his counsel as he kept his path;
    'Twas for his race, not for himself he spoke.
He knew the import of his Master's call,
And felt himself too mighty to be small.

No miser in the good he held was he,—
    His kindness followed his horizon's rim.
His heart, his talents, and his hands were free
    To all who truly needed aught of him.
Where poverty and ignorance were rife,
He gave his bounty as he gave his life.

The place and cause that first aroused his might
    Still proved its power until his latest day.
In Freedom's lists and for the aid of Right
    Still in the foremost rank he waged the fray;
Wrong lived; his occupation was not gone.
He died in action with his armor on!

We weep for him, but we have touched his hand,
    And felt the magic of his presence nigh,
The current that he sent throughout the land,
    The kindling spirit of his battle-cry.
O'er all that holds us we shall triumph yet,
And place our banner where his hopes were set!

Oh, Douglass, thou hast passed beyond the shore,
    But still thy voice is ringing o'er the gale!
Thou'st taught thy race how high her hopes may soar,
    And bade her seek the heights, nor faint, nor fail.
She will not fail, she heeds thy stirring cry,
She knows thy guardian spirit will be nigh,
And, rising from beneath the chast'ning rod,
She stretches out her bleeding hands to God!

How Shall I Woo Thee?

How shall I woo thee to win thee, mine own?
    Say in what tongue shall I tell of my love.
I who was fearless so timid have grown,
    All that was eagle has turned into dove.
The path from the meadow that leads to the bars
Is more to me now than the path of the stars.

How shall I woo thee to win thee, mine own,
    Thou who art fair and as far as the moon?
Had I the strength of the torrent's wild tone,
    Had I the sweetness of warblers in June;
The strength and the sweetness might charm and persuade,
But neither have I my petition to aid.

How shall I woo thee to win thee, mine own?
    How shall I traverse the distance between
My humble cot and your glorious throne?
    How shall a clown gain the ear of a queen?
Oh teach me the tongue that shall please thee the best,
For till I have won thee my heart may not rest.

In Summer Time

When summer time has come, and all
The world is in the magic thrall
Of perfumed airs that lull each sense
To fits of drowsy indolence;
When skies are deepest blue above,
And flow'rs aflush,—then most I love
To start, while early dews are damp,
And wend my way in woodland tramp
Where forests rustle, tree on tree,
And sing their silent songs to me;
Where pathways meet and path ways part,—
To walk with Nature heart by heart,
Till wearied out at last I lie
Where some sweet stream steals singing by
A mossy bank; where violets vie
In color with the summer sky,—
Or take my rod and line and hook,
And wander to some darkling brook,
Where all day long the willows dream,
And idly droop to kiss the stream,
And there to loll from morn till night—
Unheeding nibble, run, or bite—
Just for the joy of being there
And drinking in the summer air,
The summer sounds, and summer sights,
That set a restless mind to rights
When grief and pain and raging doubt
Of men and creeds have worn it out;
The birds' song and the water's drone,
The humming bees' low monotone,
The murmur of the passing breeze,
And all the sounds akin to these,
That make a man in summer time
Feel only fit for rest and rhyme.
Joy springs all radiant in my breast;
Though pauper poor, than king more blest,

The tide beats in my soul so strong
That happiness breaks forth in song,
And rings aloud the welkin blue
With all the songs I ever knew.
O time of rapture! time of song!
How swiftly glide thy days along
Adown the current of the years,
Above the rocks of grief and tears!
'Tis wealth enough of joy for me
In summer time to simply be.

LITTLE BROWN BABY

Little brown baby wif spa'klin' eyes,
   Come to yo' pappy an' set on his knee.
What you been doin', suh—makin' san' pies?
   Look at dat bib—you's ez du'ty ez me.
Look at dat mouf—dat's merlasses, I bet;
   Come hyeah, Maria, an' wipe off his han's.
Bees gwine to ketch you an' eat you up yit,
   Bein' so sticky an sweet—goodness lan's!

Little brown baby wif spa'klin' eyes,
   Who's pappy's darlin' an' who's pappy's chile?
Who is it all de day nevah once tries
   Fu' to be cross, er once loses dat smile?
Whah did you git dem teef? My, you's a scamp!
   Whah did dat dimple come f'om in yo' chin?
Pappy do' know you—I b'lieves you's a tramp;
   Mammy, dis hyeah's some ol' straggler got in!

Let's th'ow him outen de do' in de san',
   We do' want stragglers a-layin' 'roun' hyeah;
Let's gin him 'way to de big buggah-man;
   I know he's hidin' erroun' hyeah right neah.
Buggah-man, buggah-man, come in de do',
   Hyeah's a bad boy you kin have fu' to eat.
Mammy an' pappy do' want him no mo',
   Swaller him down f'om his haid to his feet!

Dah, now, I t'ought dat you'd hug me up close.
   Go back, ol' buggah, you sha'n't have dis boy.
He ain't no tramp, ner no straggler, of co'se;
   He's pappy's pa'dner an' play-mate an' joy.
Come to you' pallet now—go to yo' res';
   Wisht you could allus know ease an' cleah skies;
Wisht you could stay jes' a chile on my breas'—
   Little brown baby wif spa'klin' eyes!

PAUL LAURENCE DUNBAR AND ALICE DUNBAR NELSON

Love's Pictures

Like the blush upon the rose
    When the wooing south wind speaks,
Kissing soft its petals,
    Are thy cheeks.

Tender, soft, beseeching, true,
    Like the stars that deck the skies
Through the ether sparkling,
    Are thine eyes.

Like the song of happy birds,
    When the woods with spring rejoice,
In their blithe awak'ning,
    Is thy voice.

Like soft threads of clustered silk
    O'er thy face so pure and fair,
Sweet in its profusion,
    Is thy hair.

Like a fair but fragile vase,
    Triumph of the carver's art,
Graceful formed and slender,—
    Thus thou art.

Ah, thy cheek, thine eyes, thy voice,
    And thy hair's delightful wave
Make me, I'll confess it,
    Thy poor slave!

Two Little Boots

Two little boots all rough an' wo',
    Two little boots!
Law, I's kissed 'em times befo',
    Dese little boots!
Seems de toes a-peepin' thoo
Dis hyeah hole an' sayin' "Boo!"
Evah time dey looks at you—
    Dese little boots.

Membah de time he put 'em on,
    Dese little boots;
Riz an' called fu' 'em by dawn,
    Dese little boots;
Den he tromped de livelong day,
Laffin' in his happy way,
Evaht'ing he had to say,
    "My little boots!"

Kickin' de san' de whole day long,
    Dem little boots;
Good de cobblah made 'em strong,
    Dem little boots!
Rocks was fu' dat baby's use,
I'on had to stan' abuse
W'en you tu'ned dese champeens loose,
    Dese little boots!

Ust to make de ol' cat cry,
    Dese little boots;
Den you walked it mighty high,
    Proud little boots!
Ahms akimbo, stan'in' wide,

Eyes a-sayin' "Dis is pride!"
Den de manny-baby stride!
    You little boots.

Somehow, you don' seem so gay,
    Po' little boots,
Sence yo' ownah went erway,
    Po' little boots!
Yo' bright tops don' look so red,
Dese brass tips is dull an' dead;
"Goo'-by," whut de baby said;
    Deah little boots!

Ain't you kin' o' sad yo'se'f,
    You little boots?
Dis is all his mammy's lef',
    Two little boots.
Sence huh baby gone an' died.
Heav'n itse'f hit seem to hide
Des a little bit inside
    Two little boots.

ODE TO ETHIOPIA

O Mother Race! to thee I bring
This pledge of faith unwavering,
   This tribute to thy glory.
I know the pangs which thou didst feel,
When Slavery crushed thee with its heel,
   With thy dear blood all gory.

Sad days were those—ah, sad indeed!
But through the land the fruitful seed
   Of better times was growing.
The plant of freedom upward sprung,
And spread its leaves so fresh and young—
   Its blossoms now are blowing.

On every hand in this fair land,
Proud Ethiope's swarthy children stand
   Beside their fairer neighbor;
The forests flee before their stroke,
Their hammers ring, their forges smoke,—
   They stir in honest labour.

They tread the fields where honour calls;
Their voices sound through senate halls
   In majesty and power.
To right they cling; the hymns they sing
Up to the skies in beauty ring,
   And bolder grow each hour.

Be proud, my Race, in mind and soul;
Thy name is writ on Glory's scroll
   In characters of fire.
High 'mid the clouds of Fame's bright sky
Thy banner's blazoned folds now fly,
   And truth shall lift them higher.

Thou hast the right to noble pride,
Whose spotless robes were purified
    By blood's severe baptism.
Upon thy brow the cross was laid,
And labour's painful sweat-beads made
    A consecrating chrism.

No other race, or white or black,
When bound as thou wert, to the rack,
    So seldom stooped to grieving;
No other race, when free again,
Forgot the past and proved them men
    So noble in forgiving.

Go on and up! Our souls and eyes
Shall follow thy continuous rise;
    Our ears shall list thy story
From bards who from thy root shall spring,
And proudly tune their lyres to sing
    Of Ethiopia's glory.

PASSION AND LOVE

A maiden wept and, as a comforter,
Came one who cried, "I love thee," and he seized
Her in his arms and kissed her with hot breath,
That dried the tears upon her flaming cheeks.
While evermore his boldly blazing eye
Burned into hers; but she uncomforted
Shrank from his arms and only wept the more.

Then one came and gazed mutely in her face
With wide and wistful eyes; but still aloof
He held himself; as with a reverent fear,
As one who knows some sacred presence nigh.
And as she wept he mingled tear with tear,
That cheered her soul like dew a dusty flower,—
Until she smiled, approached, and touched his hand!

PHILOSOPHY

I been t'inkin' 'bout de preachah; whut he said de othah night,
    'Bout hit bein' people's dooty, fu' to keep dey faces bright;
How one ought to live so pleasant dat ouah tempah never riles,
    Meetin' evahbody roun' us wid ouah very nicest smiles.

Dat 's all right, I ain't a-sputin' not a t'ing dat soun's lak fac',
    But you don't ketch folks a-grinnin' wid a misery in de back;
An' you don't fin' dem a-smilin' w'en dey's hongry ez kin be,
    Leastways, dat 's how human natur' allus seems to 'pear to me.

We is mos' all putty likely fu' to have our little cares,
    An' I think we 'se doin' fus' rate w'en we jes' go long and bears,
Widout breakin' up ouah faces in a sickly so't o' grin,
    W'en we knows dat in ouah innards we is p'intly mad ez sin.

Oh dey's times fu' bein' pleasant an' fu' goin' smilin' roun',
    'Cause I don't believe in people allus totin' roun' a frown,
But it's easy 'nough to titter w'en de stew is smokin' hot,
    But hit's mighty ha'd to giggle w'en dey's nuffin' in de pot.

The Place Where the Rainbow Ends

There's a fabulous story
Full of splendor and glory,
   That Arabian legends transcends;
Of the wealth without measure,
The coffers of treasure,
   At the place where the rainbow ends.

Oh, many have sought it,
And all would have bought it,
   With the blood we so recklessly spend;
But none has uncovered,
The gold, nor discovered
   The spot at the rainbow's end.

They have sought it in battle,
And e'en where the rattle
   Of dice with man's blasphemy blends;
But howe'er persuasive,
It still proves evasive,
   This place where the rainbow ends.

I own for my pleasure,
I yearn not for treasure,
   Though gold has a power it lends;
And I have a notion,
To find without motion,
   The place where the rainbow ends.

The pot may hold pottage,
The place be a cottage,
   That a humble contentment defends,
Only joy fills its coffer,
But spite of the scoffer,
   There's the place where the rainbow ends.

Where care shall be quiet,
And love shall run riot,
    And I shall find wealth in my friends;
Then truce to the story,
Of riches and glory;
    There's the place where the rainbow ends.

The Plantation Child's Lullaby

Wintah time hit comin'
    Stealin' thoo de night;
Wake up in the mo'nin'
    Evah t'ing is white;
Cabin lookin' lonesome
    Stannin' in de snow,
Meks you kin' o' nervous,
    Wen de win' hit blow.

Trompin' back from feedin',
    Col' an' wet an' blue,
Homespun jacket ragged,
    Win' a-blowin' thoo.
Cabin lookin' cheerful,
    Unnerneaf de do',
Yet you kin' o' keerful
    Wen de win' hit blow.

Hickory log a-blazin'
    Light a-lookin' red,
Faith o' eyes o' peepin'
    'Rom a trun'le bed,
Little feet a-patterin'
    Cleak across de flo';
Bettah had be keerful
    Wen de win' hit blow.

Suppah done an' ovah,
    Evah t'ing is still;
Listen to de snowman
    Slippin' down de hill.
Ashes on de fiah,
    Keep it wa'm but low.
What's de use o' keerin'
    Ef de win' do blow?

Smoke house full o' bacon,
    Brown an' sweet an' good;
Taters in de cellah,
    'Possum roam de wood;
Little baby snoozin'
    Des ez ef he know.
What's de use o' keerin'
    Ef de win' do blow?

The Poet and His Song

A song is but a little thing,
And yet what joy it is to sing!
In hours of toil it gives me zest,
And when at eve I long for rest;
When cows come home along the bars,
    And in the fold I hear the bell,
As Night, the shepherd, herds his stars,
    I sing my song, and all is well.

There are no ears to hear my lays,
No lips to lift a word of praise;
But still, with faith unfaltering,
I live and laugh and love and sing.
What matters yon unheeding throng?
    They cannot feel my spirit's spell,
Since life is sweet and love is long,
    I sing my song, and all is well.

My days are never days of ease;
I till my ground and prune my trees.
When ripened gold is all the plain,
I put my sickle to the grain.
I labor hard, and toil and sweat,
    While others dream within the dell;
But even while my brow is wet,
    I sing my song, and all is well.

Sometimes the sun, unkindly hot,
My garden makes a desert spot;
Sometimes a blight upon the tree
Takes all my fruit away from me;
And then with throes of bitter pain
    Rebellious passions rise and swell;
But—life is more than fruit or grain,
    And so I sing, and all is well.

Poor Withered Rose

A Song

Poor withered rose, she gave it me,
Half in revenge and half in glee;
Its petals not so pink by half
As are her lips when curled to laugh,
As are her cheeks when dimples gay
In merry mischief o'er them play.

Chorus

    Forgive, forgive, it seems unkind
    To cast thy petals to the wind;
    But it is right, and lest I err
    So scatter I all thought of her.

Poor withered rose, so like my heart,
That wilts at sorrow's cruel dart.
Who hath not felt the winter's blight
When every hope seemed warm and bright?
Who doth not know love unreturned,
E'en when the heart most wildly burned?

Poor withered rose, thou liest dead;
Too soon thy beauty's bloom hath fled.
'Tis not without a tearful ruth
I watch decay thy blushing youth;
And though thy life goes out in dole,
Thy perfume lingers in my soul.

Sympathy

I know what the caged bird feels, alas!
 When the sun is bright on the upland slopes;
When the wind stirs soft through the springing grass,
And the river flows like a stream of glass;
 When the first bird sings and the first bud opes,
And the faint perfume from its chalice steals—
I know what the caged bird feels!

I know why the caged bird beats his wing
 Till its blood is red on the cruel bars;
For he must fly back to his perch and cling
When he fain would be on the bough a-swing;
 And a pain still throbs in the old, old scars
And they pulse again with a keener sting—
I know why he beats his wing!

I know why the caged bird sings, ah me,
 When his wing is bruised and his bosom sore,—
When he beats his bars and he would be free;
It is not a carol of joy or glee,
 But a prayer that he sends from his heart's deep core,
But a plea, that upward to Heaven he flings—
I know why the caged bird sings!

The Colored Band

Wen de colo'ed ban' comes ma'chin' down de street,
Don't you people stan' daih starin'; lif yo' feet!
    Ain't dey playin'? Hip, hooray!
    Stir yo' stumps an' cleah de way,
Fu' de music dat dey mekin' can't be beat.

Oh, de major man's a-swingin' of his stick,
An' de pickaninnies crowdin' roun' him thick;
    In his go'geous uniform,
    He's de lightnin' of de sto'm,
An' de little clouds erroun' look mighty slick.

You kin hyeah a fine perfo'mance w'en de white ban's serenade,
    An' dey play dey high-toned music mighty sweet,
But hit's Sousa played in ragtime, an' hit's Rastus on Parade,
Wen de colo'ed ban' comes ma'chin' down de street.

Wen de colo'ed ban' comes ma'chin' down de street
You kin hyeah de ladies all erroun' repeat:
    "Ain't dey handsome? Ain't dey gran'?
    Ain't dey splendid? Goodness, lan'!
Wy dey's pu'fect f'om dey fo'heads to dey feet!"
An' sich steppin' to de music down de line,
'Tain't de music by itself dat meks it fine,
    Hit's de walkin', step by step,
    An' de keepin' time wid "Hep,"
Dat it mek a common ditty soun' divine.

Oh, de white ban' play hits music, an' hit's mighty good to hyeah,
An' it sometimes leaves a ticklin' in yo' feet;
But de hea't goes into bus'ness fu' to he'p erlong de eah,
    Wen de colo'ed ban' goes ma'chin' down de street.

The Old Apple Tree

There's a memory keeps a-runnin'
    Through my weary head tonight,
An' I see a picture dancin'
    In the fire-flames' ruddy light;
'Tis the picture of an orchard
    Wrapped in autumn's purple haze,
With the tender light about it
    That I loved in other days.
An' a-standin' in a corner
    Once again I seem to see
The verdant leaves an' branches
    Of an old apple-tree.

You perhaps would call it ugly,
    An' I don't know but it's so,
When you look the tree all over
    Unadorned by memory's glow;
For its boughs are gnarled an' crooked,
    An' its leaves are gettin' thin,
An' the apples of its bearin'
    Would n't fill so large a bin
As they used to. But I tell you,
    When it comes to pleasin' me,
It's the dearest in the orchard,—
    Is that old apple-tree.

I would hide within its shelter,
    Settlin' in some cosy nook,
Where no calls nor threats could stir me
    From the pages o' my book.
Oh, that quiet, sweet seclusion
    In its fulness passeth words!
It was deeper than the deepest
    That my sanctum now affords.
Why, the jaybirds an' the robins,

They was hand in glove with me,
As they winked at me an' warbled
    In that old apple-tree.

It was on its sturdy branches
    That in summers long ago
I would tie my swing an' dangle
    In contentment to an' fro,
Idly dreamin' childish fancies,
    Buildin' castles in the air,
Makin' o' myself a hero
    Of romances rich an' rare.
I kin shet my eyes an' see it
    Jest as plain as plain kin be,
That same old swing a-danglin'
    To the old apple-tree.

There's a rustic seat beneath it
    That I never kin forget.
It's the place where me an' Hallie—
    Little sweetheart—used to set,
When we'd wander to the orchard
    So 's no listenin' ones could hear
As I whispered sugared nonsense
    Into her little willin' ear.
Now my gray old wife is Hallie,
    An' I'm grayer still than she,
But I'll not forget our courtin'
    'Neath the old apple-tree.

Life for us ain't all been summer,
    But I guess we've had our share
Of its flittin' joys an' pleasures,
    An' a sprinklin' of its care.
Oft the skies have smiled upon us;
    Then again we've seen 'em frown,
Though our load was ne'er so heavy
    That we longed to lay it down.

But when death does come a-callin',
    This my last request shall be,—
That they'll bury me an' Hallie
    'Neath the old apple tree.

The Unsung Heroes

A song for the unsung heroes who rose in the country's need,
When the life of the land was threatened by the slaver's cruel greed,
For the men who came from the cornfield, who came from the plough
  and the flail,
Who rallied round when they heard the sound of the mighty man of
  the rail.

They laid them down in the valleys, they laid them down in the wood,
And the world looked on at the work they did, and whispered, "It is
  good."
They fought their way on the hillside, they fought their way in the glen,
And God looked down on their sinews brown, and said, "I have made
  them men."

They went to the blue lines gladly, and the blue lines took them in,
And the men who saw their muskets' fire thought not of their dusky
  skin.
The gray lines rose and melted beneath their scathing showers,
And they said, "'T is true, they have force to do, these old slave boys
  of ours."

Ah, Wagner saw their glory, and Pillow knew their blood,
That poured on a nation's altar, a sacrificial flood.
Port Hudson heard their war-cry that smote its smoke-filled air,
And the old free fires of their savage sires again were kindled there.

They laid them down where the rivers the greening valleys gem.
And the song of the thund'rous cannon was their sole requiem,
And the great smoke wreath that mingled its hue with the dusky
  cloud,
Was the flag that furled o'er a saddened world, and the sheet that
  made their shroud.

Oh, Mighty God of the Battles Who held them in Thy hand,
Who gave them strength through the whole day's length, to fight for
  their native land,

They are lying dead on the hillsides, they are lying dead on the plain,
And we have not fire to smite the lyre and sing them one brief strain.

Give, Thou, some seer the power to sing them in their might,
The men who feared the master's whip, but did not fear the fight;
That he may tell of their virtues as minstrels did of old,
Till the pride of face and the hate of race grow obsolete and cold.

A song for the unsung heroes who stood the awful test,
When the humblest host that the land could boast went forth to meet
    the best;
A song for the unsung heroes who fell on the bloody sod,
Who fought their way from night today and struggled up to God.

Trouble in De Kitchen

Dey was oncet a awful quoil 'twixt de skillet an' de pot;
De pot was des a-bilin' an' de skillet sho' was hot.
Dey slurred each othah's colah an' dey called each othah names,
Wile de coal-oil can des gu-gled, po'in oil erpon de flames.

De pot, hit called de skillet des a flat, disfiggered t'ing,
An' de skillet 'plied dat all de pot could do was set an' sing,
An' he 'lowed dat dey was 'lusions dat he wouldn't stoop to mek
'Case he reckernize his juty, an' he had too much at steak.

Well, at dis de pot biled ovah, case his tempah gittin' highah,
An' de skillet got to sputterin', den de fat was in de fiah.
Mistah flan lay daih smokin' an' a-t'inkin' to hisse'f,
Wile de peppah-box us nudgin' of de gingah on de she'f.

Den dey all des lef hit to 'im, 'bout de trouble an' de talk;
An' howevah he decided, w'y dey bofe 'u'd walk de chalk;
But de fiah uz so 'sgusted how dey quoil an' dey shout
Dat he cooled 'em off, I reckon, w'en he puffed an' des went out.

Yesterday and Tomorrow

Yesterday I held your hand,
Reverently I pressed it,
And its gentle yieldingness
From my soul I blessed it.

But today I sit alone,
Sad and sore repining;
Must our gold forever know
Flames for the refining?

Yesterday I walked with you,
Could a day be sweeter?
Life was all a lyric song
Set to tricksy meter.

Ah, today is like a dirge,—
Place my arms around you,
Let me feel the same dear joy
As when first I found you.

Let me once retrace my steps,
From these roads unpleasant,
Let my heart and mind and soul
All ignore the present.

Yesterday the iron seared
And today means sorrow.
Pause, my soul, arise, arise,
Look where gleams the morrow.

PLAYS

The Author's Evening at Home

SCENE—*Library. Weather—Ninety in the shade.*
   AUTHOR, *tired, nervous.*
   WIFE, *fidgety.*
   MOTHER
   SERVANT

WIFE: *discovered lying on lounge.* AUTHOR *enters, and seats himself by her side.*
AUTHOR: Well, little girl, how are you?
WIFE: Oh, I am so sick!
AUTHOR: Let me go for a doctor.
WIFE: No, I don't need a doctor; I just have a headache.
AUTHOR: Well, lie quiet, dear.
WIFE: I don't want to lie quiet. (*Struggles to a sitting posture*)
AUTHOR: Do you want to go out for a walk, dear? (*Kisses her*)
WIFE (*crossly*): No! (*Lies down again*)
AUTHOR (*going to desk*): Well, dear, I thought over that final chapter today, and I think I will write it out.
WIFE: John!
AUTHOR: Yes, dear.
WIFE: You have kissed me only once.
AUTHOR (*dutifully rising and kissing her on her forehead*): Poor little woman! (*Goes back to desk*)
WIFE: John!
AUTHOR: Yes, dear.
WIFE: If you only knew how my head aches!
AUTHOR (*seating himself again on lounge*): I can imagine dear.
WIFE: Why don't you do something to amuse me?
AUTHOR: I, dear? What can I do?
WIFE (*petulantly*): What have you been doing today? You never tell me a thing.
AUTHOR: Well, I finished two chapters. Would you like to hear them, dear?
WIFE: Of course.
(AUTHOR *begins to read aloud*)
WIFE: John!

AUTHOR: Yes, dear.

WIFE: Mrs. De Smythe was here today, and you have no idea how elegant she looked. She wore a gray satin suit trimmed with cut steel and gray chiffon, and her hat was a gray toque with violets.

AUTHOR: Have you finished, dear?

WIFE: Oh, yes; go on.

(AUTHOR *reads to end of chapter and looks to* WIFE *for approaval*)

WIFE: John!

AUTHOR: Yes, dear.

WIFE: Do you know that bald spot on your head has changed its form completely? Now it's almost a heart-shape.

(AUTHOR *says things under his breath and goes to his desk again*)

WIFE (*pettishly*): How cross you are!

(*Silence for thirty-three seconds.* AUTHOR *writes industriously.* WIFE *sits up and begins to embroider. Enter* SERVANT)

SERVANT: I've come for the breakfast order, mum.

WIFE: Oh, yes. Well, Mary, we'll have—let me see—John, would you like a mackerel tomorrow?

(AUTHOR *mutters unpublishable things and grunts for reply*)

WIFE: All right. Well, Mary, we'll have broiled mackerel and cakes, and—well, just anything.

SERVANT: Yes, mum. (*Exit*)

(*Silence for twenty-six seconds.* WIFE *fidgets in her chair; drops scissors; hums one of Sousa's marches*)

WIFE: John!

AUTHOR: Well?

WIFE: John, if England whips the Boers, it will change things about in Africa, won't it?

AUTHOR: Yes, I suppose so.

WIFE: John, where is the Boer country?

AUTHOR: Get an atlas and find out.

(WIFE *spends some noisy moments finding an atlas on the bookshelves, drops a book on her foot and cries out.* AUTHOR *groans*)

WIFE: John!

AUTHOR: Well?

(AUTHOR *rises and seats himself beside her on the lounge*)

WIFE: I don't understand what the Orange Free State is. Tell me.

(AUTHOR *explains tersely, shuts the atlas and goes back to his desk. Enter* MOTHER; *sighs; and sits in an armchair*)

MOTHER: Oh, my, how warm it is!

AUTHOR: Let me open the window. (*Rises and opens window.* WIFE *resignedly puts on a shawl*)

AUTHOR: Are you cold, dear?

WIFE: Oh, it makes no difference about *me*. (AUTHOR *goes back to desk with lines deepening on his face.* MOTHER *and* WIFE *coverse in sibilant whispers*)

AUTHOR: For heaven's sake!

WIFE: You're disturbing John, mother. (*Exit into next room, where she can be heard moving about and humming the Sousa march*)

MOTHER: Are you busy, dear?

AUTHOR: Oh, no; just amusing myself, trying to make some bread and butter.

MOTHER: I'm sorry to disturb you, dear, but then, you know, I just like to be about and see you at work. Of course, I sha'n't bother you at all. You can go right on. I sha'n't make a bit of noise or be in your way. I don't disturb you, do I?

AUTHOR: Oh, no, mother, not at all.

MOTHER: I thought not. You see, it's just as I was saying today to Mrs. Blackwell; when John comes home in the evening, Bess and I love to sit in the library while he writers, and watch him and learn repose by keeping still.

(*enter* WIFE *on tiptoe; her shoes creak audibly. Goes to lounge, knocking against a chair on the way. Lies down with heavy sigh. Silence for three minutes, broken by the stretching of* AUTHOR's *pen and alternate sighs from* WIFE *and* MOTHER. *Bell Rings*)

WIFE: Mercy me, I hope it's no one to disturb John!

(*Enter* SERVANT)

SERVANT: Mr. and Mrs. Cartwright are in the parlor, mum, and Mrs. Cartwright says as how they've come over for a rubber of whist.

MOTHER: What a pity!

WIFE: Just as John was in such a good train of thought, too.

AUTHOR: Thank heavens!

GONE WHITE: A PLAY IN THREE ACTS

CHARACTERS

ALLAN FRANKLIN CORDELL: *The Man*
ANNA MARTIN: *The Woman*
JOHN CHAMBERLAIN: *The Buffer*
BLANCHE PARKER: *The Aunt*
GRANNY WIMBISH: *The Grandmother*
HARRY BLAKE: *The Fool*
EMMA GORDON: *The Loyal One*
JIMMY DAVIS: *The Constant Lover*
EVAN MARTIN: *The Cripple*
Time: *The Present*
Place: *Anywhere in this country*

Act I

Scene: *Anna's garden. A Small plot of ground in a small city. One tree dominates the garden. Around it is a circular wooden seat. To the right a cottage door and window, praticable. To the left, a street, separated from the garden by wooden paling fence, with a gate, sagging on its hinges. A little garden with common flowers, bravely struggling to bloom. Geraniums in earthen pots are on the window sills of the cottage window, and cheap lace curtains flutter in and out in the breeze.*

It is sunset, and a stormy red suffuses the scene. Gradually it fades, darkens, and merges into a brilliant moonlight as the action progresses.

A group of young people pass the garden on the outside of the palings, singing. Their song is of the lightest and most carefree, a popular tune. Emma and Jimmy detach themselves from the group, and enter the garden. They seat themselves, Emma swinging a little basket as she talks.

JIMMY: I wonder what's become of Anna?

EMMA: Probably singing a bedtime story to one of her charges.

JIMMY: That Evan is a pain. If I could get my hands on him once, I'd give him such a slap he'd get over his perennial peeve.

EMMA: But, Jimmy, you must remember Evan is crippled. Anna has had him since her sister died—

JIMMY: Some legacy—

EMMA: And she's been a slave to the child.

JIMMY: Not to mention her old Granny Wimbish—another pain.

EMMA: Sh, Jimmy! You're awful!

JIMMY: Well, she is and they are, both of them. Anna's too fine a
girl to be a martyr. She's given up all her life, all her prospects of
education and having the chance that other girls of her age and
class have had. She'll never collect dividends on what she's put out
in time and energy and love and devotion and sacrifice and—

EMMA: Catch your breath, Jimmy. When she marries Allan, she'll have
happiness to spare. For if ever two people loved each other——

JIMMY: Yes, when.

EMMA: Jimmy, you don't mean, you can't think, you don't imagine——

JIMMY: I don't imagine anything, Emma. I know that Allan is
ambitious. He's not making good now. He's not going to make
good here. He's picked out a profession that no colored man can
make good at, in this country——

(*Harry Blake has gradually strolled down the street outside the fence. He
leans on the gate, listening to the conversation. At the last word, he comes in
and leans against a tree*)

HARRY: You're right there, old thing. What any colored man wants
to be a civil engineer for in this dump I can't make out. About the
only engineering he'll do is to fire the furnace in an office building.

EMMA: But you must give him credit, Harry, for his ambition.

HARRY: (*Snaps fingers, lights cigarette*) Ambition! Old Stuff! 'T'ain't
going to buy no pork chops. As for me——

EMMA: (*Hotly*) Even if Allan didn't have pride, Anna's influence——

HARRY: Anna's influence! Anna's eyes! Fat chance Anna'll have of
influencing him with a half-witted cripple hanging to her and a
pesky grandmother nagging the heart out of her. Anna—(*jeers*)
As for me and my house, it's the little old job that brings in the
shekels for mine.

JIMMY: Hear! Hear!

EMMA: It's just like you men to be so sordid. I hate you all. I did
think that You, Jimmy,—but—(*Chokes and flings herself out the
gate. As she goes out, she collides with Allan Cordell. He is tall, slim, fair,
light-haired. His shoulders droop with dejection, but he catches Emma
by the arm as she falls against him. She looks up in his face, and speaks
breathlessly*)

EMMA: Oh, Allan, I'm so glad I met you. You do, you do love Anna, don't you?

ALLAN: More than my life, Emma

EMMA: (*Triumphantly*) I knew it. (*She runs happily down the street*)

ALLAN: Why the convocation, fellows?

JIMMY: Oh, nothing, just a question of values, that's all. Harry says the job's the thing. Emma says the ideal is the thing. I'm open-minded. What do you say?

ALLAN: I hope I may never come to the point where I have to choose. But I've always stuck to my ideals. I've got an ambition I want to realize for myself—and—for—Anna, and I'm going to fight it out with my back to the wall it may be, but fight I will.

HARRY: I always was the fool in the bunch, but I've got the money. When I run short of high palaver and ideals, I can always come to you two and get them. Contrariwise, when you run short of money, you'll find Harry's little old bank roll quite convenient.

(*Jimmy laughs, and pushes Harry before him out the gate, and they pass down the street laughing. Allan sinks down on the seat and puts his head in his hands. A step is heard. Anna comes into the garden from the house door. Allan rises to greet her*)

ALLAN: Anna!

ANNA: Allan!

(*Anna is young and slim, and brown and beautiful. Her manner is bit more sedate than Emma's, and her dress is almost severe in its simplicity. She is eagerly in love with Allan. Her hands caress his arms tenderly*)

ANNA: Something is wrong, dear. I saw you shake your head.

ALLAN: No, nothing more than usual. I'm disappointed. I wanted to set our wedding day—but—

ANNA: (*Catching her breath*) Yes, you can, Allan—yes. We could marry, and then you could go away and try for work somewhere else, and then send for me.

ALLAN: That's sneaky. I'm going to fight it out here. And why marry you and run away?

ANNA: You see, Allan. I—you MUST go away—you can't make good here.

ALLAN: (*Rising furiously*) Why can't I? I've got my diploma—my recommendations. I've been the best man in the university, none stood higher. Why—with all these big buildings going up—the contractors are crying for men. Here, now, is the big opportunity.

I'll stay right here; color or no color. I know what you'll say—that my race is a bar. That's nothing but damnable propaganda to keep colored men from entering the profession. If you've got the goods you'll be able to make good. You're weak-kneed, like all the rest. Crying at your shadow—

(*Anna shrinks against the tree, hiding her face in her hands. Allan sits by her and takes her in his arms*)

ALLAN: Forgive me darling. Of all women, you're the last anyone should ever call weak. But I've been nagged at everywhere until I'm sore, I guess. I WON'T run away. I'll stay right here, and with you to help me—

ANNA: And what little my love can do for you it shall do. Love may not be all, but it is my all. (*They open the garden gate and pass down the street, hand in hand. Granny Wimbish comes into the garden from the house, just as they go out the gate. She is withered, thin, yellow, a typical crone. She lends on her cane and shakes her head gloomily, as the lovers go down the street*)

GRANNY: Humph! There they go. Lovers! SHE thinks they're lovers, but he will not marry her. He's making a fool of her. No man as white as that is going to marry a brown girl. And if he does, there'll be misery! Misery! The world is full of nothing but misery!

(*She croaks and croons on the last words, rocking to and from the garden seat. Evan limps in the gate. He is little and elfish, with irons on his limps; a cruel limp and a weary scowl*)

EVAN: (*Shrilly*) I met 'em. I met 'em! They was going down to the river, and he was sayin' poetry. Silly! Silly! She thinks she's goin' to marry him, but I know better. (*He hops about in his elfish way*)

GRANNY: Shut up, you brat! After she's worked her fingers to the bone, washin' and coin' and sewin' for you, there you are makin' fun of her. What I tell you 'bout young folks? Don't care for nobody but theirselves.

EVAN: Granny, ef Anna marries, she'll leave me an' you. (*Sniffs*)

GRANNY: Anna ain't that kind. She's been all our 'pendence. And a mother to us both. Workin' at anything she could get. And never gettin' to graduate like the other girls, 'cause her poor no-count sister left her you to take keer of.

EVAN: (*Sullenly*) Well, I ain't no mo' burden den you. An' you don't want her to marry Allan needer. He ain't got a think for feeder of us to do.

(*A masculine voice heard singing up the street,* "Oh Anna, dear Anna, my love to be!" *Enter John Chamberlain, with a box of flowers. He is tall, dark, handsome. Older than Allan. He has the undisputed signs of well-being, well-doing, and an air of authority*)

JOHN: Good evening. Is Anna home?

GRANNY: No, she's gone out. (*Granny's manner is distinctly ingratiating*)

EVAN: (*Chanting*) Down by the river-side, down by de river-side. With Allan. She ain't gwine study love no mo'.

(*John looks annoyed. He turns to go, and Anna enters the gate alone*)

ANNA: John! (*She comes to him with outstretched hand*)

JOHN: Anna! I brought you some flowers. Red roses. Like the red in your sweet lips. Like the red blood in your warm heart. Like the courage in your splendid soul.

EVAN: (*Aside*) Like the red light on the tail of a car! (*Limps out into the street*)

GRANNY: (*Aside*) Like the red flag of a danger signal (*Limps into the house*)

JOHN: (*Still holding Anna's hands, oblivious of the others*)Anna, I won't wait any longer for my answer. Come to me. You know I love you—I—

ANNA: Stop, John, I can't—

JOHN: You only THINK you love Allan. But there can be no true happiness between you. Poverty. Struggle. The giving up—for you would have to give up Granny and evan, after all your struggle to hold the home together. He hasn't a start yet. And I can care for all three of you.

(*Anna's head drops. She is silent*)

JOHN: You've worked too hard, little girl. Be thoughtful of your own interests and come to me.

ANNA: Oh, John. You don't tempt me when you talk like that. You're only wasting your breath.

JOHN: And, Anna, the time will come when Allan will look upon you as a handicap, as a drag. Children. Your own family. I will be patient. I will wait until you can care for me. Just a little. But think—think—before you say no again.

ANNA: Don't, John. I'm fond of you; I respect you, but this that you ask—(*She pushes him gently toward the gate. The postman pauses and gives Anna a letter*) See, this letter has good fortune in it for me. (*John passes out into the street as Anna opens the letter*)

ANNA: From Blanche Parker. Who is Blanche Parker? Oh, I know; it's
Allan's Aunt Blanche he talks of so much. Why does she write me?
Let's see.

> My dear Miss Martin
>
> I am writing this to ask you to break off your affair
> with my nephew. He is trying to be loyal to his promise
> to you (*Anna's voice breaks as she reads*) but it is a foolish
> loyalty. He really owes something to me, his aunt, for I
> have done the most to put him through college. Allan can
> make a career for himself, if he will step aside from his race,
> and he knows it. Only a stubborn and mistaken sense of
> gratitude, and so-called race pride, is making him cling to
> the people, who have nothing but poverty to offer him. I
> feel that his engagement to you is making him still more
> determined to continue in this mistaken course. As a white
> man, and there is nothing about him to indicate color—he
> can rise in his chosen profession. As a colored man, he must
> compromise—and fail. I am sure you are too sensible to
> stand in his way. A girl of your complexion and class would
> be only a hindrance to him. If you love Allan, you will
> dismiss him from your life.
>
> Sincerely yours,
> Blanche Parker

(*During the reading of this Anna has sobbed softly to herself. She crumples
the letter in her hand*)
ANNA: Cruel. Bitter. Malicious. How could she! I hate her. I hate
them all. "As a white man he could rise—" (*She sinks on the garden
seat*)
(*Allan runs in the garden gate eagerly, a bunch of violets in his hands*)
ALLAN: Anna, see what I stopped to get you? Violets for your new
dress tomorrow. Modest and fragrant, like you. Their sweetness
hidden and lying close to the heart.
(*Anna looks up indifferently, her eyes hard, as she lays the flowers on the seat
without looking at them*)
ANNA: Allan, what are your prospects for getting taken on by the new
firm?
ALLAN: (*Slowly*) Er—well, you see—I—er—

ANNA: (*Coldly*) In other words, they've refused you?

ALLAN: (*Slowly*) Yes—but I'm sure its only a tentative refusal. I am sure they will listen to the recommendation of Prof. Auerbach.

ANNA: And all the other places have refused you?

ALLAN: Well, but a man doesn't expect immediate big jobs.

ANNA: But didn't all the other men in your class get positions immediately at the Works?

ALLAN: Yes—but—

ANNA: And didn't you stand head of your class?

ALLAN: Yes—but—

ANNA: Yet—when the positions were given out, you were overlooked?

ALLAN: But you see, Anna—

ANNA: Let's face facts, Allan. You're getting no work, because you're known to be colored?

ALLAN: Anna, it isn't fair—

ANNA: That being the case, since only white men are employed as engineers, if you want employment at your profession, you must "go white."

ALLAN: Never! I'll stick, until I compel them to admit that a Negro can be as good or better an engineer than a white man. I'll ram their damn prejudice down their throats I'll—(*He stands excitedly, fists clenched*)

ANNA: (*Stands also. Speaks coldly*) All heroics, Allan. You'll starve or wind up your career hopping bells or being Pullman George.

ALLAN: What's come over you, Anna? You're cynical. That's a new role.

ANNA: (*Laughs bitterly*) Cynical? No, I'm not cynical. I'm disgusted. I can't see where we're getting anywhere. You'll never make good. I'm tired of waiting for you. And Granny and Evan are dependent on me. You can't support yourself, much less three others.

ALLAN: (*Blustering*) Can't support myself?

ANNA: (*Wearily*) Oh, Allan, don't you suppose I know that your Aunt Blanche has been looking out for you? At least you owe her gratitude enough to try to make a living at the profession she gave you.

ALLAN: And so I will.

ANNA: But not with my help. I'm tired of being a stepladder. Go on, Go white! Take your Nordic face out of my race!

ALLAN: Anna! Anna! Little Anna! (*They stand facing each other, tensley, like animals. Then a sudden gesture on Anna's part knocks down John's box of flowers from the seat. It falls open, disclosing the red roses*)

ALLAN: Where'd those damn things come from?

ANNA: (*Stoops. Takes the flowers from the box and holds them against her breasts*) John Chamberlain brought them to me.

ALLAN: Humph! I see. Costly roses, John has money; a car. I see now why you're tired of waiting. No wonder you feel the burden of Granny and Evan. So I must be white, and get out of your way. You—you— (*Choking with rage, he seizes Anna's wrists*)

ANNA: (*Slowly, as if the words were being cut out of her heart*) You are right. It is—John Chamberlain. I shall marry him. He has money. I haven't the courage to face poverty with you. And you can be white. Be a great engineer. Have a career.

ALLAN: Damn careers! Damn you for a mercenary false thing. A prostitute sells her body for gold. You are worse; you'll sell your body, your soul and your lover to boot. Truth! Vows! What is truth? There is none in woman and none in man! (*He tears the red roses from her arms, and rending them into the crushed bits, pitches the pieces in her face. Anna cows under the blows and the lash of his fury*) Damn you. Hypocrites. Liars. All of you. White hypocrites, black liars. Lying women and thieving men. Damn you. All of you! (*He dashes out the gate and down the street. Anna sinks huddled on the seat, the rose petals clinging in her hair. Outside the gate, Emma and Jimmy pause and call to Anna. She raises her head daily*)

EMMA: Jimmy and I have had a dispute. I want him to go on to school, and I'll wait for him until he graduates in law. But he's afraid I won't wait for him.

JIMMY: (*Sullenly*) Yes, while I am away grinding at law books, she'll be spending Harry Blake's money.

EMMA: Oh, Jimmy, just as Anna is true to Allan, and will wait for him—

ANNA: (*Interrupting*) You're wrong, Emma. I'm going to marry John Chamberlain. (*Droops her head against the tree*)

JIMMY: Didn't I tell you? You women! You can't resist a dollar. Clothes. Good time. Cars. Fur coats. That's what you want. Why should a man scrimp and sacrifice to get a profession when a girl only wants money, and she doesn't care how the fellow gets it?

EMMA: You stop, Jimmy! If Anna is—(*But Jimmy slams the gate and goes out*)

ANNA: Don't let him go away like that, Emma. Your happiness is slipping through your fingers. Call it back before it is too late.

EMMA: I'm not bothered about him. It's you, Anna. Why, dear—oh, I know you loved Allan. Why? Why? (*Granny comes from the house crooning, "Nobody knows the trouble I see."*)

GRANNY: No supper ready. Nothin done. Everybody talking, talking, talking. An' what does it amount to? Just words. No sense to them.

ANNA: God knows why, Emma. And He won't tell. They press us on every side. Bitter foes. And all we can say is—Courage! (*She sobs a bit on Emma's shoulder, then dries her eyes, straightens up, smiles bravely, and says, "Courage!"*)

CURTAIN

Act II

SCENE ONE: *By the riverside in a distant city. Twelve years have passed. A park by the side of the river. Benches face a walk which runs parallel to a wooded stream. The benches are set back in trees and shrubbery, which partly hide those who sit upon them. It is twilight. A heavy, scented, brooding dusky quiet.*

Anna enters, with slow dragging steps and sinks on one of the park benches. Even in the dusk, it is seen that she has grown visibly order. Her shoulders droop with weariness, and lines of pain and worry are carved in her face. Her dress is plain, shabby. She leans her chin in her hand, and gazes dispiritedly at the water.

ANNA: We used to sit by the riverside at home, just at this hour, and watch the lights come up one by one on the island. It was so much like this.

(*In the distance a group of boys and girls sing. A stringed orchestra, apparently in a pavilion on the distant island, plays*)

ANNA: On such a night as this—oh, futile poetry of life!

(*Voices heard approaching up the river walk. A group of white men appear, walking slowly. Allan Cordell is among them. They are conventional and prosperous looking, in clothes, with lighted cigars. They stroll down the path before the hidden bench*)

FIRST VOICE: I've seldom heard a better speech, Cordell, than the one you made this afternoon.

SECOND VOICE: Yes, he's got 'em all—the three P's of a good Rotarian—Pep, Punch, and Personality.

ALLAN: Am I to understand that I am another Babbitt?

THIRD VOICE: Not so bad as that; but you mae us all feel that having you as our guest of honor at our annual luncheon, we were more than honoring ourselves!

ALLAN: (*Feigned modesty in his tone*) It was nothing but telling the truth—what I have done in the past twelve years.

FIRST VOICE: Yes, but few men have been able to do in two decades what you have done in one.

SECOND VOICE: And there's a good stretch before you yet. You have my contratulations.

THIRD VOICE: Just keep up the pace, and don't let your foot slip.

ALLAN: Thanks. I'll stop here, and finish this cigar, if you'll excuse me. This scene brings to my mind one that I knew in my earlier days. It—well—

FIRST VOICE: Nor too successful to feel the urge for sentimental and romantic memories. Well, enjoy yourself.

(*The three men laughing, pass down the walk, Allan seats himself on the bench, without seeing Anna, and relights his cigar. The flaring of the match shows him a dark, huddled form on the end of the bench*)

ALLAN: (*Starting*) I beg your pardon, I did not know anyone was on the bench. Will it annoy you if I rest here awhile?

ANNA: No, it's perfectly all right.

ALLAN: (*Under his breath*) That voice! Those rippling, golden notes! (*He moves closer, and strikes a match. The light flares over Anna. She puts her hands over her face*)

ALLAN: Anna! (*With a wild gesture, he seizes her, and crushes her in his arms. She resists, then sighs softly and relaxes in his embrace*)

ALLAN: Twelve years! And you spurned me for another man. But I have found you, at last. Tell me, Anna, have you forgotten me?

ANNA: Never, for one instant. (*She sighs contentedly. They stand silent in a gripping embrace*)

ALLAN: Anna, are you happy with him?

ANNA: You are successful, are you not, Allan?

ALLAN: Successful? Ye-es—

ANNA: Then I am content.

ALLAN: I hated you for years. I hate you this minute, when I think of the anguish you caused me. My loss of faith in women. The crushing blow to my pride—

ANNA: Your pride?

ALLAN: But underlying that hatred is a love that cries out in misery when it realizes what it has lost. I hated all women—

ANNA: But you married?

ALLAN: Expediency. The same old conventional story. Daughter of the employer, interested in the penniless youth, who sees chance for advancement by marrying into rich employer's family.

ANNA: That's a cynical way to put it.

ALLAN: Truth. Yet once I said there is no truth. God, how I suffered!

ANNA: Allan, listen. You have deposed me for twelve years. Let me square myself with you. I was not the mercenary wretch you believed me when I sent you away. My heart ever since has been a dead thing squeezed dry of everything but anguish.

ALLAN: Yet, you sent me away—

ANNA: For your own good. You could not have made a success; you could never have even made good in a small way. I should have been nothing but a hindrance to you, in every way—my color and my poverty and my responsibilities. You could only succeed on the other side of the racial wall—I could not go there with you.

ALLAN: (*Seizing her by the arm*) Look at me. (*He strikes a match. The flare shows her face drooping, averted*) Who put that fool notion in your head? I've often wondered. In one hour you swore to me that you would stand by me until death, and in the next hour you sent my packing, with some half baked reason, plus the cruelest thrust a woman can give a man.

ANNA: No one.

ALLAN: The truth, Anna. I believed that twelve years ago. I've had a chance to think it over. The truth. Who was it?

ANNA: (*Faltering*) Your—Aunt—Blanche—

ALLAN: Hm-m.

ANNA: She wrote me a letter.

ALLAN: And you let her impudent, infernal meddling wreck our lives?

ANNA: She was right. Your career has proved she was right.

ALLAN: Career? Career? But at what a sacrifice of manhood. Tell me about yourself.

ANNA: The short and simple annals of the poor. John went to war. His business failed. We have been very unfortunate. Granny's death came a year or two later. Evan lingered a bit longer. He was a great care. I have had to work hard. John was ill for a long while after he returned from overseas at the same time that Granny was. There was a baby, but it died when it was three months old. The war wrecked us. John has been in the veteran's hospital, but it has been a long, hard pull. Were you in the war?

ALLAN: Exempt. Wife and three children, and building roads and bridges. I have made much money otherwise.

ANNA: So I heard. My sacrifice was not in vain. You are a success.

ALLAN: If money and the plaudits of the world is success.

ANNA: The white world. You are one of the supreme Nordics.

ALLAN: Yes, with a constant, nagging fear in my soul that my house of cards will tumble at any moment. I did not know that you lived in this city. If I had, I should probably not have accepted the invitation of the Rotary Club to address them.

ANNA: We don't live here now; we did before the way. But we are back in the old home town—for economy's sake. I came here today to look after some business of John's.

ALLAN: Ah! I do not wish to see anyone who knew me in the old days. The haunting dread of my life is that someone will arise one day, point a finger at me and yell, "Nigger!" And I should slink away like a spectre that is shot with a silver bullet. There would not be courage enough left in me to deny, or to brazen it out. My wife tells me of her childhood, but my lips are closed on my early days. She thinks it is because there were painful scenes in my early boyhood that I do not wish to recall. There are. They are the sweet days of my youth with the boys and girls of my own people. I do not go back to class reunions at the university. Someone might begin to piece together the name of Allan Cordell, the penniless Negro student, and Franklin Cordell, the successful engineer. I am not superstitious, yet the advent of each child filled me with dread. I dared not face a possible flare-back. I knew it was all silly poppycock—the things the propagandists tell us of atavism—but who knew what my fears and dread might have induced?

ANNA: Poor boy!

ALLAN: Poverty of the direst sort!

(*Silence. The darkness has been lighted fitfully by flashes of light from boats passing on the river. A group of boys and girls go by singing and thrumming ukuleles*)

ALLAN: Anna. The past twelve years have been nothing but a horrible dream. Our love is only reality. Let us forget it all. Come away with me. Let us start life over somewhere where we can forget all this past nightmare—just you and I—

ANNA: Don't. Hush! You must not.

ALLAN: We've paid out debt to the world, to our families, to convention. We owe it to ourselves to live—to live. Do you know what that means, Anna? To love each other, and to be to each other what God intended.

ANNA: You don't realize what you are saying.

ALLAN: Yes, I do. I do realize it. The hunger of my empty heart would tell me if I did not. I've found you, and I know now what life will mean to me should I lose you again. You can't send me away again.

ANNA: You are mad—

ALLAN: Yes, mad for love of you. Anna, you think I am impracticable, but I am not. I am rich. We can go away—to South America, to Europe, anywhere, just to be with you.

ANNA: You have forgotten—

ALLAN: My wife? She will weep a bit and then divorce me and marry again, and forget me. It was a tepid sort of love between us, easily forgotten.

ANNA: That is not all.

ALLAN: Your husband? The government will take care of him, and then—you never loved him, did you, Anna? Tell me, you never really loved him? Your silence is all the answer I want. Anna, my God, you will not wreck our happiness again, will you? I want you; you want me—Anna—Anna (*His voice breaks in sobs*)

ALLAN: Beloved!

ANNA: Beloved!

(*A searchlight from a passing steamer finds them, and its beam of light rests on them. They are seated on the park bench, their forms clasped in a close embrace*)

CURTAIN

SCENE TWO: *The next morning. The same scene as in Scene One. A pitiless sunlight makes bare mockery all the romance of the night before.*

Harry and Jimmy enter from the left, and stroll up the walk. They are chatting and smoking. Just in front of the bench they pause, and face the river.

HARRY: Looks like the river front at home, doesn't it, Jim?

JIMMY: Enough to make me homesick.

HARRY: Homesick for the Main Street burg! The taste of some people.

JIMMY: Home is home.

HARRY: Yes, and a pig sty is a pig sty, and a barn is a barn. I imagine Farmer Brown would yearn for the haystack when he was in the bright lights of the big city.

JIMMY: Call me Rube. Doesn't hurt me. I'm homesick. Haven't seen the old place since before the war, when we went out together filled with zeal, patriotism, homesickness and an ineffable urge for the great adventure.

HARRY: And came back filled with bitterness, gloom, trench feet and no job. What became of Emma!

JIMMY: Threw me down. I said some bitter things when Anna turned down Allan Cordell for John Chamberlain, and Emma never forgave me. I thought she'd marry you.

HARRY: So did I. She thought otherwise. Wouldn't trust any man, and so on to the n'th degree of damfoolishness. So, it's the little old bachelor flat for mine, and a pipe and peace, and nary a skirt to disturb my bank roll.

JIMMY: So she didn't marry him, after all? (*Musingly to himself*)

HARRY: Cordell made good on the other side.

JIMMY: Hm-m. Wonder how he likes it? I had sometime connecting the two—but I pieced it all together, and doped out the great Cordell. Our old-time chum. Well, joy be with him.

HARRY: Yes. Pale face frau, 'n' everything. He's welcome to 'em. Never like 'em too pale. All wishy-washy. Brown-a-tone suits me.

JIMMY: Success is all right. I'm glad he made good. But I wonder what price he pays for it? Dread of discovery. Shifting glance when a man looks at him too hard. Fear lest his wife discover his past. Skirting around the edges of places, lest he run into an old friend. There must be silences when his wife speaks of his past.

HARRY: If he doesn't love her, should think he'd relish some silences.

JIMMY: You can't turn your back on your own people without pulling down your flag of integrity.

HARRY: Flag of integrity is a mouthful of fine words, but it doesn't pay the little old landlord. And I've noticed that this integrity business doesn't command one half the respect that a good income tax receipt does.

JIMMY: Speaking of angels—

(*Allan comes up the path from the right. Pauses awkwardly when he sees the two men in conversation. There are signs of recognition on the part of all three men, but half deprecatory nod from Allan meets no response from Jimmy or Harry. They move on down the path, right, their heads together, as if Allan did not exist*)

ALLAN: (*Looking after them*) Now how am I to interpret that? As a cut direct? As a tribute to my superior position? As a noticed served that they will not betray me? Or as a disgusted desire not to acknowledge my existence? It's not the first time've been slapped in the face this way. I've always wanted to do the cutting thing myself, but I've never been allowed the chance. They always see me and beat me to it.

(*Enter Aunt Blanche breathlessly. She is a large domineering woman, fair of skin, white of hair, expensively gowned, flashing jewels*)

AUNT BLANCHE: As soon as I heard you were coming here to speak, I drove over. I'm glad you got my telegram to meet me here. I just wanted to congratulate you. It's been years since we've seen each other. But I've taken the greatest pride in your career.

ALLAN: (*Crossly*) Why couldn't you come to my hotel to see me?

AUNT BLANCHE: Because, my dear, there are too many of the employees who know who I am. One cannot straighten the hair of half the colored girls in a county and not be known everywhere. They might wonder at your receiving a colored woman. One can't be too careful.

ALLAN: Oh careful!

AUNT BLANCHE: Yes, careful. A white man might have business calls or even social calls from colored people, and nothing would be thought of it, but a man who antecedents are not mentioned must watch every step, and shun anyone who might be connected with the other race. He is under suspicion, and there are watchful eyes. Don't tear down in one hour what it has taken twelve years to build.

ALLAN: Rot! I must meet my relatives in the park like a servant girl.

AUNT BLANCHE: I am too proud of your success to do the least thing to militate against it.

ALLAN: Success! That's all you think of. You sacrificed my manhood on the altar of your ideal of success.

AUNT BLANCHE: I? Sacrificed you?

ALLAN: Yes, you sacrificed me. You wrote the only girl I ever loved a damnably plausible letter, and drove her into poverty and obscurity and misery with a man she didn't love, and sent me into the world a misanthrope and a coward.

AUNT BLANCHE: Puppy love! Sophomoric maunderings! What more do you want? There's hardly a man in the country more respected in his profession than you. You married a beautiful woman of family and wealth. You have everything the most exacting man could want.

ALLAN: All built up on a tissue of lies. I am sick of lies. I want the woman I love. And I'm going to have her.

AUNT BLANCHE: May I ask how?

ALLAN: For once in my life I'm going to have what I want. I shall take her and fly to some country where a man can practice my profession without living a lie.

AUNT BLANCHE: More heroics. And your wife and children? Your position? Your property? Your place in the professional world? Your prospects? You are young. There are many years of honor yet for you. You are no schoolboy to throw aside material benefits for a fancied romance. Must all your struggles and sacrifices go for nothing now? Why, if you must love your face, glean what satisfaction you can out of the thought of the huge joke you're playing on the world.

ALLAN: (*Wavering*) But I love her, Aunt Blanche, I love her.

AUNT BLANCHE: Nobody objects to that. If she is as poor as you say she is, and loves you as much as you think she does, she might not object to your loving her.

ALLAN: Aunt Blanche! You are damnable!

AUNT BLANCHE: I think you'll find me damnably practical. Well, Good Luck to you. (*Exits*)

(*Allan nods indifferently. Lights a cigarette nervously. Paces up and down. Lights another. Tamps it out. Beats hands nervously together as he walks up and down. Enter Anna from left. She coughs slightly. In the daylight, her face shows even more drawn and haggard than at night*)

ANNA: I thought I should find you here. I felt that you, too, would want to see the sunlight on the rivers; feel the caress of spring on your check—with me.

ALLAN: (*Huskily*) Anna, all the world seems fairer since I have found you again.

ANNA: You never really lost me, dear. Just a pause, that's all.

ALLAN: A dreary interim, bounded by two golden epochs. (*They sit silent with clasped hands*)

ALLAN: And now, dear, we must talk of our feature.

ANNA: There is no future, Allan. A beautiful golden present. No more.

ALLAN: We love each other.

ANNA: Superfluous verbiage.

ALLAN: And there must be a future. I MUST have you; MUST posses you. I've starved for your warm beauty; for the tropical beauty and passion of your enduring love. When I was denied what I wanted as a boy, I whimpered and fled with bowed head; but I am a man now. I've been taking what I wanted with a ruthless hand. I want you, Darling, I must have you.

ANNA: Wait, dear.

ALLAN: I know what you will say—what you tried to say last night. You will tell me of your duty to John Chamberlain. I grant you that—you couldn't desert him.

(*Anna starts, and looks at him searchingly*)

ALLAN: And I have a wife and children, and a position in the world, and responsibilities and a still more brilliant future. I know you would remind me of that.

ANNA: I had not mentioned those things—had not thought of them since last night you rejected them as having no further place in your life. Today, I remembered only that I had found you. Past and future alike merged into a mist of unreality. I was dazed with the happiness of the present.

ALLAN: (*Uneasily*) Yes, but one of us must think.

ANNA: You had thought it all out last night. I have let it rest there, until I can get my confused impressions in order.

ALLAN: (*Visibly embarrased*) Anna, last night I was mad from the touch of your hands. I proposed impraticable things. Can we not love each other? What have we to do with conventions, man-made laws and all that?

ANNA: But you have just said that what you proposed last night is impracticable; that you cannot give up your famil, your place in the world; that it is not right for me to leave John?

ALLAN: I know I did. But Anna, don't you understand? I want your love; I want You.

ANNA: (*Rising slowly*) Yes—I think I do understand.

(*She leans on the bench, her hands gripping its back, until her knuckles are white. They face each other silently. Then Anna speaks through clenched teeth*)

ANNA: Yes—I understand. You are offering me the position of your mistress. You are giving me the wonderful opportunity of having a secret liaison with you. You love me, but you love your position in the world of white men more. I don't blame you for that. The measure of the world's approbation does not go to the men who have stood by their ideals, but to those who have made a successful compromise with Necessity. But that you should come to me—No, don't interrupt. To me! Who had the courage to send you into another world! But you're running true to form. Your white blood and your white training and your imbibing of the Nordic ideals are showing up through your thin veil of decency. You would keep your white wife, and all that means, for respectability's sake—but you would have a romance, a liaison with the brown woman whom you love, after dark. No Negro could stoop so low as to take on such degraded ideals of so-called racial purity. And this is the moral deterioration to which you have brought your whole race. White Man! Go on back to your white gods! Lowest and vilest of scum. White Man! Go Back!

(*Allan stands with bowed head, lashed under the fury of her scorn. Anna stands still, trembling, then sinks sobbing, with her head on the back of the bench. Allan stands shamefacedly, looking at her. He makes a gesture as it to touch her, shakes his head. The three men of the night before, come down the path, right, and looking up, hail him. Allan straightens his shoulders, and steps toward the river path*)

FIRST VOICE: I see you're enjoying the morning by our river?

SECOND VOICE: I hope you haven't been here all night. We left you here, and here we find you.

THIRD VOICE: That seems to be a woman in distress. Do you know anything about her trouble?

FIRST VOICE: Some poor colored woman she seems to be. Those people are so emotional aren't they?

ALLAN: (*Drawling*) Yes, it seems to be a racial characteristic. I would have spoken to her to see if I could help her, but she seemed to want to be alone.

SECOND VOICE: Well, this bracing air had given me an appetite! Shall we have luncheon together at the hotel?

(*Exeunt down the river path*)

CURTAIN

Act III

A few days later. Anna's garden. Same as in Act I, except that the gate has sagged more. It is spring. Blossoms struggle through the ground. The afternoon sun sends long shadows athwart the garden. Voices are heard singing in the distance, and young people pass and re-pass. Emma and Jimmy detach themselves from a group, as in Act I, and enter the garden.

JIMMY: But, Emma, twelve years of loneliness is a long and bitter punishment to inflict for a fancied wrong.

EMMA: Why fancied? It is a fancied wrong when a woman heards a man blaspheme all women? Look at me. I'm an old maid because you taught me to distrust all men.

JIMMY: Look at me. I'm an old bachelor because you taught me to look down upon all women but you.

EMMA: Well, that's your hard luck. I'm sure it didn't make any difference to me whether you married or not.

JIMMY: But it made a difference to me, Emma. How could I put another woman in my heart after having known you? She would have rattled around like a dried up pea in a shell—

EMMA: You're accurately describing your heart. I congratulate you.

JIMMY: Oh, Emma, don't be so hard. You know what I mean. I see all these wasted years—

EMMA: Wasted words.

JIMMY: Emma, you quarrelled with me because—

EMMA: you flatter yourself. I did not quarrel with you.

JIMMY: You threw me over because—

EMMA: I did not throw you over. You walked off in a huff.

JIMMY: And why did I walk off? You sent me away—

EMMA: Well, that's an old story—

JIMMY: Emma, when I was wallowing in the mud and filth near the famous poppies of poetry, I had the chance to think through a lot of things that I've been waiting a chance to tell you. I'm lucky that I ran across you today, after all these years. Values are different. You were always the biggest thing in my life. And you stayed the biggest thing, while a lot of petty foolishness dropped away. It was a long wasted period that you let me in for, because you were taking on another's quarrels—

EMMA: I take on no one's quarrels. I simply had no room in my life for any man.

JIMMY: Maybe not. But how about love and a home and little ones, and all the real things—

EMMA: Sob stuffs!

JIMMY: Life is a grab bag, Emma, and you've pulled a cheap tin whistle out of it. You're blowing on it now, trying to kid yourself into thinking it's a golden trumpet.

(*The door of the cottage opens and John Chamberlain comes wearily down the steps. He leans heavily on a cane. His hair is gray and his face seamed with pain. Emma runs to him with outstretched hands. He settles himself stiffly and awkwardly on the garden seat and sighs profoundly*)

JIMMY: (*With constraint*) How's things, old man?

JOHN: About the same. But I'll be all right in a few months, and then I can go about gathering up the loose ends of life. I'll come back, never fear. Only, it has been hard on Anna.

EMMA: She has been wonderful; hasn't she, John?

JOHN: (*Slowly*) She has. Devoted to Granny. Fine to Evan. And splendid to me. The more reverses came, the better she stuck. One woman in ten thousand. But life has played a cruel joke on us both, Emma.

(*Jimmy has wandered down the garden, left, and leans on the fence, as if not interested in the conversation. He lights a cigarette, as if not hearing, but he listens keenly behind the smoke screen*)

EMMA: Why call it a joke, John?

JOHN: Wasn't it a joke on me when I married Anna to give her ease and comfort, though I knew she didn't love me—hoping the care and luxuries I lavished on her would win her love—and then went to war and lost it all? And then I came back broken, and she had to work harder than ever? We even had to come back to her poor little home, for I had no shelter to offer her. Wasn't it a joke on me when she married me, though she loved Cordell, to give ease and comfort to Granny and Evan, and they both died, and all her sacrifice for them was in vain?

EMMA: (*Slowly*) Are you sure she didn't love you?

JOHN: Sure? (*He laught bitterly*) What woman can deceive the man who loves her? She gave her body to me, but her soul? It was an impregnable fortress, and my pitiful assaults upon it threw me back upon myself. She has given me devotion and loyalty to the highest degree but that precious ruby of her inner heart, she keeps secret, hidden, and I can only guess it is there. I have never really known her, much less possessed her.

EMMA: Poor Jonh! Poor boy!

(*Jimmy stirs uneasily, and looks out of the corner of his eyes at the two*)

JOHN: I don't know why I am whining to you. I suppose physical weakness makes a man forget he is a man at times.

EMMA: Poor John. Poor Anna. Where is she? I wanted to talk to her.

JOHN: She went to my old home where the fragments of my business were left—to look after some matters for me. If all goes as I hope, I shall be on the way to a rehabilitation of our fortunes. I could not go myself—

EMMA: Anna is very efficient—

JOHN: Yes, too much so. It has laid burdens on her that no woman should carry. Efficiency in a woman is admirable, but it makes her too impersonal. It sets her in a class apart from the female herd—she becomes a celibate, married though she be.

(*Jimmy snorts*)

EMMA: My heart bleeds for you and Anna. In a way you two are responsible for—responsible for—

(*Jimmy's tense attitude and stillness attract Emma's attention, and she falters, while her eyes cling to his beseechingly*)

JOHN: Yes, for what?

EMMA: (*Desperately*) Jimmy and I parted from each other because we quarrelled over Anna's marrying you instead of Allan Cordell. I was disappointed, frankly, but I trusted Anna to do the honorable thing. But Jimmy indulged in some cheap cynicism—and well—we parted, that's all.

JIMMY: (*Coming forward*) No, it isn't all—I was wrong. Emma, as I have told you before. Anna knew what she was doing, and if she didn't—

EMMA: It wasn't anyone's business.

JOHN: Life isn't so long that we can take time out for silly quarrels. Twelve years is quite a slice out of happiness, little as there is to go around.

JIMMY: That's what I've been trying to tell Emma.

EMMA: Allan Cordell isn't worth anyone of us thinking about.

JOHN: He's a very successful man. One of the big men in the country. He made fortune during the war that broke me. If he hadn't gone white, though, he'd probably have been by my side and been gassed with some of the same bombs that his father-in-law's factory produced.

(*Anna comes slowly down the street, and stops outside the gate. She is dressed for traveling, and carries a handbag. When she sees the group in the garden, she pauses, straightens her shoulders, and enters with a light, quick step*)

ANNA: Emma! Jimmy! The old friends. It's good to see you again. (*She stoops and kisses John's cheek lightly*) I have good news for you, dear.

(*John clasps her hands and rises painfully. His eyes search her face hungrily*)

JOHN: To see you come back is good news enough for the present.

ANNA: (*Whispering*) Didn't you expect me back, when I had gone to look after your affairs?

JOHN: I don't know. I should have, I suppose. But somehow, you always seem to be going out of my life, and I should not be surprised some day to find you gone. What's the news?

ANNA: The best in the world. Mercer will finance the business. We can start anew and build up again. He predicts that with good management, we can be back to our old status in less than five years.

JOHN: Wonderful woman!

ANNA: Not wonderful, not wonderful, John. Weak, foolish. (*She grips him by the shoulders*) Look at me. I'm not going to make any confession to you. When I tell you that I saw Allan Cordell and talked to him—you will know.

JOHN: You love him still?

ANNA: Not now.

JOHN: Thank God! I prayed, oh, how I prayed, that some day you'd see this man, this sleek, well-fed, smug hypocrite of a near-white man, with his veneer of superiority, and his soul clogged in the fat of compromise and cowardice, and seeing him, the years would drop from your life, and the scales from your eyes, and you would know that you could never take pride in him, and you would be proud of your clean-washed soul again—

ANNA: And proud of you, John. You because you have been clean, and honest, and when you have lost, you have lost like a good sport. Because you have never compromised—even though you lost the material things of the world. Yes, I'm proud of you, John—and that means life to me.

(*During this conversation, Emma and Jimmy have drifted toward the lower end of the garden, not hearing the other two. Their hands have gradually found each other*)

(*A long whistle heard from the street. Harry Blake comes briskly to the gate, leans on the top of the gate, from without, and surveys the two couples within*)

HARRY: Some love-nest; all billing and cooing, and all the rest of it.

JIMMY: Congratulate me, old man.

HARRY: So I do, thought I'd rather you'd be congratulating me. But Emma's taller than I am; she'd probably throw things at me anyway. So you're going to leave this dump, Anna, and you and John going back to God's country, and the little old business again, eh? Time, says I.

ANNA: (*Smiling at him and turning to John*) Yes, we'll leave it all here, youthful romance, ashes of the past, the restless spirit of poor, tortured Evan, the lonely soul of Granny, the poor baby who smiled at us for a brief time, your illness, our poverty, my blindness, all-all—and we'll start life anew. A new life, with no rose-colored cobwebs of the past to distort it—and who knows what the future may have in store for us?

(*As John takes her in his arms, Jimmy does the same to Emma, and Harry Blake, in the mock attitude of a preachers, bestows a blessing on the two couples*)

CURTAIN

LOVE'S DISGUISE

Synopsis

Agnes has a dual face, one side being beautiful, the other side paralyzed and disfigured. Wherever she goes to secure work, her services are at once refused because of her frightful appearance. At last she secures work in a restaurant, opening oysters and doing mean chores. Her employer, seeing an opportunity to hire a servant for the price of a marriage fee, offers to marry her, telling her that such a fright as she will never have another offer. When she refuses him he turns her out.

One day Agnes faints on the street, and is taken to a charity hospital. Later, when she is convalescent and is one day sitting with the madonna-like side of her face toward the window, Dr. Weaver, passing by, is attracted by her beauty. Coming in the room to speak with the nurse, he is startled to see the disfigured side of the profile. Many times later he thinks with interest of the strange face. One day he asks Agnes if she would like to be an attendant to his blind mother. She eagerly consents. After giving her case much study, Dr. Weaver asks her to allow him to experiment. She consents; and after an operation and patient effort, he restores her face to a normal condition. Agnes rewards him by marrying him.

CHARACTERS

AGNES, *beautiful and ugly*
ANDY LAYFIELD
DR. WEAVER
MRS. WEAVER, *his mother*
    Proprietor store
    Kitchen employees
    Nurse
    Mother
    Little boy

Scenario

1——Bedroom——
    Agnes looks at herself in the mirror, first at the beautiful side of her face, then at the ugly side—dons hat—exit—

2——Exterior mansion——

Agnes approaches—ascends steps—rings—maid admits her—

3——Living room——

Mother reads to the little boy—maid admits Agnes—Agnes explains—

Leader——"You Advertised For a Nurse Girl."

——Back to scene——

Little boy cries at the sight of Agnes—hangs on to mother in fright—mother declines services of Agnes—rings—exit Agnes with maid—

4——Interior store——

Enter Agnes—approaches proprietor—explains—

Leader——"You Advertised For a Clerk."

——Back to scene——

Proprietor regards her as curiousity—refuses her services—exit Agnes—

Leader——At Last——

5——Interior restaurant——

Enter Agnes—approaches proprietor—offers her service—Layfield finally accepts her—motions her to follow him—they exeunt into—

6——Kitchen——

Layfield puts her to work opening oysters and doing mena chores—he smiles at her coarsely—

Leader——One Night——

7——Kitchen as 6——

Agnes drudges—Layfield approaches—smiles—tries to embrace her—

Leader——"Suppose We Get Married. You Can Work Here Just the Same."

——Back to scene——

He proceeds to embrace her—she struggles to be free—he becomes angry—pushes her out the door—

Leader——One Day——

8——Street——

Agnes walks wearily along street—suddenly faints—people rush to her aid—

9——Room in hospital——

Agnes lies ill—nurse bends over her—

Leader——One Day——

10——Room in hospital——

Agnes, with disfigured side of face turned toward nurse, sits sewing at window—

11——Exterior room in hospital——

Dr. Weaver, passing by, is attracted by the beauty of face at window—

12——Room in hospital——back to 10——

Dr. Weaver enters—talks to nurse—looks at disfigured side of Agnes' face—is startled and interested—slowly exit—

Leader——THAT NIGHT——

13——Living room——

Dr. Weaver talks to blind mother—speaks of Agnes—(vision of beautiful side of face)—(vision of disfigured side of face)—mother is interested —

Leader——THE NEXT DAY——

14——Room in hospital——as 9, 10,12——

Nurse is reading to Agnes—enter Dr. Weaver—approaches Agnes—talks—

Leader——"MY MOTHER, BEING BLIND, NEEDS AN ATTENDANT. WOULD YOU LIKE TO SERVE HER?"

——Back to scene——

Agnes expresses her eagerness—

Leader——LATER——

15——Park——

Agnes guides Mrs. Weaver's steps—

Leader——ONE NIGHT——

16——Living room——

Agnes reads to Mrs. Weaver—enter Dr. Weaver—he sits near Agnes—shows her some medical books—

Leader——"I'VE STUDIED YOUR CASE UNTIRINGLY FOR MONTHS. WILL YOU LET ME PERFORM AN OPERATION ON YOUR FACE?"

——Back to scene——

Agnes hesitates—then consents—

Leader——ONE GLAD DAY——

17——Living room——as 13, 16——

Dr. Weaver removes bandage from Agnes' face, revealing it to be normal—looking into a mirror he hands her, she becomes radiant with joy—when he embraces her, she looks at him with grateful, loving eyes.

Mine Eyes Have Seen

Characters

Dan: the cripple
Chris: the younger brother
Lucy: the sister
Mrs. O'Neill: an Irish neighbor
Jake: a Jewish boy
Julia: Chris' sweetheart
Bill Harvey: a muleteer
Cornelia Lewis: a settlement worker
Time: Now (1918)
Place: A manufacturing city in the northern part of the United
    States.

(Kitchen of a tenement. All details of furnishing emphasize sordidness—laundry tubs, range, table covered with oil cloth, pine chairs. Curtain discloses Dan in a rude imitation of a steamer chair, propped by faded pillows, his feet covered with a patch-work quilt)

(Lucy is bustling about the range preparing a meal. During the conversation she moves from range to table, setting latter and making ready the noon-day meal)

(Dan is about thirty years old; face thin, pinched, bearing traces of suffering. His hair is prematurely grey; nose finely chiselled; eyes wide, as if seeing Beyond. Complexion brown)

(Lucy is slight, frail, brown-skinned, about twenty, with a pathetic face. She walks with a slight limp)

Dan: Isn't it most time for him to come home, Lucy?
Lucy: It's hard to tell, Danny, dear; Chris doesn't come home on
    time anymore. It's half-past twelve, and he ought to be here by the
    clock, but you can't tell anymore—you can't tell.
Dan: Where does he go?
Lucy: I know where he doesn't go, Dan, but where he does, I can't
    say. He's not going to Julia's anymore lately. I'm afraid, Dan, I'm
    afraid!
Dan: Of what, Little Sister?

Lucy: Of everything; oh, Dan, it's too big, too much for me—the world outside, the street—Chris going and coming home nights moody-eyed; I don't understand.

Dan: And so you're afraid? That's been the trouble from the beginning of time—we're afraid because we don't understand.

Lucy: (*coming down front, with a dish cloth in her hand*)
Oh, Dan, wasn't it better in the old days when we were back home—in the little house with the garden, and you and father coming home nights and mother getting supper, and Chris and I studying lessons in the dining-room at the table—we didn't have to eat and live in the kitchen then, and—

Dan: (*grimly*)—And the notices posted on the fence for us to leave town because niggers had no business having such a decent home.

Lucy: (*unheeding the interruption*)—And Chris and I reading the wonderful books and laying our plans—

Dan: To see them go up in the smoke of our burned home.

Lucy: (*continuing, her back to Dan, her eyes lifted, as if seeing a vision of retrospect*)—And everyone petting me because I had hurt my foot when I was little, and father—

Dan: Shot down like a dog for daring to defend his home—

Lucy: Calling me "Little Brown Princess," and telling mother—

Dan: Dead of pneumonia and heartbreak in this bleak climate.

Lucy: That when you—

Dan: Maimed for life in a factory of hell! Useless—useless—broken on the wheel.

(*His voice breaks in a dry sob*)

Lucy: (*Coming out of her trance, she throws aside the dish-cloth, and running to Dan, lays her cheek against his and strokes his hair*)
Poor Danny, poor Danny, forgive me, I'm selfish.

Dan: Not selfish, Little Sister, merely natural.

(*Enter roughly and unceremoniously Chris. He glances at the two with their arms about each other, shrugs his shoulders, hangs up his rough cap and mackinaw on a nail, then seats himself at the table, his shoulders hunched up; his face dropping on his hand. Lucy approaches him timidly*)

Lucy: Tired, Chris?

Chris: No.

Lucy: Ready for dinner?

Chris: If it's ready for me.

Lucy: (*busies herself bringing dishes to the table*)

You're late today.

CHRIS: I have bad news. My number was posted today.

LUCY: Number? Posted?

(*Pauses with a plate in her hand*)

CHRIS: I'm drafted.

LUCY: (*Drops plate with a crash. Dan leans forward tensely, his hands grasping the arms of his chair*)

Oh, it can't be! They won't take you from us! And shoot you down, too? What will Dan do?

DAN: Never mind about me, Sister. And you're drafted, boy?

CHRIS: Yes—yes—but—(*He rises and strikes the table heavily with his hand*)

I'm not going.

DAN: Your duty—

CHRIS: Is here with you. I owe none elsewhere, I'll pay none.

LUCY: Chris! Treason! I'm afraid!

CHRIS: Yes, of course, you're afraid, Little Sister, why shouldn't you be? Haven't you had your soul shrivelled with fear since we were driven like dogs from our home? And for what? Because we were living like Christians. Must I go and fight for the nation that let my father's murder go unpunished? That killed my mother—that took away my chances for making a man out of myself? Look at us—you—Dan, a shell of a man—

DAN: Useless—useless—

LUCY: Hush, Chris!

CHRIS: And me, with a fragment of an education, and no chance—only half a man. And you, poor Little Sister, there's no chance for you; what is there in life for you? No, if others want to fight, let them. I'll claim exemption.

DAN: On what grounds?

CHRIS: You—and Sister. I am all you have; I support you.

DAN: (*half rising in his chair*)

Hush! Have I come to this, that I should be the excuse, the woman's skirts for a slacker to hide behind?

CHRIS: (*clenching his fists*)

You call me that? You, whom I'd lay down my life for? I'm no slacker when I hear the real call of duty. Shall I desert the cause that needs me—you—Sister—home? For a fancied glory? Am I to take up the cause of a lot of kings and politicians who play with men's souls, as if they are cards—dealing them out, a hand here, in the Somme—a hand there, in Palestine—a hand there, in the Alps—a hand there, in Russia—and because the cards don't match well, call it a misdeal, gather them up, throw them in the discard, and call for a new deal of a million human, suffering souls? And I must be the Deuce of Spades?

(*During the speech, the door opens slowly and Jake lounges in. He is a slight, pale youth, Hebraic, thin-lipped, eager-eyed. His hands are in his pockets, his narrow shoulders drawn forward. At the end of Chris' speech he applauds softly*)

JAKE: Bravo! You've learned the patter well. Talk like the fellows at the Socialist meetings.

DAN and LUCY: Socialist meetings!

CHRIS: (*defiantly*)
Well?

DAN: Oh, nothing; it explains. All right, go on—anymore?

JAKE: Guess he's said all he's got breath for. I'll go; it's too muggy in here. What's the row?

CHRIS: I'm drafted.

JAKE: Get exempt. Easy—if you don't want to go. As for me—
(*Door opens, and Mrs. O'Neill bustles in. She is in deep mourning, plump, Irish, shrewd-looking, bright-eyed*)

MRS. O'NEILL: Lucy, they do be sayin' as how down by the chain stores they be a raid on the potatoes, an' ef ye'er wantin' some, ye'd better be after gittin' into yer things an' comin' wid me. I kin kape the crowd off yer game foot—an' what's the matter wid youse all?

LUCY: Oh, Mrs. O'Neill, Chris has got to go to war.

MRS. O'NEILL: An' ef he has, what of it? Ye'll starve, that's all.

DAN: Starve? Never! He'll go, we'll live.

(*Lucy wrings her hands impotently. Mrs. O'Neill drops a protecting arm about the girl's shoulder*)

MRS. O'NEILL: An' it's hard it seems to yer? But they took me man from me year before last, an' he wint afore I came over here, an' it's a widder I am wid me five kiddies, an' I've niver a word to say but—

CHRIS: He went to fight for his own. What do they do for my people? They don't want us, except in extremity. They treat us like—like—like—

JAKE: Like Jews in Russia, eh?

(He slouches forward, then his frame straightens itself electrically)

Like Jews in Russia, eh? Denied the right of honor in men, eh? Or the right of virtue in women, eh? There isn't a wrong you can name that your race has endured that mine has not suffered, too. But there's a future, Chris—a big one. We younger ones must be in that future—ready for it, ready for it—

(His voice trails off, and he sinks despondently into a chair)

Chris: Future? Where? Not in this country? Where?

(The door opens and Julia rushes in impulsively. She is small, slightly built, eager-eyed, light-brown skin, wealth of black hair; full of sudden shyness)

Julia: Oh, Chris, someone has just told me—I was passing by—one of the girls said your number was called. Oh, Chris, will you have to go?

(She puts her arms up to Chris' neck; he removes them gently, and makes a slight gesture toward Dan's chair)

Julia: Oh, I forgot. Dan, excuse me. Lucy, it's terrible, isn't it?

Chris: I'm not going, Julia.

Mrs. O'Neill: Not going!

Dan: Our men have always gone, Chris. They went in 1776.

Chris: Yes, as slaves. Promised a freedom they never got.

Dan: No, gladly, and saved the day, too, many a time. Ours was the first blood shed on the altar of National liberty. We went in 1812, on land and sea. Our men were through the struggles of 1861—

Chris: When the Nation was afraid not to call them. Didn't want 'em at first.

Dan: Never mind; they helped work out their own salvation. And they were there in 1898—

Chris: Only to have their valor disputed.

Dan: And they were at Carrizal, my boy, and now—

Mrs. O'Neill: An' sure, wid a record like that—ah, 'tis me ould man who said at first 'twasn't his quarrel. His Oireland bled an' the work of thim divils to try to make him a traitor nearly broke his heart—but he said he'd go to do his bit—an' here I am.

(There is a sound of noise and bustle without, and with a loud laugh, Bill Harvey enters. He is big, muscular, rough, his voice thunderous. He emits cries of joy at seeing the group, shakes hands and claps Chris and Dan on their backs)

Dan: And so you weren't torpedoed?

HARVEY: No, I'm here for a while—to get more mules and carry them to the front to kick their bit.

MRS. O'NEILL: You've been—over there?

HARVEY: Yes, over the top, too. Mules, rough-necks, wires, mud, dead bodies, stench, terror!

JULIA: (*horror-stricken*)
Ah—Chris!

CHRIS: Never, mind, not for mine.

HARVEY: It's a great life—not. But I'm off again, first chance.

MRS. O'NEILL: They're brutes, eh?

HARVEY: Don't remind me.

MRS. O'NEILL: (*whispering*)
They maimed my man, before he died.

JULIA: (*clinging to Chris*)
Not you, oh, not you!

HARVEY: They crucified children.

DAN: Little children? They crucified little children.

CHRIS: Well, what's that to us? They're little white children. But here our fellow countrymen throw our little black babies in the flames— as did the worshippers of Moloch, only they haven't the excuse of a religious rite.

JAKE: (*slouches out of his chair, in which he has been sitting brooding*)
Say, don't you get tired sitting around grieving because you're colored? I'd be ashamed to be—

DAN: Stop! Who's ashamed of his race? Ours the glorious inheritance; ours the price of achievement. Ashamed! I'm proud. And you, too, Chris, smouldering in youthful wrath, you, too, are proud to be numbered with the darker ones, soon to come into their inheritance.

MRS. O'NEILL: Aye, but you've got to fight to keep yer inheritance. Ye can't lay down when someone else has done the work, and expect it to go on. Ye've got to fight.

JAKE: If you're proud, show it. All of your people—well, look at us! Is there a greater race than ours? Have any people had more horrible persecutions—and yet—we're loyal always to the country where we live and serve.

MRS. O'NEILL: And us! Look at us!

DAN: (*half tears himself from the chair, the upper part of his body writhing, while the lower part is inert, dead*)

Oh, God! If I were but whole and strong! If I could only prove to a doubting world of what stuff my people are made!

JULIA: But why, Dan, it isn't our quarrel? What have we to do with their affairs? These white people, they hate us. Only today I was sneered at when I went to help with some of their relief work. Why should you, my Chris, go to help those who hate you?

(*Chris clasps her in his arms, and they stand, defying the others*)

HARVEY: If you could have seen the babies and girls—and old women—if you could have—

(*Covers his eyes with his hand*)

CHRIS: Well, it's good for things to be evened up somewhere.

DAN: Hush, Chris! It is not for us to visit retribution. Nor to wish hatred on others. Let us rather remember the good that has come to us. Love of humanity is above the small considerations of time or place or race or sect. Can't you be big enough to feel pity for the little crucified French children—for the ravished Polish girls, even as their mothers must have felt sorrow, if they had known, for our burned and maimed little ones? Oh, Mothers of Europe, we be of one blood, you and I!

(*There is a tense silence. Julia turns from Chris, and drops her hand. He moves slowly to the window and looks out. The door opens quietly, and Cornelia Lewis comes in. She stands still a moment, as if sensing a difficult situation*)

CORNELIA: I've heard about it, Chris, your country calls you.

(*Chris turns from the window and waves hopeless hands at Dan and Lucy*)

Yes, I understand; they do need you, don't they?

DAN: (*fiercely*)

No!

LUCY: Yes, we do, Chris, we do need you, but your country needs you more. And, above that, your race is calling you to carry on its good name, and with that, the voice of humanity is calling to us all—we can manage without you, Chris.

CHRIS: You? Poor little crippled Sister. Poor Dan—

DAN: Don't pity me, pity your poor, weak self.

CHRIS: (*clenching his fist*)

Brother, you've called me two names today that no man ought to have to take—a slacker and a weakling!

DAN: True. Aren't you both?

(*Leans back and looks at Chris speculatively*)

CHRIS: (*Makes an angry lunge towards the chair, then flings his hands above his head in an impatient gesture*)

Oh, God!

(*Turns back to the window*)

JULIA: Chris, it's wicked for them to taunt you so—but Chris—it is our country—our race—

(*Outside the strains of music from a passing band are heard. The music comes faintly, gradually growing louder and louder until it reaches a crescendo. The tune is "The Battle Hymn of the Republic," played in stirring march time*)

DAN: (*singing softly*)

"Mine eyes have seen the glory of the coming of the Lord!"

CHRIS: (*turns from the window and straightens his shoulders*)

And Mine!

CORNELIA: "As he died to make men holy, let us die to make them free!"

MRS. O'NEILL: An' ye'll make the sacrifice, me boy, an' ye'll be the happier.

JAKE: Sacrifice! No sacrifice for him, it's those who stay behind. Ah, if they would only call me, and call me soon!

LUCY: We'll get on, never fear. I'm proud! Proud!

(*Her voice breaks a little, but her head is thrown back*)

(*As the music draws nearer, the group breaks up, and the whole roomful rushes to the window and looks out. Chris remains in the center of the floor, rigidly at attention, a rapt look on his face. Dan strains at his chair, as if he would rise, then sinks back, his hand feebly beating time to the music, which swells to a martial crash*)

CURTAIN

PROSE

ALICE

A Story of Vengeance

Yes, Eleanor, I have grown grayer. I am younger than you, you know, but then, what have you to age you? A kind husband, lovely children, while I—I am nothing but a lonely woman. Time goes slowly, slowly for me now.

Why did I never marry? Move that screen a little to one side, please; my eyes can scarcely bear a strong light. Bernard? Oh, that's a long story. I'll tell you if you wish; it might pass an hour.

Do you ever think to go over the old school-days? We thought such foolish things then, didn't we? There wasn't one of us but imagined we would have only to knock ever so faintly on the portals of fame and they would fly wide for our entrance into the magic realms. On Commencement night we whispered merrily among ourselves on the stage to see our favorite planet, Venus, of course, smiling at us through a high, open window, "bidding adieu to her astronomy class," we said.

Then you went away to plunge into the most brilliant whirl of society, and I stayed in the beautiful old city to work.

Bernard was very much *en evidence* those days. He liked you a great deal, because in school-girl parlance you were my "chum." You say,— thanks, no tea, it reminds me that I'm an old maid; you say you know what happiness means—maybe, but I don't think any living soul could experience the joy I felt in those days; it was absolutely painful at times.

Byron and his counterparts are ever dear to the womanly heart, whether young or old. Such a man was he, gloomy, misanthropical, tired of the world, with a few dozen broken love-affairs among his varied experiences. Of course, I worshipped him secretly, what romantic, silly girl of my age, would not, being thrown in such constant contact with him.

One day he folded me tightly in his arms, and said:

"Little girl, I have nothing to give you in exchange for that priceless love of yours but a heart that has already been at another's feet, and a wrecked life, but may I ask for it?"

"It is already yours," I answered. I'll draw the veil over the scene which followed; you know, you've "been there."

Then began some of the happiest hours that ever the jolly old sun beamed upon, or the love-sick moon clothed in her rays of silver. Deceived me? No, no. He admitted that the old love for Blanche was still in his heart, but that he had lost all faith and respect for her, and could nevermore be other than a friend. Well, I was fool enough to be content with such crumbs.

We had five months of happiness. I tamed down beautifully in that time,—even consented to adopt the peerless Blanche as a model. I gave up all my most ambitious plans and cherished schemes, because he disliked women whose names were constantly in the mouth of the public. In fact, I became quiet, sedate, dignified, renounced too some of my best and dearest friends. I lived, breathed, thought, acted only for him; for me there was but one soul in the universe—Bernard's. Still, for all the suffering I've experienced, I'd be willing to go through it all again just to go over those five months. Everyday together, at nights on the lake-shore listening to the soft lap of the waters as the silver sheen of the moon spread over the dainty curled waves; sometimes in a hammock swinging among the trees talking of love and reading poetry. Talk about Heaven! I just think there can't he a better time among the angels.

But there is an end to all things. A violent illness, and his father relenting, sent for the wayward son. I will always believe he loved me, but he was eager to get home to his mother, and anxious to view Blanche in the light of their new relationship. We had a whole series of parting scenes,—tears and vows and kisses exchanged. We clung to each other after the regulation fashion, and swore never to forget, and to write everyday. Then there was a final wrench. I went back to my old life—he, away home.

For a while I was content, there were daily letters from him to read; his constant admonitions to practice; his many little tokens to adore—until there came a change,—letters less frequent, more mention of Blanche and her love for him, less of his love for me, until the truth was forced upon me. Then I grew cold and proud, and with an iron will crushed and stamped all love for him out of my tortured heart and cried for vengeance.

Yes, quite melo-dramatic, wasn't it? It is a dramatic tale, though.

So I threw off my habits of seclusion and mingled again with men and women, and took up all my long-forgotten plans. It's no use telling you how I succeeded. It was really wonderful, wasn't it? It seems as though that fickle goddess, Fortune, showered every blessing, save one, on my path. Success followed success, triumph succeeded triumph. I was lionized, feted, petted, caressed by the social and literary world.

You often used to wonder how I stood it in all those years. God knows; with the heart-sick weariness and the fierce loathing that possessed me, I don't know myself.

But, mind you, Eleanor, I schemed well. I had everything seemingly that humanity craved for, but I suffered, and by all the gods, I swore that he should suffer too. Blanche turned against him and married his brother. An unfortunate chain of circumstances drove him from his father's home branded as a forger. Strange, wasn't it? But money is a strong weapon, and its long arm reaches over leagues and leagues of land and water.

One day he found me in a distant city, and begged for my love again, and for mercy and pity. Blanche was only a mistake, he said, and he loved me alone, and so on. I remembered all his thrilling tones and tender glances, but they might have moved granite now sooner than me. He knelt at my feet and pleaded like a criminal suing for life. I laughed at him and sneered at his misery, and told him what he had done for my happiness, and what I in turn had done for his.

Eleanor, to my dying day, I shall never forget his face as he rose from his knees, and with one awful, indescribable look of hate, anguish and scorn, walked from the room. As he neared the door, all the old love rose in me like a flood, drowning the sorrows of past years, and overwhelming me in a deluge of pity. Strive as I did, I could not repress it; a woman's love is too mighty to be put down with little reasonings. I called to him in terror, "Bernard, Bernard!" He did not turn; gave no sign of having heard.

"Bernard, come back; I didn't mean it!"

He passed slowly away with bent head, out of the house and out of my life. I've never seen him since, never heard of him. Somewhere, perhaps on God's earth he wanders outcast, forsaken, loveless. I have my vengeance, but it is like Dead Sea fruit, all bitter ashes to the taste. I am a miserable, heart-weary wreck,—a woman with fame, without love.

"Vengeance is an arrow that often falleth and smiteth the hand of him that sent it."

The Goodness of Saint Rocque

Manuela was tall and slender and graceful, and once you knew her the lithe form could never be mistaken. She walked with the easy spring that comes from a perfectly arched foot. Today she swept swiftly down Marais Street, casting a quick glance here and there from under her heavy veil as if she feared she was being followed. If you had peered under the veil, you would have seen that Manuela's dark eyes were swollen and discoloured about the lids, as though they had known a sleepless, tearful night. There had been a picnic the day before, and as merry a crowd of giddy, chattering Creole girls and boys as ever you could see boarded the ramshackle dummy-train that puffed its way wheezily out wide Elysian Fields Street, around the lily-covered bayous, to Milneburg-on-the-Lake. Now, a picnic at Milneburg is a thing to be remembered forever. One charters a rickety-looking, weather-beaten dancing-pavilion, built over the water, and after storing the children—for your true Creole never leaves the small folks at home—and the baskets and mothers downstairs, the young folks go up-stairs and dance to the tune of the best band you ever heard. For what can equal the music of a violin, a guitar, a cornet, and a bass viol to trip the quadrille to at a picnic?

Then one can fish in the lake and go bathing under the prim bath-houses, so severely separated sexually, and go rowing on the lake in a trim boat, followed by the shrill warnings of anxious mamans. And in the evening one comes home, hat crowned with cool gray Spanish moss, hands burdened with fantastic latanier baskets woven by the brown bayou boys, hand in hand with your dearest one, tired but happy.

At this particular picnic, however, there had been bitterness of spirit. Theophile was Manuela's own especial property, and Theophile had proven false. He had not danced a single waltz or quadrille with Manuela, but had deserted her for Claralie, blonde and petite. It was Claralie whom Theophile had rowed out on the lake; it was Claralie whom Theophile had gallantly led to dinner; it was Claralie's hat that he wreathed with Spanish moss, and Claralie whom he escorted home after the jolly singing ride in town on the little dummy-train.

Not that Manuela lacked partners or admirers. Dear no! she was too graceful and beautiful for that. There had been more than enough for her. But Manuela loved Theophile, you see, and no one could take his place. Still, she had tossed her head and let her silvery laughter ring out in the dance, as though she were the happiest of mortals, and had tripped home with Henri, leaning on his arm, and looking up into his eyes as though she adored him.

This morning she showed the traces of a sleepless night and an aching heart as she walked down Marais Street. Across wide St. Rocque Avenue she hastened. "Two blocks to the river and one below—" she repeated to herself breathlessly. Then she stood on the corner gazing about her, until with a final summoning of a desperate courage she dived through a small wicket gate into a garden of weed-choked flowers.

There was a hoarse, rusty little bell on the gate that gave querulous tongue as she pushed it open. The house that sat back in the yard was little and old and weather-beaten. Its one-story frame had once been painted, but that was a memory remote and traditional. A straggling morning-glory strove to conceal its time-ravaged face. The little walk of broken bits of brick was reddened carefully, and the one little step was scrupulously yellow-washed, which denoted that the occupants were cleanly as well as religious.

Manuela's timid knock was answered by a harsh "Entrez."

It was a small sombre room within, with a bare yellow-washed floor and ragged curtains at the little window. In a corner was a diminutive altar draped with threadbare lace. The red glow of the taper lighted a cheap print of St. Joseph and a brazen crucifix. The human element in the room was furnished by a little, wizened yellow woman, who, black-robed, turbaned, and stern, sat before an uncertain table whereon were greasy cards.

Manuela paused, her eyes blinking at the semi-obscurity within. The Wizened One called in croaking tones:

"An' fo' w'y you come here? Assiez-la, ma'amzelle."

Timidly Manuela sat at the table facing the owner of the voice.

"I want," she began faintly; but the Mistress of the Cards understood: she had had much experience. The cards were shuffled in her long grimy talons and stacked before Manuela.

"Now you cut dem in t'ree part, so—un, deux, trois, bien! You mek' you' weesh wid all you' heart, bien! Yaas, I see, I see!"

Breathlessly did Manuela learn that her lover was true, but "dat light gal, yaas, she mek' nouvena in St. Rocque fo' hees love."

"I give you one lil' charm, yaas," said the Wizened One when the seance was over, and Manuela, all white and nervous, leaned back in the rickety chair. "I give you one lil' charm fo' to ween him back, yaas.

You wear h'it 'roun' you' wais', an' he come back. Den you mek prayer at St. Rocque an' burn can'le. Den you come back an' tell me, yaas. Cinquante sous, ma'amzelle. Merci. Good luck go wid you."

Readjusting her veil, Manuela passed out the little wicket gate, treading on air. Again the sun shone, and the breath of the swamps came as healthful sea-breeze unto her nostrils. She fairly flew in the direction of St. Rocque.

There were quite a number of persons entering the white gates of the cemetery, for this was Friday, when all those who wish good luck pray to the saint, and wash their steps promptly at twelve o'clock with a wondrous mixture to guard the house. Manuela bought a candle from the keeper of the little lodge at the entrance, and pausing one instant by the great sun-dial to see if the heavens and the hour were propitious, glided into the tiny chapel, dim and stifling with heavy air from myriad wish-candles blazing on the wide table before the altar-rail. She said her prayer and lighting her candle placed it with the others.

Mon Dieu! how brightly the sun seemed to shine now, she thought, pausing at the door on her way out. Her small finger-tips, still bedewed with holy water, rested caressingly on a gamin's head. The ivy which enfolds the quaint chapel never seemed so green; the shrines which serve as the Way of the Cross never seemed so artistic; the baby graves, even, seemed cheerful.

Theophile called Sunday. Manuela's heart leaped. He had been spending his Sundays with Claralie. His stay was short and he was plainly bored. But Manuela knelt to thank the good St. Rocque that night, and fondled the charm about her slim waist. There came a box of bonbons during the week, with a decorative card all roses and fringe, from Theophile; but being a Creole, and therefore superstitiously careful, and having been reared by a wise and experienced maman to mistrust the gifts of a recreant lover, Manuela quietly thrust bonbons, box, and card into the kitchen fire, and the Friday following placed the second candle of her nouvena in St. Rocque.

Those of Manuela's friends who had watched with indignation Theophile gallantly leading Claralie home from High Mass on Sundays, gasped with astonishment when the next Sunday, with his usual bow, the young man offered Manuela his arm as the worshippers filed out in step to the organ's march. Claralie tossed her head as she crossed herself with holy water, and the pink in her cheeks was brighter than usual.

Manuela smiled a bright good-morning when she met Claralie in

St. Rocque the next Friday. The little blonde blushed furiously, and Manuela rushed post-haste to the Wizened One to confer upon this new issue.

"H'it ees good," said the dame, shaking her turbaned head. "She ees 'fraid, she will work, mais you' charm, h'it weel beat her."

And Manuela departed with radiant eyes.

Theophile was not at Mass Sunday morning, and murderous glances flashed from Claralie to Manuela before the tinkling of the Host-Bell. Nor did Theophile call at either house. Two hearts beat furiously at the sound of every passing footstep, and two minds wondered if the other were enjoying the beloved one's smiles. Two pair of eyes, however, blue and black, smiled on others, and their owners laughed and seemed none the less happy. For your Creole girls are proud, and would die rather than let the world see their sorrows.

Monday evening Theophile, the missing, showed his rather sheepish countenance in Manuela's parlour, and explained that he, with some chosen spirits, had gone for a trip—"over the Lake."

"I did not ask you where you were yesterday," replied the girl, saucily.

Theophile shrugged his shoulders and changed the conversation.

The next week there was a birthday fete in honour of Louise, Theophile's young sister. Everyone was bidden, and no one thought of refusing, for Louise was young, and this would be her first party. So, though the night was hot, the dancing went on as merrily as light young feet could make it go. Claralie fluffed her dainty white skirts, and cast mischievous sparkles in the direction of Theophile, who with the maman and Louise was bravely trying not to look self-conscious. Manuela, tall and calm and proud-looking, in a cool, pale yellow gown was apparently enjoying herself without paying the slightest attention to her young host.

"Have I the pleasure of this dance?" he asked her finally, in a lull of the music.

She bowed assent, and as if moved by a common impulse they strolled out of the dancing-room into the cool, quaint garden, where jessamines gave out an overpowering perfume, and a caged mocking-bird complained melodiously to the full moon in the sky.

It must have been an engrossing tete-a-tete, for the call to supper had sounded twice before they heard and hurried into the house. The march had formed with Louise radiantly leading on the arm of papa. Claralie tripped by with Leon. Of course, nothing remained for Theophile and

Manuela to do but to bring up the rear, for which they received much good-natured chaffing.

But when the party reached the dining-room, Theophile proudly led his partner to the head of the table, at the right hand of maman, and smiled benignly about at the delighted assemblage. Now you know, when a Creole young man places a girl at his mother's right hand at his own table, there is but one conclusion to be deduced therefrom.

If you had asked Manuela, after the wedding was over, how it happened, she would have said nothing, but looked wise.

If you had asked Claralie, she would have laughed and said she always preferred Leon.

If you had asked Theophile, he would have wondered that you thought he had ever meant more than to tease Manuela.

If you had asked the Wizened One, she would have offered you a charm.

But St. Rocque knows, for he is a good saint, and if you believe in him and are true and good, and make your nouvenas with a clean heart, he will grant your wish.

In Our Neighborhood

The Harts were going to give a party. Neither Mrs. Hart, nor the Misses Hart, nor the small and busy Harts who amused themselves and the neighborhood by continually falling in the gutter on special occasions, had mentioned this fact to anyone, but all the interested denizens of that particular square could tell by the unusual air of bustle and activity which pervaded the Hart domicile. Lillian, the æsthetic, who furnished theme for many spirited discussions, leaned airily out of the window; her auburn (red) tresses carefully done in curl papers. Martha, the practical, flourished the broom and duster with unwonted activity, which the small boys of the neighborhood, peering through the green shutters of the front door, duly reported to their mammas, busily engaged in holding down their respective door-steps by patiently sitting thereon.

Pretty soon, the junior Harts,—two in number—began to travel to and fro, soliciting the loan of a "few chairs," "some nice dishes," and such like things, indispensable to every decent, self-respecting party. But to all inquiries as to the use to which these articles were to be put, they only vouchsafed one reply, "Ma told us as we wasn't to tell, just ask for the things, that's all."

Mrs. Tuckley the dress-maker, brought her sewing out on the front-steps, and entered a vigorous protest to her next-door neighbor.

"Humph," she sniffed, "mighty funny they can't say what's up. Must be something in it. Couldn't get none o' *my* things, and not invite *me!*"

"Did she ask you for any?" absent-mindedly inquired Mrs. Luke, shielding her eyes from the sun.

"No-o—, but she'd better sense, she knows *me*—she ain't—mercy me, Stella! Just look at that child tumbling in the mud! You, Stella, come here, I say! Look at you now, there—and there—and there?"

The luckless Stella having been soundly cuffed, and sent whimpering in the back-yard, Mrs. Tuckley continued,

"Yes as I was saying, 'course, taint none o' my business, but I always did wonder how them Harts do keep up. Why, them girls dress just as fine as any lady on the Avenue and that there Lillian wears real diamond ear-rings. 'Pears mighty, mighty funny to me, and Lord the airs they do put on! Holdin' up their heads like nobody's good enough to speak to. I don't like to talk about people, you know, yourself, Mrs. Luke I never speak about anybody, but mark my word, girls that cut up capers like them Hartses' girls never come to any good."

Mrs. Luke heaved a deep sigh of appreciation at the wisdom of her neighbor, but before she could reply a re-inforcement in the person of little Mrs. Peters, apron over her head, hands shrivelled and soap-sudsy from washing, appeared.

"Did you ever see the like?" she asked in her usual, rapid breathless way. "Why, my Louis says they're putting canvass cloths on the floor, and taking down the bed in the back-room; and putting greenery and such like trash about. Some style about them, eh?"

Mrs. Tuckley tossed her head and sniffed contemptuously, Mrs. Luke began to rehearse a time worn tale, how once a carriage had driven up to the Hart house at nine o'clock at night, and a distinguished looking man alighted, went in, stayed about ten minutes and finally drove off with a great clatter. Heads that had shaken ominously over this story before began to shake again, and tongues that had wagged themselves tired with conjectures started now with some brand new ideas and theories. The children of the square, tired of fishing for minnows in the ditches, and making mud-pies in the street, clustered about their mother's skirts receiving occasional slaps, when their attempts at taking part in the conversation became too pronounced.

Meanwhile, in the Hart household, all was bustle and preparation. To and fro the members of the house flitted, arranging chairs, putting little touches here and there, washing saucers and glasses, chasing the Hart Juniors about, losing things and calling frantically for each other's assistance to find them. Mama Hart, big, plump and perspiring, puffed here and there like a large, rosy engine, giving impossible orders, and receiving sharp answers to foolish questions. Lillian, the æsthetic, practiced her most graceful poses before the large mirror in the parlor; Martha rushed about, changing the order of the furniture, and Papa Hart, just come in from work, paced the rooms disconsolately, asking for dinner.

"Dinner!" screamed Mama Hart, "Dinner, who's got time to fool with dinner this evening? Look in the sideboard and you'll see some bread and ham; eat that and shut up."

Eight o'clock finally arrived, and with it, the music and some straggling guests. When the first faint chee-chee of the violin floated out into the murky atmosphere, the smaller portion of the neighborhood went straightway into ecstasies. Boys and girls in all stages of deshabille clustered about the door-steps and gave vent to audible exclamations of approval or disapprobation concerning the state of affairs behind the green shutters. It was a warm night and the big round moon sailed serenely in a cloudless, blue sky. Mrs. Tuckley had put on a clean calico wrapper, and planted herself with the indomitable Stella on her steps, "to watch the purceedings."

The party was a grand success. Even the intensely critical small fry dancing on the pavement without to the scraping and fiddling of the string band, had to admit that. So far as they were concerned it was all right, but what shall we say of the guests within? They who glided easily over the canvassed floors, bowed, and scraped and simpered, "just like the big folks on the Avenue," who ate the ice-cream and cake, and drank the sweet, weak Catawba wine amid boisterous healths to Mr. and Mrs. Hart and the Misses Hart; who smirked and perspired and cracked ancient jokes and heart-rending puns during the intervals of the dances, who shall say that they did not enjoy themselves as thoroughly and as fully as those who frequented the wealthier entertainments up-town.

Lillian and Martha in gossamer gowns of pink and blue flitted to and fro attending to the wants of their guests. Mrs. Hart, gorgeous in a black satin affair, all folds and lace and drapery, made desperate efforts to appear cool and collected—and failed miserably. Papa Hart spent one half his time standing in front of the mantle, spreading out his coat-tails, and benignly smiling upon the young people, while the other half was devoted to initiating the male portion of the guests into the mysteries of "snake killing."

Everybody had said that he or she had had a splendid time, and finally, when the last kisses had been kissed, the last goodbyes been said, the whole Hart family sat down in the now deserted and disordered rooms, and sighed with relief that the great event was over at last.

"Nice crowd, eh?" remarked Papa Hart. He was brimful of joy and second-class whiskey, so no one paid any attention to him.

"But did you see how shamefully Maude flirted with Willie Howard?" said Lillian. Martha tossed her head in disdain; Mr. Howard she had always considered her especial property, so Lillian's observation had a rather disturbing effect.

"I'm so warm and tired," cried Mama Hart, plaintively, "children how are we going to sleep tonight?"

Thereupon the whole family arose to devise ways and means for wooing the drowsy god. As for the Hart Juniors they had long since solved the problem by falling asleep with sticky hands and faces upon a pile of bed-clothing behind the kitchen door.

It was late in the next day before the house had begun to resume anything like its former appearance. The little Harts were kept busy all morning returning chairs and dishes, and distributing the remnants of the feast to the vicinity. The ice-cream had melted into a warm custard, and the cakes had a rather worse for wear appearance, but they were appreciated as much as though just from the confectioner. No one was forgotten, even Mrs. Tuckley, busily stitching on a muslin garment on the steps, and unctuously rolling the latest morsel of scandal under her tongue, was obliged to confess that "them Hartses wasn't such bad people after all, just a bit queer at times."

About two o'clock, just as Lillian was re-draping the tidies on the stiff, common plush chairs in the parlor, someone pulled the bell violently. The visitor, a rather good-looking young fellow, with a worried expression smiled somewhat sarcastically as he heard a sound of scuffling and running within the house.

Presently Mrs. Hart opened the door wiping her hand, red and smoking with dish-water, upon her apron. The worried expression deepened on the visitor's face as he addressed the woman with visible embarrassment.

"Er—I—I—suppose you are Mrs. Hart?" he inquired awkwardly.

"That's my name, sir," replied she with pretentious dignity.

"Er—your-er—may I come in madam?"

"Certainly," and she opened the door to admit him, and offered a chair.

"Your husband is an employee in the Fisher Oil Mills, is he not?"

Mrs. Hart straightened herself with pride as she replied in the affirmative. She had always been proud of Mr. Hart's position as foreman of the big oil mills, and was never so happy as when he was expounding to someone in her presence, the difficulties and intricacies of machine-work.

"Well you see my dear Mrs. Hart," continued the visitor. "Now pray don't get excited—there has been an accident, and your husband—has—er—been hurt, you know."

But for a painful whitening in her usually rosy face, and a quick compression of her lips, the wife made no sign.

"What was the accident?" she queried, leaning her elbows on her knees.

"Well, you see, I don't understand machinery and the like, but there was something about a wheel out of gear, and a band bursted, or something, anyhow a big wheel flew to pieces, and as he was standing near, he was hit."

"Where?"

"Well—well, I may as well tell you the truth, madam; a large piece of the wheel struck him on the head—and—he was killed instantly."

She did not faint, nor make any outcry, nor tear her hair as he had partly expected, but sat still staring at him, with a sort of helpless, dumb horror shining out her eyes, then with a low moan, bowed her head on her knees and shuddered, just as Lillian came in, curious to know what the handsome stranger had to say to her mother.

THE POOR MUTILATED BODY CAME home at last, and was laid in a stiff, silver-decorated, black coffin in the middle of the sitting-room, which had been made to look as uncomfortable and unnatural as mirrors and furniture shrouded in sheets and mantel and tables divested of ornaments would permit.

There was a wake that night to the unconfined joy of the neighbors, who would rather a burial than a wedding. The friends of the family sat about the coffin, and through the house with long pulled faces. Mrs. Tuckley officiated in the kitchen, making coffee and dispensing cheese and crackers to those who were hungry. As the night wore on, and the first restraint disappeared, jokes were cracked, and quiet laughter indulged in, while the young folks congregated in the kitchen, were hilariously happy, until some member of the family would appear, when every face would sober down.

The older persons contented themselves with recounting the virtues of the deceased, and telling anecdotes wherein he figured largely. It was astonishing how many intimate friends of his had suddenly come to light. Every other man present had either attended school with him, or was a close companion until he died. Proverbs and tales and witty sayings were palmed off as having emanated from his lips. In fact, the dead man would have been surprised himself, had he suddenly come to life and discovered what an important, what a modern solomon he had become.

The long night dragged on, and the people departed in groups of twos and threes, until when the gray dawn crept slowly over the blackness of night shrouding the electric lights in mists of cloudy blue, and sending cold chills of dampness through the house, but a few of the great crowd remained.

The day seemed so gray in contrast to the softening influence of the night, the grief which could be hidden then, must now come forth and parade itself before all eyes. There was the funeral to prepare for; the dismal black dresses and bonnets with their long crape veils to don; there were the condolences of sorrowing friends to receive; the floral offerings to be looked at. The little Harts strutted about resplendent in stiff black cravats, and high crape bands about their hats. They were divided between two conflicting emotions—joy at belonging to a family so noteworthy and important, and sorrow at the death. As the time for the funeral approached, and Lillian began to indulge in a series of fainting fits, the latter feeling predominated.

WELL IT WAS ALL OVER at last, the family had returned, and as on two nights previous, sat once more in the deserted and dismantled parlor. Mrs. Tuckley and Mrs. Luke, having rendered all assistance possible, had repaired to their respective front steps to keep count of the number of visitors who returned to condole with the family.

"A real nice funeral," remarked the dress-maker at last, "a nice funeral. Everybody took it so hard, and Lillian fainted real beautiful. She's a good girl that Lillian. Poor things, I wonder what they'll do now."

Stella, the irrepressible, was busily engaged balancing herself on one toe, *a la* ballet.

"Mebbe she's goin' to get married," she volunteered eagerly, "'cos I saw that yeller-haired young man what comes there all the time, wif his arms around her waist, and a tellin' her not to grieve as he'd take care of her. I was a peepin' in the dinin'-room."

"How dare you peep at other folks, and pry into people's affairs? I can't imagine where you get your meddlesome ways from. There aint none in *my family*. Next time I catch you at it, I'll spank you good." Then, after a pause, "Well what else did he say?"

In Unconsciousness

There was a big booming in my ears, great heavy iron bells that swung to-and-fro on either side, and sent out deafening reverberations that steeped the senses in a musical melody of sonorous sound; to-and-fro, backward and forward, yet ever receding in a gradually widening circle, monotonous, mournful, weird, suffusing the soul with an unutterable sadness, as images of wailing processions, of weeping, empty-armed women, and widowed maidens flashed through the mind, and settled on the soul with a crushing, o'er-pressing weight of sorrow.

Now I lay floating, arms outstretched, on an illimitable waste of calm tranquil waters. Far away as eye could reach, there was naught but the pale, white-flecked, green waters of this ocean of eternity, and above the tender blue sky arched down in perfect love of its mistress, the ocean. Sky and sea, sea and sky, blue, calm, infinite, perfect sea, heaving its womanly bosom to the passionate kisses of its ardent sun-lover. Away into infinity stretched this perfectibility of love; into eternity, I was drifting, alone, silent, yet burdened still with the remembrance of the sadness of the bells.

Far away, they tolled out the incessant dirge, grown resignedly sweet now; so intense in its infinite peace, that a calm of love, beyond all human understanding and above all earthly passions, sank deep into my soul, and so permeated my whole being with rest and peace, that my lips smiled and my eyes drooped in access of fulsome joy. Into the illimitable space of infinity we drifted, my soul and I, borne along only by the network of auburn hair that floated about me in the green waters.

But now, a rude grasp from somewhere is laid upon me, pressing upon my face. Instantly the air grows gloomy, gray, and the ocean rocks menacingly, while the great bells grow harsh and strident, as they hint of a dark fate. I clasp my hands appealingly to the heavens; I moan and struggle with the unknown grasp; then there is peace and the sweet content of the infinite Nirvana.

Then slowly, softly, the net of auburn hair begins to drag me down below the surface of the sea. Oh! the skies are so sweet, and now that the tender stars are looking upon us, how fair to stay and sway upon the breast of eternity! But the net is inexorable, and gently, slowly pulls me down. Now we sink straight, now we whirl in slow, eddying circles, spiral-like; while at each turn those bells ring out clanging now in wild crescendo, then whispering dread secrets of the ocean's depths. Oh, ye mighty bells, tell me from your learned lore of the hopes of mankind! Tell me what fruit he beareth from his strivings and yearnings; know not ye? Why ring ye now so joyful, so hopeful; then toll your dismal prophecies of o'er-cast skies?

Years have passed, and now centuries, too, are swallowed in the gulf of eternity, yet the auburn net still whirls me in eddying circles, down, down to the very womb of time; to the innermost recesses of the mighty ocean.

AND NOW, PEACE, PERFECT, UNCONDITIONED, sublime peace, and rest, and silence. For to the great depths of the mighty ocean the solemn bells cannot penetrate, and no sound, not even the beatings of one's own heart, is heard. In the heart of eternity there can be nothing to break the calm of frozen æons. In the great white hall I lay, silent, unexpectant, calm, and smiled in perfect content at the web of auburn hair which trailed across my couch. No passionate longing for life or love, no doubting question of heaven or hell, no strife for carnal needs,—only rest, content, peace—happiness, perfect, whole, complete, sublime.

And thus passed ages and ages, æons and æons. The great earth there in the dim distance above the ocean has toiled wearily about the sun, until its mechanism was failing, and the warm ardor of the lover's eye was becoming pale and cold from age, while the air all about the fast dwindling sphere was heavy and thick with the sorrows and heartaches and woes of the humans upon its face. Heavy with the screams and roar of war; with the curses of the deceived of traitors; with the passionate sighs of unlawful love; with the crushing unrest of blighted hopes. Knowledge and contempt of all these things permeated even to the inmost depths of time, as I lay in the halls of rest and smiled at the web floating through my white fingers.

BUT HARK! DISCORD BEGINS. THERE is a vague fear which springs from an unknown source and drifts into the depths of rest; fear, indefinable, unaccountable, unknowable, shuddering. Pain begins, for the heart springs into life, and fills the silence with the terror of its beatings, thick, knifing, frightful in its intense longing. Power of mind over soul, power of calm over fear avail nothing; suspense and misery, locked arm in arm, pervade æonic stillness, till all things else become subordinate, unnoticed.

Centuries drift away, and the giddy, old reprobate—earth, dying a hideous, ghastly death, with but one solitary human to shudder in unison with its last throes, to bask in the last pale rays of a cold sun, to inhale the last breath of a metallic atmosphere; totters, reels, falls into space, and is no more. Peal out, ye brazen bells, peal out the requiem of the sinner! Roll your mournful tones into the ears of the saddened angels, weeping with wing-covered eyes! Toll the requiem of the sinner, sinking swiftly, sobbingly into the depths of time's ocean. Down, down, until the great groans which arose from the domes and Ionic roofs about me told that the sad old earth sought rest in eternity, while the universe shrugged its shoulders over the loss of another star.

And now, the great invisible fear became apparent, tangible, for all the sins, the woes, the miseries, the dreads, the dismal achings and throbbings, the dreariness and gloom of the lost star came together and like a huge geni took form and hideous shape—octopus-like—which slowly approached me, erstwhile happy—and hovered about my couch in fearful menace.

OH, SHINING WEB OF HAIR, burst loose your bonds and bid me move! Oh, time, cease not your calculations, but speed me on to deliverance! Oh, silence, vast, immense, infuse into your soul some sound other than the heavy throbbing of this fast disintegrating heart! Oh, pitiless stone arches, let fall your crushing weight upon this Stygian monster!

I pray to time, to eternity, to the frozen æons of the past. Useless. I am seized, forced to open my cold lips; there is agony,—supreme, mortal agony of nerve tension, and wrenching of vitality. I struggle, scream, and clutching the monster with superhuman strength, fling him aside, and rise, bleeding, screaming—but triumphant, and keenly mortal in every vein, alive and throbbing with consciousness and pain.

NO, IT WAS NOT OPIUM, nor night-mare, but chloroform, a dentist, three obstinate molars, a pair of forceps, and a lively set of nerves.

La Juanita

If you never lived in Mandeville, you cannot appreciate the thrill of wholesome, satisfied joy which sweeps over its inhabitants every evening at five o'clock. It is the hour for the arrival of the "New Camelia," the happening of the day. As early as four o'clock the trailing smoke across the horizon of the treacherous Lake Pontchartrain appears, and Mandeville knows then that the hour for its siesta has passed, and that it must array itself in its coolest and fluffiest garments, and go down to the pier to meet this sole connection between itself and the outside world; the little, puffy, side-wheel steamer that comes daily from New Orleans and brings the mail and the news.

On this particular day there was an air of suppressed excitement about the little knot of people which gathered on the pier. To be sure, there were no outward signs to show that anything unusual had occurred. The small folks danced with the same glee over the worn boards, and peered down with daring excitement into the perilous depths of the water below. The sun, fast sinking in a gorgeous glow behind the pines of the Tchefuncta region far away, danced his mischievous rays in much the same manner that he did every other day. But there was a something in the air, a something not tangible, but mysterious, subtle. You could catch an indescribable whiff of it in your inner senses, by the half-eager, furtive glances that the small crowd cast at La Juanita.

"Gar, gar, le bateau!" said one dark-tressed mother to the wide-eyed baby. "Et, oui," she added, in an undertone to her companion. "Voila, La Juanita!"

La Juanita, you must know, was the pride of Mandeville, the adored, the admired of all, with her petite, half-Spanish, half-French beauty. Whether rocking in the shade of the Cherokee-rose-covered gallery of Grandpere Colomes' big house, her fair face bonnet-shaded, her dainty hands gloved to keep the sun from too close an acquaintance, or splashing the spray from the bow of her little pirogue, or fluffing her skirts about her tiny feet on the pier, she was the pet and ward of Mandeville, as it were, La Juanita Alvarez, since Madame Alvarez was a widow, and Grandpere Colomes was strict and stern.

And now La Juanita had set her small foot down with a passionate stamp before Grandpere Colomes' very face, and tossed her black curls about her wilful head, and said she would go to the pier this evening to meet her Mercer. All Mandeville knew this, and cast its furtive glances alternately at La Juanita with two big pink spots in her cheeks, and at the entrance to the pier, expecting Grandpere Colomes and a scene.

The sun cast red glows and violet shadows over the pier, and the pines murmured a soft little vesper hymn among themselves up on the beach, as the "New Camelia" swung herself in, crabby, sidewise, like a fat old gentleman going into a small door. There was the clang of an important bell, the scream of a hoarse little whistle, and Mandeville rushed to the gang-plank to welcome the outside world. Juanita put her hand through a waiting arm, and tripped away with her Mercer, big and blond and brawny. "Un Americain, pah!" said the little mother of the black eyes. And Mandeville sighed sadly, and shook its head, and was sorry for Grandpere Colomes.

This was Saturday, and the big regatta would be Monday. Ah, that regatta, such a one as Mandeville had never seen! There were to be boats from Madisonville and Amite, from Lewisburg and Covington, and even far-away Nott's Point. There was to be a Class A and Class B and Class C, and the little French girls of the town flaunted their ribbons down the one oak-shaded, lake-kissed street, and dared anyone to say theirs were not the favourite colours.

In Class A was entered, "La Juanita', captain Mercer Grangeman, colours pink and gold." Her name, her colours; what impudence!

Of course, not being a Mandevillian, you could not understand the shame of Grandpere Colomes at this. Was it not bad enough for his petite Juanita, his Spanish blossom, his hope of a family that had held itself proudly aloof from "dose Americain" from time immemorial, to have smiled upon this Mercer, this pale-eyed youth? Was it not bad enough for her to demean herself by walking upon the pier with him? But for a boat, his boat, "un bateau Americain," to be named La Juanita! Oh, the shame of it! Grandpere Colomes prayed a devout prayer to the Virgin that "La Juanita" should be capsized.

Monday came, clear and blue and stifling. The waves of hot air danced on the sands and adown the one street merrily. Glassily calm lay the Pontchartrain, heavily still hung the atmosphere. Madame Alvarez cast an inquiring glance toward the sky. Grandpere Colomes chuckled. He had not lived on the shores of the treacherous Lake Pontchartrain for nothing. He knew its every mood, its petulances and passions; he knew this glassy warmth and what it meant. Chuckling again and again, he stepped to the gallery and looked out over the lake, and at the pier, where lay the boats rocking and idly tugging at their moorings. La Juanita in her rose-scented room tied the pink ribbons on her dainty frock, and fastened cloth of gold roses at her lithe waist.

It was said that just before the crack of the pistol La Juanita's tiny hand lay in Mercer's, and that he bent his head, and whispered softly, so that the surrounding crowd could not hear,—

"Juanita mine, if I win, you will?"

"Oui, mon Mercere, eef you win."

In another instant the white wings were off scudding before the rising breeze, dipping their glossy boat-sides into the clear water, straining their cordage in their tense efforts to reach the stake boats. Mandeville indiscriminately distributed itself on piers, large and small, bath-house tops, trees, and craft of all kinds, from pirogue, dory, and pine-raft to pretentious cat-boat and shell-schooner. Mandeville cheered and strained its eyes after all the boats, but chiefly was its attention directed to "La Juanita."

"Ah, voila, eet is ahead!"

"Mais non, c'est un autre!"

"La Juanita! La Juanita!"

"Regardez Grandpere Colomes!"

Old Colomes on the big pier with Madame Alvarez and his granddaughter was intently straining his weather-beaten face in the direction of Nott's Point, his back resolutely turned upon the scudding white wings. A sudden chuckle of grim satisfaction caused La Petite's head to toss petulantly.

But only for a minute, for Grandpere Colomes' chuckle was followed by a shout of dismay from those whose glance had followed his. You must know that it is around Nott's Point that the storm king shows his wings first, for the little peninsula guards the entrance which leads into the southeast waters of the stormy Rigolets and the blustering Gulf. You would know, if you lived in Mandeville, that when the pines on Nott's Point darken and when the water shows white beyond like the teeth of a hungry wolf, it is time to steer your boat into the mouth of someone of the many calm bayous which flow silently throughout St. Tammany parish into the lake. Small wonder that the cry of dismay went up now, for Nott's Point was black, with a lurid light overhead, and the roar of the grim southeast wind came ominously over the water.

La Juanita clasped her hands and strained her eyes for her namesake.

The racers had rounded the second stake-boat, and the course of the triangle headed them directly for the lurid cloud.

You should have seen Grandpere Colomes then. He danced up and down the pier in a perfect frenzy. The thin pale lips of Madame Alvarez moved in a silent prayer; La Juanita stood coldly silent.

And now you could see that the advance guard of the southeast force had struck the little fleet. They dipped and scurried and rocked, and you could see the sails being reefed hurriedly, and almost hear the rigging creak and moan under the strain. Then the wind came up the lake, and struck the town with a tumultuous force. The waters rose and heaved in the long, sullen ground-swell, which betokened serious trouble. There was a rush of lake-craft to shelter. Heavy gray waves boomed against the breakwaters and piers, dashing their brackish spray upon the strained watchers; then with a shriek and a howl the storm burst full, with blinding sheets of rain, and a great hurricane of Gulf wind that threatened to blow the little town away.

La Juanita was proud. When Grandpere and Madame led her away in the storm, though her face was white, and the rose mouth pressed close, not a word did she say, and her eyes were as bright as ever before. It was foolish to hope that the frail boats could survive such a storm. There was not even the merest excuse for shelter out in the waters, and when Lake Pontchartrain grows angry, it devours without pity.

Your tropical storm is soon over, however, and in an hour the sun struggled through a gray and misty sky, over which the wind was sweeping great clouds. The rain-drops hung diamond-like on the thick foliage, but the long ground-swell still boomed against the breakwaters and showed white teeth, far to the south.

As chickens creep from under shelter after a rain, so the people of Mandeville crept out again on the piers, on the bath-houses, on the breakwater edge, and watched eagerly for the boats. Slowly upon the horizon appeared white sails, and the little craft swung into sight. One, two, three, four, five, six, seven, eight, nine, counted Mandeville. Everyone coming in! Bravo! And a great cheer that swept the whole length of the town from the post-office to Black Bayou went up. Bravo! Every boat was coming in. But—was every man?

This was a sobering thought, and in the hush which followed it you could hear the Q. and C. train thundering over the great lake-bridge, miles away.

Well, they came into the pier at last, "La Juanita" in the lead; and as Captain Mercer landed, he was surrounded by a voluble, chattering, anxious throng that loaded him with questions in patois, in broken English, and in French. He was no longer "un Americain" now, he was a hero.

When the other eight boats came in, and Mandeville saw that no one was lost, there was another ringing bravo, and more chattering of questions.

We heard the truth finally. When the storm burst, Captain Mercer suddenly promoted himself to an admiralship and assumed command of his little fleet. He had led them through the teeth of the gale to a small inlet on the coast between Bayou Lacombe and Nott's Point, and there they had waited until the storm passed. Loud were the praises of the other captains for Admiral Mercer, profuse were the thanks of the sisters and sweethearts, as he was carried triumphantly on the shoulders of the sailors adown the wharf to the Maison Colomes.

The crispness had gone from Juanita's pink frock, and the cloth of gold roses were wellnigh petalless, but the hand that she slipped into his was warm and soft, and the eyes that were upturned to Mercer's blue ones were shining with admiring tears. And even Grandpere Colomes, as he brewed on the Cherokee-rose-covered gallery, a fiery punch for the heroes, was heard to admit that "sometime dose Americain can mos' be lak one Frenchman."

And we danced at the betrothal supper the next week.

M'sieu Fortier's Violin

Slowly, one by one, the lights in the French Opera go out, until there is but a single glimmer of pale yellow flickering in the great dark space, a few moments ago all a-glitter with jewels and the radiance of womanhood and a-clash with music. Darkness now, and silence, and a great haunted hush over all, save for the distant cheery voice of a stage hand humming a bar of the opera.

The glimmer of gas makes a halo about the bowed white head of a little old man putting his violin carefully away in its case with aged, trembling, nervous fingers. Old M'sieu Fortier was the last one out every night.

Outside the air was murky, foggy. Gas and electricity were but faint splotches of light on the thick curtain of fog and mist. Around the opera was a mighty bustle of carriages and drivers and footmen, with a car gaining headway in the street now and then, a howling of names and numbers, the laughter and small talk of cloaked society stepping slowly to its carriages, and the more bourgeoisie vocalisation of the foot passengers who streamed along and hummed little bits of music. The fog's denseness was confusing, too, and at one moment it seemed that the little narrow street would become inextricably choked and remain so until some mighty engine would blow the crowd into atoms. It had been a crowded night. From around Toulouse Street, where led the entrance to the troisiemes, from the grand stairway, from the entrance to the quatriemes, the human stream poured into the street, nearly all with a song on their lips.

M'sieu Fortier stood at the corner, blinking at the beautiful ladies in their carriages. He exchanged a hearty salutation with the saloon-keeper at the corner, then, tenderly carrying his violin case, he trudged down Bourbon Street, a little old, bent, withered figure, with shoulders shrugged up to keep warm, as though the faded brown overcoat were not thick enough.

Down on Bayou Road, not so far from Claiborne Street, was a house, little and old and queer, but quite large enough to hold M'sieu Fortier, a wrinkled dame, and a white cat. He was home but little, for on nearly everyday there were rehearsals; then on Tuesday, Thursday, and Saturday nights, and twice Sundays there were performances, so Ma'am Jeanne and the white cat kept house almost always alone. Then, when

M'sieu Fortier was at home, why, it was practice, practice all the day, and smoke, snore, sleep at night. Altogether it was not very exhilarating.

M'sieu Fortier had played first violin in the orchestra ever since—well, no one remembered his not playing there. Sometimes there would come breaks in the seasons, and for a year the great building would be dark and silent. Then M'sieu Fortier would do jobs of playing here and there, one night for this ball, another night for that soiree dansante, and in the day, work at his trade,—that of a cigar-maker. But now for seven years there had been no break in the season, and the little old violinist was happy. There is nothing sweeter than a regular job and good music to play, music into which one can put some soul, some expression, and which one must study to understand. Dance music, of the frivolous, frothy kind deemed essential to soirees, is trivial, easy, uninteresting.

So M'sieu Fortier, Ma'am Jeanne, and the white cat lived a peaceful, uneventful existence out on Bayou Road. When the opera season was over in February, M'sieu went back to cigar-making, and the white cat purred none the less contentedly.

It had been a benefit tonight for the leading tenor, and he had chosen "Roland a Ronceveaux," a favourite this season, for his farewell. And, mon Dieu, mused the little M'sieu, but how his voice had rung out bell-like, piercing above the chorus of the first act! Encore after encore was given, and the bravos of the troisiemes were enough to stir the most sluggish of pulses.

"Superbes Pyrenees
Qui dressez dans le ciel,
Vos cimes couronnees
D'un hiver eternelle,
Pour nous livrer passage
Ouvrez vos larges flancs,
Faites faire l'orage,
Voici, venir les Francs!"

M'sieu quickened his pace down Bourbon Street as he sang the chorus to himself in a thin old voice, and then, before he could see in the thick fog, he had run into two young men.

"I—I—beg your pardon,—messieurs," he stammered.

"Most certainly," was the careless response; then the speaker, taking a second glance at the object of the rencontre, cried joyfully:

"Oh, M'sieu Fortier, is it you? Why, you are so happy, singing your love sonnet to your lady's eyebrow, that you didn't see a thing but the moon, did you? And who is the fair one who should clog your senses so?"

There was a deprecating shrug from the little man.

"Ma foi, but monsieur must know fo' sho', dat I am too old for love songs!"

"I know nothing save that I want that violin of yours. When is it to be mine, M'sieu Fortier?"

"Nevare, nevare!" exclaimed M'sieu, gripping on as tightly to the case as if he feared it might be wrenched from him. "Me a lovere, and to sell mon violon! Ah, so ver' foolish!"

"Martel," said the first speaker to his companion as they moved on up town, "I wish you knew that little Frenchman. He's a unique specimen. He has the most exquisite violin I've seen in years; beautiful and mellow as a genuine Cremona, and he can make the music leap, sing, laugh, sob, skip, wail, anything you like from under his bow when he wishes. It's something wonderful. We are good friends. Picked him up in my French-town rambles. I've been trying to buy that instrument since—"

"To throw it aside a week later?" lazily inquired Martel. "You are like the rest of these nineteenth-century vandals, you can see nothing picturesque that you do not wish to deface for a souvenir; you cannot even let simple happiness alone, but must needs destroy it in a vain attempt to make it your own or parade it as an advertisement."

As for M'sieu Fortier, he went right on with his song and turned into Bayou Road, his shoulders still shrugged high as though he were cold, and into the quaint little house, where Ma'am Jeanne and the white cat, who always waited up for him at nights, were both nodding over the fire.

It was not long after this that the opera closed, and M'sieu went back to his old out-of-season job. But somehow he did not do as well this spring and summer as always. There is a certain amount of cunning and finesse required to roll a cigar just so, that M'sieu seemed to be losing, whether from age or deterioration it was hard to tell. Nevertheless, there was just about half as much money coming in as formerly, and the quaint little pucker between M'sieu's eyebrows which served for a frown came oftener and stayed longer than ever before.

"Minesse," he said one day to the white cat,—he told all his troubles to her; it was of no use to talk to Ma'am Jeanne, she was too deaf to understand,—"Minesse, we are gettin' po'. You' pere git h'old, an' hees han's dey go no mo' rapidement, an' dere be no mo' soirees dese day. Minesse, eef la saison don' hurry up, we shall eat ver' lil' meat."

And Minesse curled her tail and purred.

Before the summer had fairly begun, strange rumours began to float about in musical circles. M. Mauge would no longer manage the opera, but it would be turned into the hands of Americans, a syndicate. Bah! These English-speaking people could do nothing unless there was a trust, a syndicate, a company immense and dishonest. It was going to be a guarantee business, with a strictly financial basis. But worse than all this, the new manager, who was now in France, would not only procure the artists, but a new orchestra, a new leader. M'sieu Fortier grew apprehensive at this, for he knew what the loss of his place would mean to him.

September and October came, and the papers were filled with accounts of the new artists from France and of the new orchestra leader too. He was described as a most talented, progressive, energetic young man. M'sieu Fortier's heart sank at the word "progressive." He was anything but that. The New Orleans Creole blood flowed too sluggishly in his old veins.

November came; the opera reopened. M'sieu Fortier was not re-engaged.

"Minesse," he said with a catch in his voice that strongly resembled a sob, "Minesse, we mus' go hongry sometime. Ah, mon pauvre violon! Ah, mon Dieu, dey put us h'out, an' dey will not have us. Nev' min', we will sing anyhow." And drawing his bow across the strings, he sang in his thin, quavering voice, "Salut demeure, chaste et pure."

It is strange what a peculiar power of fascination former haunts have for the human mind. The criminal, after he has fled from justice, steals back and skulks about the scene of his crime; the employee thrown from work hangs about the place of his former industry; the schoolboy, truant or expelled, peeps in at the school-gate and taunts the good boys within. M'sieu Fortier was no exception. Night after night of the performances he climbed the stairs of the opera and sat, an attentive listener to the orchestra, with one ear inclined to the stage, and a quizzical expression on his wrinkled face. Then he would go home, and pat Minesse, and fondle the violin.

"Ah, Minesse, dose new player! Not one bit can dey play. Such tones, Minesse, such tones! All the time portemento, oh, so ver' bad! Ah, mon chere violon, we can play." And he would play and sing a romance, and smile tenderly to himself.

At first it used to be into the deuxiemes that M'sieu Fortier went, into the front seats. But soon they were too expensive, and after all, one could hear just as well in the fourth row as in the first. After a while even the rear row of the deuxiemes was too costly, and the little musician wended his way with the plebeians around on Toulouse Street, and climbed the long, tedious flight of stairs into the troisiemes. It makes no difference to be one row higher. It was more to the liking, after all. One felt more at home up here among the people. If one was thirsty, one could drink a glass of wine or beer being passed about by the libretto boys, and the music sounded just as well.

But it happened one night that M'sieu could not even afford to climb the Toulouse Street stairs. To be sure, there was yet another gallery, the quatriemes, where the peanut boys went for a dime, but M'sieu could not get down to that yet. So he stayed outside until all the beautiful women in their warm wraps, a bright-hued chattering throng, came down the grand staircase to their carriages.

It was on one of these nights that Courcey and Martel found him shivering at the corner.

"Hello, M'sieu Fortier," cried Courcey, "are you ready to let me have that violin yet?"

"For shame!" interrupted Martel.

"Fifty dollars, you know," continued Courcey, taking no heed of his friend's interpolation.

M'sieu Fortier made a courtly bow. "Eef Monsieur will call at my 'ouse on de morrow, he may have mon violon," he said huskily; then turned abruptly on his heel, and went down Bourbon Street, his shoulders drawn high as though he were cold.

When Courcey and Martel entered the gate of the little house on Bayou Road the next day, there floated out to their ears a wordless song thrilling from the violin, a song that told more than speech or tears or gestures could have done of the utter sorrow and desolation of the little old man. They walked softly up the short red brick walk and tapped at the door. Within, M'sieu Fortier was caressing the violin, with silent tears streaming down his wrinkled gray face.

There was not much said on either side. Courcey came away with the instrument, leaving the money behind, while Martel grumbled at the essentially sordid, mercenary spirit of the world. M'sieu Fortier turned back into the room, after bowing his visitors out with old-time French courtliness, and turning to the sleepy white cat, said with a dry sob:

"Minesse, dere's only me an' you now."

About six days later, Courcey's morning dreams were disturbed by the announcement of a visitor. Hastily doing a toilet, he descended the stairs to find M'sieu Fortier nervously pacing the hall floor.

"I come fo' bring back you' money, yaas. I cannot sleep, I cannot eat, I only cry, and t'ink, and weesh fo' mon violon; and Minesse, an' de ol' woman too, dey mope an' look bad too, all for mon violon. I try fo' to use dat money, but eet burn an' sting lak blood money. I feel lak' I done sol' my child. I cannot go at l'opera no mo', I t'ink of mon violon. I starve befo' I live widout. My heart, he is broke, I die for mon violon."

Courcey left the room and returned with the instrument.

"M'sieu Fortier," he said, bowing low, as he handed the case to the little man, "take your violin; it was a whim with me, a passion with you. And as for the money, why, keep that too; it was worth a hundred dollars to have possessed such an instrument even for six days."

SISTER JOSEPHA

Sister Josepha told her beads mechanically, her fingers numb with the accustomed exercise. The little organ creaked a dismal "O Salutaris," and she still knelt on the floor, her white-bonneted head nodding suspiciously. The Mother Superior gave a sharp glance at the tired figure; then, as a sudden lurch forward brought the little sister back to consciousness, Mother's eyes relaxed into a genuine smile.

The bell tolled the end of vespers, and the sombre-robed nuns filed out of the chapel to go about their evening duties. Little Sister Josepha's work was to attend to the household lamps, but there must have been as much oil spilled upon the table tonight as was put in the vessels. The small brown hands trembled so that most of the wicks were trimmed with points at one corner which caused them to smoke that night.

"Oh, cher Seigneur," she sighed, giving an impatient polish to a refractory chimney, "it is wicked and sinful, I know, but I am so tired. I can't be happy and sing anymore. It doesn't seem right for le bon Dieu to have me all cooped up here with nothing to see but stray visitors, and always the same old work, teaching those mean little girls to sew, and washing and filling the same old lamps. Pah!" And she polished the chimney with a sudden vigorous jerk which threatened destruction.

They were rebellious prayers that the red mouth murmured that night, and a restless figure that tossed on the hard dormitory bed. Sister Dominica called from her couch to know if Sister Josepha were ill.

"No," was the somewhat short response; then a muttered, "Why can't they let me alone for a minute? That pale-eyed Sister Dominica never sleeps; that's why she is so ugly."

About fifteen years before this night someone had brought to the orphan asylum connected with this convent, du Sacre Coeur, a round, dimpled bit of three-year-old humanity, who regarded the world from a pair of gravely twinkling black eyes, and only took a chubby thumb out of a rosy mouth long enough to answer in monosyllabic French. It was a child without an identity; there was but one name that anyone seemed to know, and that, too, was vague,—Camille.

She grew up with the rest of the waifs; scraps of French and American civilization thrown together to develop a seemingly inconsistent miniature world. Mademoiselle Camille was a queen among them, a pretty little tyrant who ruled the children and dominated the more timid sisters in charge.

One day an awakening came. When she was fifteen, and almost fully ripened into a glorious tropical beauty of the type that matures early, some visitors to the convent were fascinated by her and asked the Mother Superior to give the girl into their keeping.

Camille fled like a frightened fawn into the yard, and was only unearthed with some difficulty from behind a group of palms. Sulky and pouting, she was led into the parlour, picking at her blue pinafore like a spoiled infant.

"The lady and gentleman wish you to go home with them, Camille," said the Mother Superior, in the language of the convent. Her voice was kind and gentle apparently; but the child, accustomed to its various inflections, detected a steely ring behind its softness, like the proverbial iron hand in the velvet glove.

"You must understand, madame," continued Mother, in stilted English, "that we never force children from us. We are ever glad to place them in comfortable—how you say that?—quarters—maisons— homes—bien! But we will not make them go if they do not wish."

Camille stole a glance at her would-be guardians, and decided instantly, impulsively, finally. The woman suited her; but the man! It was doubtless intuition of the quick, vivacious sort which belonged to her blood that served her. Untutored in worldly knowledge, she could not divine the meaning of the pronounced leers and admiration of her physical charms which gleamed in the man's face, but she knew it made her feel creepy, and stoutly refused to go. Next day Camille was summoned from a task to the Mother Superior's parlour. The other girls gazed with envy upon her as she dashed down the courtyard with impetuous movement. Camille, they decided crossly, received too much notice. It was Camille this, Camille that; she was pretty, it was to be expected. Even Father Ray lingered longer in his blessing when his hands pressed her silky black hair.

As she entered the parlour, a strange chill swept over the girl. The room was not an unaccustomed one, for she had swept it many times, but today the stiff black chairs, the dismal crucifixes, the gleaming whiteness of the walls, even the cheap lithograph of the Madonna which Camille had always regarded as a perfect specimen of art, seemed cold and mean.

"Camille, ma chere," said Mother, "I am extremely displeased with you. Why did you not wish to go with Monsieur and Madame Lafaye yesterday?"

The girl uncrossed her hands from her bosom, and spread them out in a deprecating gesture.

"Mais, ma mere, I was afraid."

Mother's face grew stern. "No foolishness now," she exclaimed.

"It is not foolishness, ma mere; I could not help it, but that man looked at me so funny, I felt all cold chills down my back. Oh, dear Mother, I love the convent and the sisters so, I just want to stay and be a sister too, may I?"

And thus it was that Camille took the white veil at sixteen years. Now that the period of novitiate was over, it was just beginning to dawn upon her that she had made a mistake.

"Maybe it would have been better had I gone with the funny-looking lady and gentleman," she mused bitterly one night. "Oh, Seigneur, I'm so tired and impatient; it's so dull here, and, dear God, I'm so young."

There was no help for it. One must arise in the morning, and help in the refectory with the stupid Sister Francesca, and go about one's duties with a prayerful mien, and not even let a sigh escape when one's head ached with the eternal telling of beads.

A great fete day was coming, and an atmosphere of preparation and mild excitement pervaded the brown walls of the convent like a delicate aroma. The old Cathedral around the corner had stood a hundred years, and all the city was rising to do honour to its age and time-softened beauty. There would be a service, oh, but such a one! with two Cardinals, and Archbishops and Bishops, and all the accompanying glitter of soldiers and orchestras. The little sisters of the Convent du Sacre Coeur clasped their hands in anticipation of the holy joy. Sister Josepha curled her lip, she was so tired of churchly pleasures.

The day came, a gold and blue spring day, when the air hung heavy with the scent of roses and magnolias, and the sunbeams fairly laughed as they kissed the houses. The old Cathedral stood gray and solemn, and the flowers in Jackson Square smiled cheery birthday greetings across the way. The crowd around the door surged and pressed and pushed in its eagerness to get within. Ribbons stretched across the banquette were of no avail to repress it, and important ushers with cardinal colours could do little more.

The Sacred Heart sisters filed slowly in at the side door, creating a momentary flutter as they paced reverently to their seats, guarding the blue-bonneted orphans. Sister Josepha, determined to see as much of the world as she could, kept her big black eyes opened wide, as the church rapidly filled with the fashionably dressed, perfumed, rustling, and self-conscious throng.

Her heart beat quickly. The rebellious thoughts that will arise in the most philosophical of us surged in her small heavily gowned bosom. For her were the gray things, the neutral tinted skies, the ugly garb, the coarse meats; for them the rainbow, the ethereal airiness of earthly joys, the bonbons and glaces of the world. Sister Josepha did not know that the rainbow is elusive, and its colours but the illumination of tears; she had never been told that earthly ethereality is necessarily ephemeral, nor that bonbons and glaces, whether of the palate or of the soul, nauseate and pall upon the taste. Dear God, forgive her, for she bent with contrite tears over her worn rosary, and glanced no more at the worldly glitter of femininity.

The sunbeams streamed through the high windows in purple and crimson lights upon a veritable fugue of colour. Within the seats, crush upon crush of spring millinery; within the aisles erect lines of gold-braided, gold-buttoned military. Upon the altar, broad sweeps of golden robes, great dashes of crimson skirts, mitres and gleaming crosses, the soft neutral hue of rich lace vestments; the tender heads of childhood in picturesque attire; the proud, golden magnificence of the domed altar with its weighting mass of lilies and wide-eyed roses, and the long candles that sparkled their yellow star points above the reverent throng within the altar rails.

The soft baritone of the Cardinal intoned a single phrase in the suspended silence. The censer took up the note in its delicate clink clink, as it swung to and fro in the hands of a fair-haired child. Then the organ, pausing an instant in a deep, mellow, long-drawn note, burst suddenly into a magnificent strain, and the choir sang forth, "Kyrie Eleison, Christe Eleison." One voice, flute-like, piercing, sweet, rang high over the rest. Sister Josepha heard and trembled, as she buried her face in her hands, and let her tears fall, like other beads, through her rosary.

It was when the final word of the service had been intoned, the last peal of the exit march had died away, that she looked up meekly, to encounter a pair of youthful brown eyes gazing pityingly upon her. That was all she remembered for a moment, that the eyes were youthful and handsome and tender. Later, she saw that they were placed in a rather beautiful boyish face, surmounted by waves of brown hair, curling and soft, and that the head was set on a pair of shoulders decked in military uniform. Then the brown eyes marched away with the rest of the rear guard, and the white-bonneted sisters filed out the side door, through the narrow court, back into the brown convent.

That night Sister Josepha tossed more than usual on her hard bed, and clasped her fingers often in prayer to quell the wickedness in her heart. Turn where she would, pray as she might, there was ever a pair of tender, pitying brown eyes, haunting her persistently. The squeaky organ at vespers intoned the clank of military accoutrements to her ears, the white bonnets of the sisters about her faded into mists of curling brown hair. Briefly, Sister Josepha was in love.

The days went on pretty much as before, save for the one little heart that beat rebelliously now and then, though it tried so hard to be submissive. There was the morning work in the refectory, the stupid little girls to teach sewing, and the insatiable lamps that were so greedy for oil. And always the tender, boyish brown eyes, that looked so sorrowfully at the fragile, beautiful little sister, haunting, following, pleading.

Perchance, had Sister Josepha been in the world, the eyes would have been an incident. But in this home of self-repression and retrospection, it was a life-story. The eyes had gone their way, doubtless forgetting the little sister they pitied; but the little sister?

The days glided into weeks, the weeks into months. Thoughts of escape had come to Sister Josepha, to flee into the world, to merge in the great city where recognition was impossible, and, working her way like the rest of humanity, perchance encounter the eyes again.

It was all planned and ready. She would wait until some morning when the little band of black-robed sisters wended their way to mass at the Cathedral. When it was time to file out the side-door into the courtway, she would linger at prayers, then slip out another door, and unseen glide up Chartres Street to Canal, and once there, mingle in the throng that filled the wide thoroughfare. Beyond this first plan she could think no further.

Penniless, garbed, and shaven though she would be, other difficulties never presented themselves to her. She would rely on the mercies of the world to help her escape from this torturing life of inertia. It seemed easy now that the first step of decision had been taken.

The Saturday night before the final day had come, and she lay feverishly nervous in her narrow little bed, wondering with wide-eyed fear at the morrow. Pale-eyed Sister Dominica and Sister Francesca were whispering together in the dark silence, and Sister Josepha's ears pricked up as she heard her name.

"She is not well, poor child," said Francesca. "I fear the life is too confining."

"It is best for her," was the reply. "You know, sister, how hard it would be for her in the world, with no name but Camille, no friends, and her beauty; and then—"

Sister Josepha heard no more, for her heart beating tumultuously in her bosom drowned the rest. Like the rush of the bitter salt tide over a drowning man clinging to a spar, came the complete submerging of her hopes of another life. No name but Camille, that was true; no nationality, for she could never tell from whom or whence she came; no friends, and a beauty that not even an ungainly bonnet and shaven head could hide. In a flash she realised the deception of the life she would lead, and the cruel self-torture of wonder at her own identity. Already, as if in anticipation of the world's questionings, she was asking herself, "Who am I? What am I?"

The next morning the sisters du Sacre Coeur filed into the Cathedral at High Mass, and bent devout knees at the general confession. "Confiteor Deo omnipotenti," murmured the priest; and tremblingly one little sister followed the words, "Je confesse a Dieu, tout puissant—que j'ai beaucoup peche par pensees—c'est ma faute—c'est ma faute—c'est ma tres grande faute."

The organ pealed forth as mass ended, the throng slowly filed out, and the sisters paced through the courtway back into the brown convent walls. One paused at the entrance, and gazed with swift longing eyes in the direction of narrow, squalid Chartres Street, then, with a gulping sob, followed the rest, and vanished behind the heavy door.

Ten Minutes' Musing

There was a terrible noise in the school-yard at intermission; peeping out the windows the boys could be seen huddled in an immense bunch, in the middle of the yard. It looked like a fight, a mob, a knock-down,—anything, so we rushed out to the door hastily, fearfully, ready to scold, punish, console, frown, bind up broken heads or drag wounded forms from the melee as the case might be. Nearly every boy in the school was in that seething, swarming mass, and those who weren't were standing around on the edges, screaming and throwing up their hats in hilarious excitement. It was a mob, a fearful mob, but a mob apparently with a vigorous and well-defined purpose. It was a mob that screamed and howled, and kicked, and yelled, and shouted, and perspired, and squirmed, and wriggled, and pushed, and threatened, and poured itself all seemingly upon some central object. It was a mob that had an aim, that was determined to accomplish that aim, even though the whole azure expanse of sky fell upon them. It was a mob with set muscles, straining like whip-cords, eyes on that central object and with heads inward and sturdy legs outward, like prairie horses reversed in a battle. The cheerers and hat throwers on the outside were mirthful, but the mob was not; it howled, but howled without any cachinnation; it struggled for mastery. Some fell and were trampled over, some weaker ones were even tossed in the air, but the mob never deigned to trouble itself about such trivialities. It was an interesting, nervous whole, with divers parts of separate vitality.

In alarm I looked about for the principal. He was standing at a safe distance with his hands in his pockets watching the seething mass with a broad smile. At sight of my perplexed expression someone was about to venture an explanation, when there was a wild yell, a sudden vehement disintegration of the mass, a mighty rush and clutch at a dark object bobbing in the air—and the mist cleared from my intellect—as I realized it all—football.

Did you ever stop to see the analogy between a game of football and the interesting little game called life which we play everyday? There is one, far-fetched as it may seem, though, for that matter, life's game, being one of desperate chances and strategic moves, is analogous to anything.

But, if we could get out of ourselves and soar above the world, far enough to view the mass beneath in its daily struggles, and near enough the hearts of the people to feel the throbs beneath their boldly carried exteriors, the whole would seem naught but such a maddening rush and senseless-looking crushing. "We are but children of a larger growth" after all, and our ceaseless pursuing after the baubles of this earth are but the struggles for precedence in the business play-ground.

The football is money. See how the mass rushes after it! Everyone so intent upon his pursuit until all else dwindles into a ridiculous nonentity. The weaker ones go down in the mad pursuit, and are unmercifully trampled upon, but no matter, what is the difference if the foremost win the coveted prize and carry it off. See the big boy in front, he with iron grip, and determined, compressed lips? That boy is a type of the big, merciless man, the Gradgrind of the latter century. His face is set towards the ball, and even though he may crush a dozen small boys, he'll make his way through the mob and come out triumphant. And he'll be the victor longer than anyone else, in spite of the envy and fighting and pushing about him.

To an observer, alike unintelligent about the rules of a football game, and the conditions which govern the barter and exchange and fluctuations of the world's money market, there is as much difference between the sight of a mass of boys on a play-ground losing their equilibrium over a spheroid of rubber and a mass of men losing their coolness and temper and mental and nervous balance on change as there is between a pine sapling and a mighty forest king—merely a difference of age. The mighty, seething, intensely concentrated mass in its emphatic tendency to one point is the same, in the utter disregard of mental and physical welfare. The momentary triumphs of transitory possessions impress a casual looker-on with the same fearful idea—that the human race, after all, is savage to the core, and cultivates its savagery in an inflated happiness at own nearness to perfection.

But the bell clangs sharply, the overheated, nervous, tingling boys fall into line, and the sudden transition from massing disorder to military precision cuts short the ten minutes' musing.

The Bee-Man

We were glancing over the mental photograph album, and commenting on the great lack of dissimilarity in tastes. Nearly everyone preferred spring to any other season, with a very few exceptions in favor of autumn. The women loved Mrs. Browning and Longfellow; the men showed decided preferences after Emerson and Macauley. Conceit stuck out when the majority wanted to be themselves and none other, and only two did not want to live in the 19th century. But in one place, in answer to the question, "Whom would you rather be, if not yourself?" the answer was,

"A baby!"

"Why would you rather be a baby than any other personage?" queried someone glancing at the writer, who blushed as she replied.

"Because then I might be able to live a better life, I might have better opportunities and better chances for improving them, and it would bring me nearer the 20th century."

"About eight or nine years ago," said the first speaker, "I remember reading a story in a magazine for young folks. It was merely a fairy story, and perhaps was not intended to point a moral, but only to amuse the little ones. It was something on this order:—"

Once upon a time, there lived in an out of the way spot an ancient decrepit Bee-man. How old he was no one knew; whence he came, no one could tell: to the memory of the oldest inhabitant he had always lived in his dirty hut, surrounded by myriads of hives, attended always by a swarm of bees. He was good to the bits of children, and always ready with a sweet morsel of honeycomb for them. All his ambitions, sympathies and hopes were centered in his hives; until one day a fairy crept into his hut and whispered:

"You have not always been a common bee-man. Once you were something else."

"Tell me what I was," he asked eagerly.

"Nay, that I cannot do," replied the fairy, "our queen sent me to tell you this, and if you wished to search for your former self, I am to assist you. You must search the entire valley, and the first thing you meet to which you become violently attached, that is what you formerly were, and I shall give you back your correct form."

So the next morning the Bee-man, strapping his usual hive upon his back, and accompanied by the fairy in the form of a queen bee, set out upon his search throughout the valley. At first he became violently attached to the handsome person and fine castle of the Lord of the Realm, but on being kicked out of the lord's domains, his love turned to dislike.

The Bee-man and the fairy travelled far and wide and carefully inspected everything they met. The very Imp, the Languid young man, the Hippogriffith, the Thousand Tailed Hippopotamus, and many other types, until the Bee-man grew weary and was about to give up the search in disgust.

But suddenly amid all the vast halls of the enchanted domains through which they were wandering, there sounded shrieks and wails, and the inmates were thrown into the greatest confusion by the sight of the hideous hippogriffith dashing through, a million sparks emanating from his great eyes, his barbed tail waving high in the air, and holding in his talons a tiny infant.

Now, as soon as the Bee-man saw this, a great wave of sorrow and pity filled his breast, and he hastily followed the monster, arriving at his cave just in time to see him preparing to devour his prey. Madly dashing his hive of bees into the hippogriffith's face, and seizing the infant while the disturbed and angry bees stung and swarmed, the Bee-man rushed out followed by the Very Imp, the Languid young man and the fairy, and made his way to the child's mother. Just as soon as the baby was safely restored, the Bee-man ruminated thoughtfully awhile and finally remarked to the fairy:

"Do you know of all the things I have met so far, I liked the baby best of all, so I think I must have been a baby once!"

"Right you are," assented the fairy, "I knew it before, but, of course, I couldn't tell. Now I shall change you into your former shape, but remember, you must try to be something better than a Bee-man."

The Bee-man promised and was instantly changed into a baby. The fairy inoculated him from harm with a bee-sting, and gave him to the rescued infant's mother.

Nearly a cycle passed by, and one day the fairy having business in the valley, thought she would make inquiries concerning her protege. In her way she happened to pass a little, low, curious hut, with many bee hives about it, and swarms of bees flying in and out. The fairy, tired as well as curious, peeped in and discovered an ancient man attending to the wants of his pets. Upon a closer inspection, she recognized her infant of years ago. He had become a bee-man again!

"IT POINTS A PRETTY LITTLE moral," said the Fatalist, "for it certainly proves that do what we will, we cannot get away from our natures. It was inherent in that man's nature to tend bees. Bee-ing was the occupation chosen for him by Fate, and had the beneficent Fairy changed him a dozen times, he would ultimately have gone to bee-ing in some form or other."

The Fatalist was doubtless right, for it seems as though the inherent things in our nature must come out. But if we want to dig deep into the child's story for metaphysical morals, does it not also uphold the theory of re-incarnation? the ancient bee-man, perhaps is but a type of humanity growing old, and settled in its mode of living, while the fairy is but thought, whispering into our souls things half dread half pleasant.

There are moments when the consciousness of a former life comes sharply upon us, in swift, lightning flashes, too sudden to be tangible, too dazzling to leave an impress, or mayhap, in troubled dreams that bewilder and confuse with vague remembrances. If only a burst of memory would come upon some mortal, that the tale might be fully told, and these theories established as facts. It would unfold great possibilities of historical lore; of literary life; of religious speculation.

The Maiden's Dream

The maid had been reading love-poetry, where the world lay bathed in moon-light, fragrant with dew-wet roses and jasmine, harmonious with the clear tinkle of mandolin and guitar. Then a lethargy, like unto that which steeps the senses, and benumbs the faculties of the lotus-eaters, enveloped her brain, and she lay as one in a trance,—awake, yet sleeping; conscious, yet unburdened with care.

And there stole into her consciousness, words, thoughts, not of her own, yet she read them not, nor heard them spoken; they fell deep into her heart and soul, softer and more caressing than the over-shadowing wing of a mother-dove, sweeter and more thrilling than the last high notes of a violin, and they were these:—

Love, most potent, most tyrannical, and most gentle of the passions which sway the human mind, thou art the invisible agency which rules mens' souls, which governs mens' kingdoms, which controls the universe. By thy mighty will do the silent, eternal hosts of Heaven sweep in sublime procession across the unmeasured blue. The perfect harmony of the spheres is attuned for thee, and by thee; the perfect coloring of the clouds, than which no mortal pigment can dare equal, are thy handiwork. Most ancient of the heathen deities, Eros; powerful God of the Christians, Jehovah, all hail! For a brief possession of thy divine fire have kingdoms waxed and waned; men in all the bitterness of hatred fought, bled, died by millions, their grosser selves to be swept into the bosom of their ancient mother, an immense holocaust to thee. For thee and thee alone does the world prosper, for thee do men strive to become better than their fellow-men; for thee, and through thee have they sunk to such depths of degradation as causes a blush to be painted upon the faces of those that see. All things are subservient to thee. All the delicate intricate workings of that marvellous machine, the human brain; all the passions and desires of the human heart,—ambition, desire, greed, hatred, envy, jealousy, all others. Thou breedst them all, O love, thou art all-potent, all-wise, infinite, eternal! Thy power is felt by mortals in all ages, all climes, all conditions. Behold!

A picture came into the maiden's eye: a broad and fertile plain, tender verdure, soft blue sky overhead, with white billowy clouds nearing the horizon like great airy, snow-capped mountains. The soft warm breeze from the south whispered faintly through the tall, slender palms and sent a thrill of joy through the frisky lambkins, who capered by the sides of their graver dams. And there among the riches of the flock stood Laban, haughty, stern, yet withal a kindly gleam in the glance which rested upon the group about him. Hoary the beard that rested upon his breast, but steady the hand that stretched in blessing. Leah, the tender-eyed, the slighted, is there; and Rachel, young and beautiful and blushing beneath the ardent gaze of her handsome lover. "And Jacob loved Rachel, and said, I will serve thee seven years for Rachel, thy younger daughter."

How different the next scene! Heaven's wrath burst loose upon a single community. Fire, the red-winged demon with brazen throat wide opened, hangs his brooding wings upon an erstwhile happy city. Hades has climbed through the crater of Vesuvius, and leaps in fiendish waves along the land. Few the souls escaping, and God have mercy upon those who stumble through the blinding darkness, made more torturingly hideous by the intermittent flashes of lurid light. And yet there come three, whom the darkness seems not to deter, nor obstacles impede. Only a blind person, accustomed to constant darkness, and familiarized with these streets could walk that way. Nearer they come, a burst of flames thrown into the inky firmament by impish hands, reveals Glaucus, supporting the half-fainting Ione, following Nydia, frail, blind, flower-loving Nydia, sacrificing life for her unloving beloved.

And then the burning southern sun shone bright and golden o'er the silken sails of the Nile serpent's ships; glinted on the armor and weapons of the famous galley; shone with a warm caressing touch upon her beauty, as though it loved this queen, as powerful in her sphere as he in his. It is at Actium, and the fate of nations and generations yet unborn hang, as the sword of Damocles hung, upon the tiny thread of destiny. Egypt herself, her splendid barbaric beauty acting like an inspiration upon the craven followers, leads on, foremost in this fierce struggle. Then, the tide turns, and overpowered, they fly before disgrace and defeat. Antony is there, the traitor, dishonored, false to his country, yet true to his love; Antony, whom ambition could not lure from her passionate caresses; Antony, murmuring softly,—

> *Egypt, thou knowest too well*
> *My heart was to thy rudder tied by the strings,*
> *And thou should'st tow me after.*
> *Over my spirit*

Thy full supremacy thou knewest,
And that thy beck might from the bidding of the gods
Command me.

Picture after picture flashed through the maiden's mind. Agnes, the gentle, sacrificing, burrowing like some frantic animal through the ruins of Lisbon, saving her lover, Franklin, by teeth and bleeding hands. Dora, the patient, serving a loveless existence, saving her rival from starvation and destitution. The stern, dark, exiled Florentine poet, with that one silver ray in his clouded life—Beatrice.

She heard the piping of an elfish voice, "Mother, why does the minister keep his hands over his heart?" and the white drawn face of Hester Prynne, with her scarlet elf-child, passed slowly across her vision. The wretched misery of deluded Lucius and his mysterious Lamia she saw, and watched with breathless interest the formation of that "Brotherhood of the Rose." There was radiant Armorel, from sea-blown, wave-washed Lyonesse, her perfect head poised in loving caress over the magic violin. Dark-eyed Corinne, head drooped gently as she improvised those Rome-famed world symphonies passed, almost ere Edna and St. Elmo had crossed the threshold of the church happy in the love now consecrated through her to God. Oh, the pictures, the forms, the love-words which crowded her mind! They thrilled her heart, crushed out all else save a crushing, over-powering sense of perfect, complete joy. A joy that sought to express itself in wondrous melodies and silences, filled with thoughts too deep and sacred for words. Overpowered with the magnificence of his reign, overwhelmed with the complete subjugation of all things unto him, do you wonder that she awoke and placing both hands into those of the lover at her side, whispered:—

Take all of me—I am thine own, heart, soul,
Brain, body, all; all that I am or dream
Is thine forever; yea, though space should teem
With thy conditions, I'd fulfil the whole,
Were to fulfil them to be loved by thee.

Violets

I

"And she tied a bunch of violets with a tress of her pretty brown hair."

She sat in the yellow glow of the lamplight softly humming these words. It was Easter evening, and the newly risen spring world was slowly sinking to a gentle, rosy, opalescent slumber, sweetly tired of the joy which had pervaded it all day. For in the dawn of the perfect morn, it had arisen, stretched out its arms in glorious happiness to greet the Saviour and said its hallelujahs, merrily trilling out carols of bird, and organ and flower-song. But the evening had come, and rest.

There was a letter lying on the table, it read:

Dear,

"I send you this little bunch of flowers as my Easter token. Perhaps you may not be able to read their meaning, so I'll tell you. Violets, you know, are my favorite flowers. Dear, little, human-faced things! They seem always as if about to whisper a love-word; and then they signify that thought which passes always between you and me. The orange blossoms—you know their meaning; the little pinks are the flowers you love; the evergreen leaf is the symbol of the endurance of our affection; the tube-roses I put in, because once when you kissed and pressed me close in your arms, I had a bunch of tube-roses on my bosom, and the heavy fragrance of their crushed loveliness has always lived in my memory. The violets and pinks are from a bunch I wore today, and when kneeling at the altar, during communion, did I sin, dear, when I thought of you? The tube-roses and orange-blossoms I wore Friday night; you always wished for a lock of my hair, so I'll tie these flowers with them—but there, it is not stable enough; let me wrap them with a bit of ribbon, pale blue, from that little dress I wore last winter to the dance, when we had such a long, sweet talk in that forgotten nook. You always loved that dress, it fell in such soft ruffles away from the throat and bosom,—you called me your little forget-me-not, that night. I laid the flowers away for awhile in our favorite book,—Byron—just at the poem we loved best, and now I send them to you. Keep them always in remembrance of me, and if aught should occur to separate us, press these flowers to your lips, and I will be with you in spirit, permeating your heart with unutterable love and happiness."

II

IT IS EASTER AGAIN. As of old, the joyous bells clang out the glad news of the resurrection. The giddy, dancing sunbeams laugh riotously in field and street; birds carol their sweet twitterings everywhere, and the heavy perfume of flowers scents the golden atmosphere with inspiring fragrance. One long, golden sunbeam steals silently into the white-curtained window of a quiet room, and lay athwart a sleeping face. Cold, pale, still, its fair, young face pressed against the satin-lined casket. Slender, white fingers, idle now, they that had never known rest; locked softly over a bunch of violets; violets and tube-roses in her soft, brown hair, violets in the bosom of her long, white gown; violets and tube-roses and orange-blossoms banked everywhere, until the air was filled with the ascending souls of the human flowers. Some whispered that a broken heart had ceased to flutter in that still, young form, and that it was a mercy for the soul to ascend on the slender sunbeam. Today she kneels at the throne of heaven, where one year ago she had communed at an earthly altar.

III

FAR AWAY IN A DISTANT city, a man, carelessly looking among some papers, turned over a faded bunch of flowers tied with a blue ribbon and a lock of hair. He paused meditatively awhile, then turning to the regal-looking woman lounging before the fire, he asked:

"Wife, did you ever send me these?"

She raised her great, black eyes to his with a gesture of ineffable disdain, and replied languidly:

"You know very well I can't bear flowers. How could I ever send such sentimental trash to anyone? Throw them into the fire."

And the Easter bells chimed a solemn requiem as the flames slowly licked up the faded violets. Was it merely fancy on the wife's part, or did the husband really sigh,—a long, quivering breath of remembrance?

When the Bayou Overflows

When the sun goes down behind the great oaks along the Bayou Teche near Franklin, it throws red needles of light into the dark woods, and leaves a great glow on the still bayou. Ma'am Mouton paused at her gate and cast a contemplative look at the red sky.

"Hit will rain tomorrow, sho'. I mus' git in my t'ings."

Ma'am Mouton's remark must have been addressed to herself or to the lean dog, for no one else was visible. She moved briskly about the yard, taking things from the line, when Louisette's voice called cheerily:

"Ah, Ma'am Mouton, can I help?"

Louisette was petite and plump and black-haired. Louisette's eyes danced, and her lips were red and tempting. Ma'am Mouton's face relaxed as the small brown hands relieved hers of their burden.

"Sylves', has he come yet?" asked the red mouth.

"Mais non, ma chere," said Ma'am Mouton, sadly, "I can' tell fo' w'y he no come home soon dese day. Ah me, I feel lak' somet'ing goin' happen. He so strange."

Even as she spoke a quick nervous step was heard crunching up the brick walk. Sylves' paused an instant without the kitchen door, his face turned to the setting sun. He was tall and slim and agile; a true 'cajan.

"Bon jour, Louisette," he laughed. "Eh, maman!"

"Ah, my son, you are ver' late."

Sylves' frowned, but said nothing. It was a silent supper that followed. Louisette was sad, Ma'am Mouton sighed now and then, Sylves' was constrained.

"Maman," he said at length, "I am goin' away."

Ma'am Mouton dropped her fork and stared at him with unseeing eyes; then, as she comprehended his remark, she put her hand out to him with a pitiful gesture.

"Sylves'!" cried Louisette, springing to her feet.

"Maman, don't, don't!" he said weakly; then gathering strength from the silence, he burst forth:

"Yaas, I'm goin' away to work. I'm tired of dis, jus' dig, dig, work in de fiel', nothin' to see but de cloud, de tree, de bayou. I don't lak' New Orleans; it too near here, dere no mo' money dere. I go up fo' Mardi Gras, an' de same people, de same strit'. I'm goin' to Chicago!"

"Sylves'!" screamed both women at once.

Chicago! That vast, far-off city that seemed in another world. Chicago! A name to conjure with for wickedness.

"W'y, yaas," continued Sylves', "lots of boys I know dere. Henri an' Joseph Lascaud an' Arthur, dey write me what money dey mek' in cigar. I can mek' a livin' too. I can mek' fine cigar. See how I do in New Orleans in de winter."

"Oh, Sylves'," wailed Louisette, "den you'll forget me!"

"Non, non, ma chere," he answered tenderly. "I will come back when the bayou overflows again, an' maman an' Louisette will have fine present."

Ma'am Mouton had bowed her head on her hands, and was rocking to and fro in an agony of dry-eyed misery.

Sylves' went to her side and knelt. "Maman," he said softly, "maman, you mus' not cry. All de boys go 'way, an' I will come back reech, an' you won't have fo' to work no mo'."

But Ma'am Mouton was inconsolable.

It was even as Sylves' had said. In the summer-time the boys of the Bayou Teche would work in the field or in the town of Franklin, hack-driving and doing odd jobs. When winter came, there was a general exodus to New Orleans, a hundred miles away, where work was to be had as cigar-makers. There is money, plenty of it, in cigar-making, if one can get in the right place. Of late, however, there had been a general slackness of the trade. Last winter oftentimes Sylves' had walked the streets out of work. Many were the Creole boys who had gone to Chicago to earn a living, for the cigar-making trade flourishes there wonderfully. Friends of Sylves' had gone, and written home glowing accounts of the money to be had almost for the asking. When one's blood leaps for new scenes, new adventures, and one needs money, what is the use of frittering away time alternately between the Bayou Teche and New Orleans? Sylves' had brooded all summer, and now that September had come, he was determined to go.

Louisette, the orphan, the girl-lover, whom everyone in Franklin knew would some day be Ma'am Mouton's daughter-in-law, wept and pleaded in vain. Sylves' kissed her quivering lips.

"Ma chere," he would say, "t'ink, I will bring you one fine diamon' ring, nex' spring, when de bayou overflows again."

Louisette would fain be content with this promise. As for Ma'am Mouton, she seemed to have grown ages older. Her Sylves' was going from her; Sylves', whose trips to New Orleans had been a yearly source of heart-break, was going far away for months to that mistily wicked city, a thousand miles away.

October came, and Sylves' had gone. Ma'am Mouton had kept up bravely until the last, when with one final cry she extended her arms to the pitiless train bearing him northward. Then she and Louisette went home drearily, the one leaning upon the other.

Ah, that was a great day when the first letter came from Chicago!

Louisette came running in breathlessly from the post-office, and together they read it again and again. Chicago was such a wonderful city, said Sylves'. Why, it was always like New Orleans at Mardi Gras with the people. He had seen Joseph Lascaud, and he had a place to work promised him. He was well, but he wanted, oh, so much, to see maman and Louisette. But then, he could wait.

Was ever such a wonderful letter? Louisette sat for an hour afterwards building gorgeous air-castles, while Ma'am Mouton fingered the paper and murmured prayers to the Virgin for Sylves'. When the bayou overflowed again? That would be in April. Then Louisette caught herself looking critically at her slender brown fingers, and blushed furiously, though Ma'am Mouton could not see her in the gathering twilight.

Next week there was another letter, even more wonderful than the first. Sylves' had found work. He was making cigars, and was earning two dollars a day. Such wages! Ma'am Mouton and Louisette began to plan pretty things for the brown cottage on the Teche.

That was a pleasant winter, after all. True, there was no Sylves', but then he was always in New Orleans for a few months anyway. There were his letters, full of wondrous tales of the great queer city, where cars went by ropes underground, and where there was no Mardi Gras and the people did not mind Lent. Now and then there would be a present, a keepsake for Louisette, and some money for maman. They would plan improvements for the cottage, and Louisette began to do sewing and dainty crochet, which she would hide with a blush if anyone hinted at a trousseau.

It was March now, and Spring-time. The bayou began to sweep down between its banks less sluggishly than before; it was rising, and soon would spread over its tiny levees. The doors could be left open now, though the trees were not yet green; but then down here the trees do not swell and bud slowly and tease you for weeks with promises of greenness. Dear no, they simply look mysterious, and their twigs shake against each other and tell secrets of the leaves that will soon be born.

Then one morning you awake, and lo, it is a green world! The boughs have suddenly clothed themselves all in a wondrous garment, and you feel the blood run riot in your veins out of pure sympathy.

One day in March, it was warm and sweet. Underfoot were violets, and wee white star flowers peering through the baby-grass. The sky was blue, with flecks of white clouds reflecting themselves in the brown bayou. Louisette tripped up the red brick walk with the Chicago letter in her hand, and paused a minute at the door to look upon the leaping waters, her eyes dancing.

"I know the bayou must be ready to overflow," went the letter in the carefully phrased French that the brothers taught at the parochial school, "and I am glad, for I want to see the dear maman and my Louisette. I am not so well, and Monsieur le docteur says it is well for me to go to the South again."

Monsieur le docteur! Sylves' not well! The thought struck a chill to the hearts of Ma'am Mouton and Louisette, but not for long. Of course, Sylves' was not well, he needed some of maman's tisanes. Then he was homesick; it was to be expected.

At last the great day came, Sylves' would be home. The brown waters of the bayou had spread until they were seemingly trying to rival the Mississippi in width. The little house was scrubbed and cleaned until it shone again. Louisette had looked her dainty little dress over and over to be sure that there was not a flaw to be found wherein Sylves' could compare her unfavourably to the stylish Chicago girls.

The train rumbled in on the platform, and two pair of eyes opened wide for the first glimpse of Sylves'. The porter, all officiousness and brass buttons, bustled up to Ma'am Mouton.

"This is Mrs. Mouton?" he inquired deferentially.

Ma'am Mouton nodded, her heart sinking. "Where is Sylves'?"

"He is here, madam."

There appeared Joseph Lascaud, then some men bearing Something. Louisette put her hands up to her eyes to hide the sight, but Ma'am Mouton was rigid.

"It was too cold for him," Joseph was saying to almost deaf ears, "and he took the consumption. He thought he could get well when he come home. He talk all the way down about the bayou, and about you and Louisette. Just three hours ago he had a bad hemorrhage, and he died from weakness. Just three hours ago. He said he wanted to get home and give Louisette her diamond ring, when the bayou overflowed."

The Woman

The literary manager of the club arose, cleared his throat, adjusted his cravat, fixed his eyes sternly upon the young man, and in a sonorous voice, a little marred by his habitual lisp, asked: "Mr.——, will you please tell us your opinion upon the question, whether woman's chances for matrimony are increased or decreased when she becomes man's equal as a wage earner?"

The secretary adjusted her eye-glass, and held her pencil alertly poised above her book, ready to note which side Mr.—— took. Mr.—— fidgeted, pulled himself together with a violent jerk, and finally spoke his mind. Someone else did likewise, also someone else, then the women interposed, and jumped on the men, the men retaliated, a wordy war ensued, and the whole matter ended by nothing being decided, pro or con—generally the case in wordy discussions. *Moi?* Well, I sawed wood and said nothing, but all the while there was forming in my mind, no, I won't say forming, it was there already. It was this, *Why should well-salaried women marry?* Take the average working-woman of today. She works from five to ten hours a day, doing extra night work, sometimes, of course. Her work over, she goes home or to her boarding-house, as the case may be. Her meals are prepared for her, she has no household cares upon her shoulders, no troublesome dinners to prepare for a fault-finding husband, no fretful children to try her patience, no petty bread and meat economies to adjust. She has her cares, her money-troubles, her debts, and her scrimpings, it is true, but they only make her independent, instead of reducing her to a dead level of despair. Her day's work ends at the office, school, factory or store; the rest of the time is hers, undisturbed by the restless going to and fro of housewifely cares, and she can employ it in mental or social diversions. She does not incessantly rely upon the whims of a cross man to take her to such amusements as she desires. In this nineteenth century she is free to go where she pleases—provided it be in a moral atmosphere—without comment. Theatres, concerts, lectures, and the lighter amusements of social affairs among her associates, are open to her, and there she can go, see, and be seen, admire and be admired, enjoy and be enjoyed, without a single harrowing thought of the baby's milk or the husband's coffee.

Her earnings are her own, indisputably, unreservedly, undividedly. She knows to a certainty just how much she can spend, how well she can dress, how far her earnings will go. If there is a dress, a book, a bit of music, a bunch of flowers, or a bit of furniture that she wants, she can get it, and there is no need of asking anyone's advice, or gently hinting to John that Mrs. So and So has a lovely new hat, and there is one ever so much prettier and cheaper down at Thus & Co.'s. To an independent spirit there is a certain sense of humiliation and wounded pride in asking for money, be it five cents or five hundred dollars. The working woman knows no such pang; she has but to question her account and all is over. In the summer she takes her savings of the winter, packs her trunk and takes a trip more or less extensive, and there is none to say her nay,—nothing to bother her save the accumulation of her own baggage. There is an independent, happy, free-and-easy swing about the motion of her life. Her mind is constantly being broadened by contact with the world in its working clothes; in her leisure moments by the better thoughts of dead and living men which she meets in her applications to books and periodicals; in her vacations, by her studies of nature, or it may be other communities than her own. The freedom which she enjoys she does not trespass upon, for if she did not learn at school she has acquired since habits of strong self-reliance, self-support, earnest thinking, deep discriminations, and firmly believes that the most perfect liberty is that state in which humanity conforms itself to and obeys strictly, without deviation, those laws which are best fitted for their mutual self-advancement.

And so your independent working woman of today comes as near being ideal in her equable self poise as can be imagined. So why should she hasten to give this liberty up in exchange for a serfdom, sweet sometimes, it is true, but which too often becomes galling and unendurable.

It is not marriage that I decry, for I don't think any really sane person would do this, but it is this wholesale marrying of girls in their teens, this rushing into an unknown plane of life to avoid work. Avoid work! What housewife dares call a moment her own?

Marriages might be made in Heaven, but too often they are consummated right here on earth, based on a desire to possess the physical attractions of the woman by the man, pretty much as a child desires a toy, and an innate love of man, a wild desire not to be ridiculed by the foolish as an "old maid," and a certain delicate shrinking from the work of the world—laziness is a good name for it—by the woman. The attraction of mind to mind, the ability of one to compliment the lights and shadows in the other, the capacity of either to fulfil the duties of wife or husband—these do not enter into the contract. That is why we have divorce courts.

And so our independent woman in every year of her full, rich, well-rounded life, gaining fresh knowledge and experience, learning humanity, and particularly that portion of it which is the other gender, so well as to avoid clay-footed idols, and finally when she does consent to bear the yoke upon her shoulders, does so with perhaps less romance and glamor than her younger scoffing sisters, but with an assurance of solid and more lasting happiness. Why should she have hastened this; was aught lost by the delay?

"They say" that men don't admire this type of woman, that they prefer the soft, dainty, winning, mindless creature who cuddles into men's arms, agrees to everything they say, and looks upon them as a race of gods turned loose upon this earth for the edification of womankind. Well, may be so, but there is one thing positive, they certainly respect the independent one, and admire her, too, even if it is at a distance, and that in itself is something. As to the other part, no matter how sensible a woman is on other questions, when she falls in love she is fool enough to believe her adored one a veritable Solomon. Cuddling? Well, she may preside over conventions, brandish her umbrella at board meetings, tramp the streets soliciting subscriptions, wield the blue pencil in an editorial sanctum, hammer a type-writer, smear her nose with ink from a galley full of pied type, lead infant ideas through the tortuous mazes of c-a-t and r-a-t, plead at the bar, or wield the scalpel in a dissecting room, yet when the right moment comes, she will sink as gracefully into his manly embrace, throw her arms as lovingly around his neck, and cuddle as warmly and sweetly to his bosom as her little sister who has done nothing else but think, dream, and practice for that hour. It comes natural, you see.

The Poet and His Song

O ur notions upon the subject of Biography," says Carlyle, "may perhaps appear extravagant; but if an individual is really of consequence enough to have his life and character for public remembrance, we have always been of opinion that the public ought to be made acquainted with all the inward springs and relations of his character. How did the world and the man's life, from his particular position, represent themselves to his mind? How did coexisting circumstances modify him from without; how did he modify these from within? With what endeavors and what efficacy rule over them; with what resistance and what suffering sink under them? . . . Few individuals, indeed, can deserve such a study; and many *lives* will be written, and, for the gratification of innocent curiosity, ought to be written, and read and forgotten, which are not, in this sense, *biographies*."

Thus Carlyle. It would seem then, that if one must write about a poet, the world would wish to know how and in what manner the great phenomena of Nature impressed him, for Nature is the mother of all poets and there can be no true poetry unless inspired deeply by the external world which men do not touch. If the poet was an urban child, if the wonder of star-filled nights, the mystery of the sea, the beauty of sunrise and sunset, the freshness of dewy morns, and the warm scent of the upturned sod filled him with no rapture, then he was no true poet, howsoever he rhymed. So if one wishes to get a correct idea of any poet whatever, he must delve beneath the mere sordid facts of life and its happenings; of so many volumes published in such and such a time; of the influence upon him of this or that author or school of poetry; of the friends who took up his time, or gave him inspiration, and, above all, one must see what the love of Nature has done for the poet.

Mere looking into the printed words may not always do this. Who knows what heart-full of suggestion may lie in one expression? Who can tell in how much one word may be, as Higginson has expressed it, "palaces to dwell in," "years of crowded passion in a phrase," "half a life concentrated in a sentence?" To the banal mind a phrase may be nothing but a sweet rhythm of language, a well-turned, well-chosen expression. To the one who may have had the chance of communion with the creative mind, ere it expressed its longings in words, the phrase may be all pregnant with suggestion.

Your true poet is a child of Nature and lies close to the great Mother-heart. Even though he were born in the city, where his outlook on trees and fields is an incidental and sporadic occurrence in his life, he senses the divine heart pulsing beneath all things, and when he is finally brought face to face with the wonders of out-of-doors, untouched by the desecrating hand of man, he bursts forth into song, released from the conventionalities of other men's verse.

This was true of Paul Dunbar. He was a child of the city, a small city, true, where Nature was not so ruthlessly crushed away from the lives of men. There were trees and flowers near home, and a never-to-be-forgotten mill-race, which swirled through all his dreams of boyhood and manhood. Like the true poet that he was, he reached out and groped for the bigness of out-of-doors, divining all that he was afterwards to see, and in his earlier verse expressing his intuitions, rather than his observations.

Love of nature was there, but the power to express this love was not. Instead, he harked back to the feeling of the race, and intuitively put their aspirations into song. Tennyson and Lowell meant much to him, because they had expressed his yearnings for the natural world, and his soul yearned toward their verse. The exquisite line, "When cows come home along the bars—" how much of the English poet went into that line, and how much of the reminiscences of the earlier life of his family? More of the former, he always confessed.

Children love "The Seedling." It is good for them who are being initiated, city-wise, into the mysteries of planting and growth. It is scientific, without being technical—it is Tennyson's "Flower in the crannied wall," Americanized, brought down to the minds of little folks. The poet loved Tennyson, he walked with him in his earlier years, he confessed his indebtedness to him in his later days; he always praised him, and defended him hotly against the accusation of too much mere academic phrasing.

In the poem "Preparation" we see more of this groping toward the light; the urban child trying to throw off the meretriciousness of city life. Say what you will, or what Mr. Howells wills, about the "feeling the Negro life esthetically, and expressing it lyrically," it was in the pure English poems that the poet expressed *himself*. He may have expressed his race in the dialect poems; they were to him the side issues of his work, the overflowing of a life apart from his dearest dreams. His deepest sorrow he told in "The Poet."

He sang of life serenely sweet,
With now and then a deeper note.
From some high peak, nigh, yet remote,
He voiced the world's absorbing heat.

He sang of love when earth was young,
And love itself, was in its lays,
But, ah, the world, it turned to praise
A jingle in a broken tongues.

This is a digression. "Preparation" is contemporaneous with "Discovered" and "Delinquent," but in the latter poems, he is feeling his way to make the laughter that the world will like; in the former, he is feeling his way to that true upward expression of the best in him. "A little bird sits in the nest and sings" is too much of Lowell to be true, "But the note is a prelude to better things," reflecting as in solution the thought of the "Vision of Sir Làkunfal." Our poet cast the poem aside as a thing of no worth, nor is it, except as it glimpses a bit of the soul within, like Lowell's clod "reaching up to a soul in grass and flowers."

Then came the experience on the lake. It was a never-to-be-forgotten summer. Opportunity and youth combined with poetry and the unsuspected beauty of the inland sea. Nature burst upon him with a surge. He knew now to the full the beauty of the gray days that he had dimly sung; the wind rising along the lake reeds and shivering premonition into them; the moon scudding before the wind clouds like a pale wraith with flung-back hair; the storm, never so swift in its wrath as on the shores of a lake; these things entered into his soul like a revelation. This, then, was what it all meant—these quivering fears and wonders of the early spring. From a little boy, he confessed, the spring filled him with longings, unexpressed, vague, terrible, like the fears, of the night, which persisted long after manhood. What did it mean, this terrible loneliness, this longing for companionship, and disgust with mere human company? He knew now. Nature had called him, and he had not been able to heed her call, until the Lake told him how.

He had sung about "Merry Autumn" in the conventional manner; he had enumerated pictures in the "Song of Summah," and he had written many conventional spring poems, dialect and otherwise, from the point of view of the spectator, but now began that passionate oneness with

Nature, that was not to leave him until he deliberately turned his back upon her.

Beginning with that summer, he began to learn how to store up pictures in the mind as Wordsworth did. He began, mind you, only began to learn how to accumulate experiences that would later burst red-hot in one phrase, one line, one stanza that combined a month's experiences, a season's joy, a year's longing in them. It is only the true poet-heart that can do this. Whether or not it may be able to express it in rhythm, or metre, or music, or painting, or express it at all, is a mere matter of no moment. If these accumulated experiences be stifled in the sweet darkness of the heart, that is no matter, they have been; it is enough.

This faculty of stored experiences swiftly phrased may be exquisitely traced in many a poem. There was in Washington a bare, red-clay hill, open to the sun, barren of shade on its highest point, steep of ascent, boldly near the sky—truly, almost a "heaven-kissing hill." Daily walks on the hill fulminate in one line in "Love's Apotheosis—the sun-kissed hill." The white arc light of the corner lamp, filtering through the arches of the maples on Spruce street, make for the tender suggestion in "Lover's Lane," where the lovers walk side by side under the "shadder-mekin'" trees. Up in the mountains of the Catskills, where the rain fell often in July days, more often than the lover of out-door sports would relish, there was one little phoebe-bird, who would sing plaintively through all the rain, ending with a mournful chirp when the sun shone out at last. His little song through the disappointing storm was infinitely cheering, and often finds expression in the song of the human bird who listened to him.

> *An' it's moughty ha'd a-hopin'*
> *W'en de clouds is big an' black,*
> *An' all de t'ings you's waited fu'*
> *Has failed—er gone to wrack—*
> *But des keep on a joggin' wid a little bit of song,*
> *De mo'n is alius brightah w'en de night's been long.*

"Keep a Song Up on De Way" enshrines both the little bird and the beloved water-fall that boomed all night under the windows. The first and third stanzas were merrily conceived and merrily written, a "compliment to the persistent bird."

Oh, de clouds is mighty heavy—

(The cloud wraiths used to creep down the mountain side and literally, camp in the front yard, so that one went stumbling about in the mixture of cloud.and mist),

An' de rain is mighty thick;
Keep a song up on de way.
And de waters is a rumblin'
On de boulders in de crick,
Keep a song up on de way.
Fu' a bird ercross de road
Is a-singin' lak he knowed
Dat we people didn't daih
Fu' to try de rainy aih
Wid a song up on de way.

The power of keen observation grows in arithmetical ratio as the soul divests itself of the littlenesses of life, the mere man-made ambitions, the ignoble strivings after place. The poet found new joy in the patch-work greenery of the mountains spread out at his feet; in the lights and shades on the fields of rye and corn and wheat and buckwheat, making the mountains seem as if Mother Nature had cunningly embroidered a huge cover for her summer dress. When he discovered, on the first visit, that the ground of the potato fields was violet, he cried aloud for joy. It had been a hard struggle to see that the light turned violet in the shadows under the vines, but when the realization came home, it was an exquisite sensation, worthy to be enshrined in a tender line. Thereafter, the mountains meant more than they had before, and subsequent visits always held out a promise of new things to be keenly detected and shoutingly announced. The waterfall that droned all night, save when, swollen with pride by the rain, it roared; the rain pouring down slantwise through the skies across the fields; the clouds casting great shadows athwart the mountain sides may have been forgotten those summers, yet, trick-like, they return here and there in unexpected places, showing how deeply they had become a part of "that inward eye, which is the bliss of solitude," of which Wordsworth sings. "The bird's call and the water's drone," and the "water-fall that sang all night," from "The Lost Dream," were but single instances of the stored-up memories expressed years after the summers in the Catskills were themselves fragments of forgotten days.

In the little poem "Rain-Songs" he sings:

> *The rain streams down like harp-strings from the sky,*
> *The wind, that world-old harpist, sitteth by;*
> *And ever, as he sings his low refrain,*
> *He plays upon the harp-strings of the rain.*

This came long after the simile of the harp-strings had been discovered, exulted over and laid aside on the tables of his memory. One more recollection of those days in the mountains is worth recording. The first time the song of the whip-poor-will came to him, he was amused. Plaintive it is to all who hear it for the first time, but to him it suggested tattling, from its nervous haste, its gasping intake of breath, like a little boy trying to clear himself from fault, yet half pleading that his companion in misdeeds be let go unpunished. The poet queried with much anxiety of everyone on the place, was the cry "Whip-poor-will" a command, or was it "Whip-poor-will" a pathetic question and hoping of Will's final exoneration? It was a whimsical turn that he gave to the cry of the night-bird, and the shrill insistence of the katy-did in the little poem "Whip-poor-Will and Katy-Did," when he wants to know why one must "Whip-poor-Will," when we know from the song of the insect that it was Katy who did?

This humorous outlook on Nature is a quaint turn of mind that few poets posses. Nature is stern, awful, sweet, sympathetic, lovable, but hardly humorous, so the world thinks. Yet where are there such exquisite manifestations of humor to be found in the man-made world about us? Nature's humor is grim sometimes, tricksy sometimes, dainty ofttimes, and sternly practical many times. To view life with humor is as Nature intended us to do. The gods must laugh, else where did men learn how?

This apropos of West Medford, Massachusetts. Here he visited thrice, and confessed that the place held for him the charm of hallowed association, which all the country near Boston must have for the world born outside Massachusetts, which still rules the minds of the *hoi polloi* with the potent sway of the nearest approach in this country to anything like reposeful ease and culture. But historic spots and monuments and powder mills of Revolutionary fame and battlefields meant but little after a while to the poet. Middlesex county abounds in rivers—were they fishable? Fishing was his one pastime, which he loved ardently, passionately, with the devotion of the true fisherman. Was there a river? Then the next question, "How is the fishing?" Walton's "Compleat Angler," is all right to read, but better to live. Anyhow it contains too many recipes for cooking. Van Dyke's "Fisherman's Luck" is better, particularly as the book is dedicated to the "Lady in Gray." Fishing and the color gray! His favorite sport and color; an unforgettable combination.

So the streams in the Catskills were deliciously suggestive of mountain trout, and even native indolence and poor health did not prevent him from arising one Fourth of July morning at three o'clock, and taking with him all the valiant souls who would go, to hie them to an over-fished stream, where the most carefully chosen flies only made the trout sniff and flirt themselves arrogantly; and where the unsportsmanlike women, having found a cool pool to use as a refrigerator, were stupid enough to try to tempt sophisticated suckers to bite—and that after a fierce cannonading of fire-crackers in honor of their early patriotism.

So West Medford suggested fishing, wonderful possibilities. What though Longfellow had enshrined the Mystic in the Hall of Fame by the lines in Paul Revere's Ride? That was no matter. Anything as brown and dimpled and slow as that river must be fishable. Thus he decided on his first visit and came back to investigate when there was more time, and lo! The result he humorously enshrined in the "Ballade."

> By Mystic's bank I held my dream,
> (I held my fishing rod as well);
> The vision was of dace and bream,
> A fruitless vision, sooth to tell.
>
> * * * * *
>
> Oh, once loved, sluggish, darkling stream,
> For me no more thy waters swell,
> Thy music now the engines' scream,
> Thy fragrance now the factory's smell.
>
> * * * * *
>
> Thy wooded lanes with shade and gleam
> Where bloomed the fragrant asphodel.
>
> * * * * *

Poor Mystic! "Arcadia now has trolley lines," mourns the poet, and so wends his way home to put up his fishing rod, and pack away the reel until the streams of the Rocky Mountains lure the basket and rod out again.

To the soul born inland, the sea is always a revelation, and a wonder-working experience in the life. The man born near the sea, who has been reared near its beauty and wonder, whose soul has learned early in life to enter into its moods, to understand its gentleness and not to fear its grimness, whose life has been attuned to the roar of the breakers and the purl of its littlest white waves, such a man can scarcely understand the rush and uplift that comes to the inland man who sees the ocean in his maturity for the first time. Such was the tidal wave that swept over the poet when the ocean burst upon his view. And like all those born inland, when once the fascination of the sea possesses them, it becomes more exquisitely a part of the whole nature than even it does in the case of the one born on the shores of the sea. When the sea became a part of the poet's life, it wrapped itself naturally into his verse—but hardly ever disassociated from the human element. Humanity and the ocean melted into one indistinguishable mist, even as Wordsworth's moors were always peopled with one shadowy figure so indistinct that it merged into the grayness of the horizon. There is no hint of the sea, save from the hearsay point, in the first published volume of poems, but before the second came, Narragansett Pier had opened his eyes to the mystic beauty of the ocean, and his soul to its turbulence. The journey to England made him familiar with the gray nothingness of mid-ocean, and life subsequently meant frequent pilgrimages to the seashore. Gray skies and gray sea; these meant most to him; sombreness and gloom seemed part of the real meaning of the ocean. One need not seek in the life of the poet a kinship between love of the serious aspects of nature and a fancied wrong or injury in life. Because Milton always loved the moon veiled in clouds is no reason why we should conclude that early and unfortunate loves left him unable to view skies moonlit and cloudless without sorrow. Because Keats found passionate intensity of emotion in the mere aspect of Grecian beauty, a passion that saddened him, is no reason why we should conclude that Greece had wronged him or that beauty had wrecked his life. A poet is a poet because he *understands*; because he is born with a divine kinship with all things, and he is a poet in direct ratio to his power of sympathy.

Something of this, emanating from his own experience the poet shows in his poem "Sympathy."

"I know what the caged bird feel, alas!"

The iron grating of the book stacks in the Library of Congress suggested to him the bars of the bird's cage. June and July days are hot. All out of doors called and the trees of the shaded streets of Washington were tantalizingly suggestive of his beloved streams and fields. The torrid sun poured its rays down into the courtyard of the library and heated the iron grilling of the book stacks until they were like prison bars in more senses than one. The dry dust of the dry books (ironic incongruity!—a poet shut up in an iron cage with medical works), rasped sharply in his hot throat, and he understood how the bird felt when it beat its wings against its cage.

When he went down to Arundel-on-the-Bay—picturesque name of a picturesque place—he was thrilled as though stepping on hallowed ground. This was the Eastern Shore that gave birth to Douglass. More than the Boston Common, which memorized Attucks and deified Robert Gould Shaw and inspired his best sonnets, this was near the home of the idol of his youthful dreams, the true friend of his enthusiastic youth. The place was wild after the fashion of the shore of the Chesapeake; it seemed almost home to him—and the fishing was excellent. He enshrined it in his memory, and later came the poem "The Eastern Shore." It was written months after the lure of the bay had been forgotten when the skies swirled snow down on a shivering city, and the mind warmed the body as it harked back to the hot days of July under the burning skies and over the clean-washed sands of the Chesapeake Bay. One more poem the eastern shore inspired, "The Memory of Martha." The story "The Memory of Martha" being finished, the poet found himself rushed onward with a mighty sympathy for the man he had created, whose wife had left him for the unknown. It was the poet-heart throbbing in sympathy with the woes of the universe. He *was* the old husband, mourning his loss, even as when he wrote "Two Little Boots"; he *was*, for the time being, the broken-hearted mother, mourning over the little shoes. He wept as he wrote the poem, both poems in fact, and then laughed at his own tears—no immediate animus for either poem, just the overflowing of an understanding soul over a fancied grief.

Sometimes with him the memory of the words of another author commingled with a landscape, and then there is a rare combination of verse. It was when in the dire grip of pneumonia that the oft-reiterated desire, perhaps delirious, certainly comic, came for "A bear story, just one little bear story," to be read aloud to him. Blessed fortune it was then that Ernest Thompson-Seton was just giving to the world his inimitable "Wild Animals I Have Known," and fever or no fever, the poet must revel into forgetfulness of pain in listening to the woes of Raggy-lug, and the too canny wolves and bears. It made a review of the "Jungle Book" a delightful process, and invited a re-persual of Bliss Carman's poems. When the Catskills burst upon his delighted vision a while later, what more natural than that "To the Road," with its hint of Carman should enshrine the little white road winding up the mountain side?

> Cool is the wind, for the summer is waning—
> Who's for the road?
> Sun-flecked and soft where the dead leaves are raining,
> Knapsack and alpenstock press hand and shoulder—

Merriment here, loud and long, because any old dead branch when carried on a walk became dignified by the name of alpenstock, and the leather chatelaine purse of the companion in tramping became a knapsack.

The "Forest Greeting" enshrined both Kipling and Thompson-Seton. "Good Hunting," from the cry of the wood brothers in the "Jungle Book," but the mourning was for the wounded animals, the funeral wail of the little ones left alone to whose sufferings Thompson-Seton was the first to call attention in an unsentimental way.

All this newly-acquired love of the wee things of Nature and life had taught him to let the smallest suggestions find expression in the quaintest turns of comic verse. The east winds from the Massachusetts Bay howl around the houses of West Medford, and their piercing "Woo—oo—ee!" suggested the "Boogah Man," written for the very tiny maiden of two years, who persisted in hugging his avuncular shoes when he wanted to write sonnets about Harriet Beecher Stowe and Robert Gould Shaw. How can one work? he asked fretfully, and then burst laughingly into "How's a poet to write a sonnet, can you tell?" And so dashed off the poem on scrap paper, and read it aloud to the small maiden, who thereupon suggested that the "Woo—oo" of the wind was a "Boogah Man." So that was written immediately, dramatizing it as he wrote, much to her delight.

The dramatic instinct was strong behind the delicate perception of the power of suggestion. One must dramatize the poems as they were written, white hot. So, when "The Dance" and "The Valse" were penned, the metre must be dramatized in order to get it right; anapestic tetrameter admits of no limping lines; so one must waltz, humming the lines in order that there be no faulty rhythm. It was well that there were good dancers in the household to be sure there would be correct metre. "Whistling Sam" was troublesome. All had to whistle Sam's tunes, and then the music teacher must come and play them out on the piano, and transcribe the musical notation to be sure there were no mistakes.

Suggestion—that power of making one idea bring out a poem apparently foreign to the original thought—was never more humorously exemplified than in "Lias" and "Dat Ol' Mare o' Mine," both products of that winter in Colorado. "Dat Ol' Mare" was a weird and eccentric maiden horse of uncertain age and dubious ancestry, whose ideas were diametrically opposed to any preconceived notions one might suppose horses in general and Colorado horses in particular to have. But she would come home "on de ve'y da'kest night," without guidance, even if she did betray doubtful pre-ownership in the day-time when an exasperated and embarrassed woman drove her into Arapahoe street, the end of the ranch road, upon which street she would make frequent, unpsychological and embarrassing stops. But she would come home unguided and sure, hence "Dat Ol' Mare o' Mine."

There never was a "Lias," except generically, but maternal adjurations as to the beauty of the life of the despised early worm, and the "early to rise" maxim generally was greeted with Homeric laughter, and culminated in poor abused "Lias."

Colorado! As much of a revelation of Nature as the sea! But here was a new mother, more stern, less sure, never so capable of intimacy. Magnificent sweep of mountain range visible from the windows of the tiny house on the ranch—one hundred and fifty miles of Rocky Mountains, from Pil e's Peak to Long's Peak, with all the unnamed spurs in between! Unsurpassed sunsets, wonderful sunrises that flushed the eastern prairies, and reflected back on the snows of the mountains in the west so that the universe went suffused in a riotous prismatic color scheme; the meadow lark perched on the eaves of the house, tossing golden liquid sweetness to the high clear heavens; cowboys herding unwilling cattle across the horizon, miles and miles away; clear ozone, thin air which pierced the lungs and made them expand, sharp extremes in January from 60 degrees above to 30 degrees below. Here was Nature, untamed, unconfined, unfamiliar, wild. It went to the head like new wine, and ideas came rushing, fulminating, fructifying. One forgot sometimes, and it became comic when forgetting that the altitude of Denver and the surrounding land of 5200 feet or more was just becoming familiar; one rushed fearlessly into the higher strata of other towns, like Leadville and Colorado Springs, and was brought sharp up against the stubborn fact that rarity of air is not to be tampered with by the tenderfoot.

But the longing for the beloved East persisted, and though two novels and some short stories came forth that winter, the verse halted because the heart was elsewhere. "A Warm Day in Winter" and "Spring Fever" are both suggestive of the East, yet both were descriptive of days in Harmon. In the darkness of the night came the sound of a herd of cattle, padding 1 feet echoing through closed doors, and so the simile of a race struggling slowly through the dark was born, and the poem "Slow Through the Dark" came to life:

> *Slow moves the pageant of a climbing race;*
> *Their footsteps drag far, far below the height—*

The spectacle of a small caravan climbing the heights of the mountains in the far distance, up the steep winding road that crept whitely out of sight across the snow-capped boulders, was pregnant with the same suggestion. So came to his mind "By Rugged Ways":

> *By rugged ways and through the night*
> *We struggle blindly toward the light.*

These two poems were always among his favorites. The darker side of the problems of the race life was being brought home more and more forcibly to him as he grew older, and the stern ruggedness of nature in the Rocky Mountains forced him to a realization of the grim problems of the world's work.

As the herd of cattle climbing the sides of the mountain suggested something more than insensate animals struggling toward food and shelter, so the trifle of a brick side yard, damp and shut in by high brick walls of the two houses on each side, made for a riot of odd little poems. There were many poems born out of the fulness of the heart, out of a suggestion of long ago, from a picture, from a book, from a chance expression. Many were truly lyrical in that they were the record of the "best and happiest moments," as Shelley puts it. So many were truly poetic in that they were the record of the divine oneness with all mankind and all nature, and so many were like that group of November poems in that they were merely experiments in the power of suggestion.

If a short brick walk between two brick walls of two city houses does not suggest a cloistered walk of a monastery, what, then, does it suggest? And if that walk be damp, as perforce it must be, and if violet beds grow on the side, wild rank things, pushing through the brick crevices and allowed to remain because the inmates of the house are sentimentally fond of violets—even wild ones that grow in city back yards—what more natural than that all kinds of cool, damp, cloistered ideas will emanate from the tiny spot? So in one *dies mirabilis* were born "To a Violet Found on All Saint's Day," "The Monk's Walk," "The Murdered Lover," "Love's Castle," "Weltschmertz," "My Lady of Castle Grand," and "In the Tents at Akbar."

It is a base libel, much advertised and bruited abroad, to label the exquisite "Violet Found on All Saints' Day" as a vulgar premonition, Within the one little flower was all the lesson of "The Seedling," fruition now, less Tennyson, more filled with the understanding of maturity. The poet had been told by those near him, who once had lived in a Roman Catholic community, that on All Saints' Day everyone goes to the cemeteries laden with flowers to lay on the graves of the loved lost ones. He had always loved the custom and he remembered each All Saints' Day with a tender sympathy. So he saw in the violet not a premonition of despair, but a sweet effort on its part to bloom in memory of man's sorrows.

The chill November winds, following an unusually riotously beautiful Indian summer, waved the bird's nest in the Virginia creeper on the house next door, and "Weltschmertz" came forth, his deepest sympathy with all the woe of the world—complete universality of the true poet, nothing personal, merely infinite. The line "Count me a priest" betrays its cloister sisterhood. "The Monk's Walk" was near enough to the original idea of a monastery, but it evolved into the "Murdered Lover." The little walk grew to mean cloisters, castles, priests, knights—even "My Lady of Castle Grand," by the process of suggestion comes to life, for what so medieval as a castle with an inverted Lady of Shalott?

The medieval fancy ran riot then, and though it seems a far cry from Tennyson's "Lady of Shalott" to Bayard Taylor's "Bedouin Love Song," yet such a bridge does the poet's fancy make from reality to dreamland, that all strange fancies clustered about that cloistered walk, and his imagination careened out into the desert sands "In the Tents of Akbar," because the "Murdered Lover" of the poem, written in the morning, suggested the murdered dancing girl under the burning skies, and the grief of Akbar rent his heart in the evening. It is the exceptional mind that drags its pitifully methodical way through conventional, well-worn grooves of thought. One who thinks at all thinks by leaps and bounds, ranging all the universe, touching but tangentially the thought suggested by the last thought, and then winging swift flight elsewhere. Else wherefore think? One might as well ruminate. The poet puts wings to his words, as Homer phrases it, "winged words," and lo, a poem is born. And three or four great poems may have the same trivial place of conception, or a great soul-shaking experience may culminate in a line. Else why write poetry?

The power of Mother Nature having once entered into the poet-soul, it could never leave altogether. When the day came that he turned his back upon her deliberately, she did not avenge herself, but persisted in the haunting line, the pregnant phrase, the tender mood, albeit dimmer in each succeeding poem. For she gathers all her children to her breast and croons them melodies that will last through all eternity, if they will have them last; and even when the petulant children stop their ears, the inward ear listens to the great mother heart and heeds its call.

PAUL

A FAMILY FEUD

I wish I could tell you the story as I heard it from the lips of the old black woman as she sat bobbing her turbaned head to and fro with the motion of her creaky little rocking-chair, and droning the tale forth in the mellow voice of her race. So much of the charm of the story was in that voice, which even the cares of age had not hardened.

It was a sunny afternoon in late November, one of those days that come like a backward glance from a reluctantly departing summer. I had taken advantage of the warmth and brightness to go up and sit with old Aunt Doshy on the little porch that fronted her cottage. The old woman had been a trusted house-servant in one of the wealthiest of the old Kentucky families, and a visit to her never failed to elicit some reminiscence of the interesting past. Aunt Doshy was inordinately proud of her family, as she designated the Venables, and was never weary of detailing accounts of their grandeur and generosity. What if some of the harshness of reality was softened by the distance through which she looked back upon them; what if the glamour of memory did put a halo round the heads of some people who were never meant to be canonised? It was all plain fact to Aunt Doshy, and it was good to hear her talk. That day she began:—

"I reckon I hain't never tol' you 'bout ole Mas' an' young Mas' fallin' out, has I? Hit's all over now, an' things is done change so dat I reckon eben ef ole Mas' was libin', he would n't keer ef I tol', an' I knows young Mas' Tho'nton wouldn't. Dey ain't nuffin' to hide 'bout it no-how, 'ca'se all quality families has de same kin' o' 'spectable fusses.

"Hit all happened 'long o' dem Jamiesons whut libed jinin' places to our people, an' whut ole Mas' ain't spoke to fu' nigh onto thutty years. Long while ago, when Mas' Tom Jamieson an' Mas' Jack Venable was bofe young mans, dey had a qua'l 'bout de young lady dey bofe was a-cou'tin', an' by-an'-by dey had a du'l an' Mas' Jamieson shot Mas' Jack in de shouldah, but Mas' Jack ma'ied de lady, so dey was eben.

"Mas' Jamieson ma'ied too, an' after so many years dey was bofe wid'ers, but dey ain't fu'give one another yit. When Mas' Tho'nton was big enough to run erroun', ole Mas' used to try to 'press on him dat a Venable mus' n' never put his foot on de Jamieson lan'; an' many a tongue-lashin' an' sometimes wuss de han's on our place got fu' mixin' wif de Jamieson servants. But, la! young Mas' Tho'nton was wuss 'n de niggers. Evah time he got a chance he was out an' gone, over lots an' fiel's an' into de Jamieson ya'd a-playin' wif little Miss Nellie, whut was Mas' Tom's little gal. I never did see two chillun so 'tached to one another. Dey used to wander erroun', han' in han', lak brother an' sister, an' dey 'd cry lak dey little hea'ts 'u'd brek ef either one of dey pappys seed 'em an' pa'ted 'em."

"I 'member once when de young Mastah was erbout eight year ole, he was a-settin' at de table one mo'nin' eatin' wif his pappy, when all of er sudden he pause an' say, jes' ez solerm-lak, 'When I gits big, I gwine to ma'y Nellie.' His pappy jump lak he was shot, an' tu'n right pale, den he say kin' o' slow an' gaspy-lak, 'Don't evah let me hyeah you say sich a thing ergin, Tho'nton Venable. Why, boy, I 'd raver let evah drap o' blood outen you, dan to see a Venable cross his blood wif a Jamieson.'

"I was jes' a-bringin' in de cakes whut Mastah was pow'ful fon' of, an' I could see bofe dey faces. But, la! honey, dat chile did n't look a bit skeered. He jes' sot dah lookin' in his pappy's face,—he was de spittin' image of him, all 'cept his eyes, dey was his mother's,—den he say, 'Why, Nellie's nice,' an' went on eatin' a aig. His pappy laid his napkin down an' got up an' went erway f'om de table. Mas' Tho'nton say,' Why, father did n't eat his cakes.' 'I reckon yo' pa ain't well,' says I, fu' I knowed de chile was innercent.

"Well, after dat day, ole Mas' tuk extry pains to keep de chillun apa't—but 'twa'n't no use. 'Tain't never no use in a case lak dat. Dey jes' would be together, an' ez de boy got older, it seemed to grieve his pappy mighty. I reckon he did n't lak to jes' fu'bid him seein' Miss Nellie, fu' he know how haidstrong Mas' Tho'nton was, anyhow. So things kep' on dis way, an' de boy got handsomer evah day. My, but his pappy did set a lot o' sto' by him. Dey was n't nuffin' dat boy eben wished fu' dat his pappy didn't gin him. Seemed lak he fa'ly wusshipped him. He 'd jes' watch him ez he went erroun' de house lak he was a baby yit. So hit mus' 'a' been putty ha'd wif Mas' Jack when hit come time to sen' Mas' Tho'nton off to college. But he never showed it. He seed him off wif a cheerful face, an' nobidy would 'a' ever guessed dat it hu't him; but dat afternoon he shet hisse'f up an' hit was th'ee days befo' anybody 'cept me seed him, an' nobidy 'cept me knowed how his vittels come back not teched. But after de fus' letter come, he got better. I hyeahd him a-laffin' to hisse'f ez he read it, an' dat day he et his dinner."

"Well, honey, dey ain't no tellin' whut Mas' Jack's plans was, an' hit ain't fu' me to try an' guess 'em; but ef he had sont Mas' Tho'nton erway to brek him off f'om Miss Nellie, he mout ez well 'a' let him stayed at home; fu' Jamieson's Sal whut nussed Miss Nellie tol' me dat huh mistis got a letter f'om Mas' Tho'nton evah day er so. An' when he was home fu' holidays, you never seed nuffin' lak it. Hit was jes' walkin' er ridin' er dribin' wif dat young lady evah day of his life. An' dey did look so sweet together dat it seemed a shame to pa't 'em—him wif his big brown eyes an' sof' curly hair an' huh all white an' gentle lak a little dove. But de ole Mas' could n't see hit dat erway, an' I knowed dat hit was a-troublin' him mighty bad. Ez well ez he loved his son, hit alius seemed lak he was glad when de holidays was over an' de boy was back at college."

"Endurin' de las' year dat de young Mastah was to be erway, his pappy seemed lak he was jes' too happy an' res'less fu' anything. He was dat proud of his son, he did n't know whut to do. He was alius tellin' visitors dat come to de house erbout him, how he was a 'markable boy an' was a-gwine to be a honour to his name. An' when 'long to'ds de ve'y end of de term, a letter come sayin' dat Mas' Tho'nton had done tuk some big honour at de college, I jes' thought sho Mas' Jack 'u'd plum bus' hisse'f, he was so proud an' tickled. I hyeahd him talkin' to his ole frien' Cunnel Mandrey an' mekin' great plans 'bout whut he gwine to do when his son come home. He gwine tek him trav'lin' fus' in Eur'p, so 's to 'finish him lak a Venable ought to be finished by seein' somep'n' of de worl'—' dem 's his ve'y words. Den he was a-gwine to come home an' 'model de house an' fit it up, 'fu' '—I never shell fu'git how he said it,— 'fu' I 'spec' my son to tek a high place in de society of ole Kintucky an' to mo' dan surstain de reputation of de Venables.' Den when de las' day come an' young Mastah was home fu' sho, so fine an' clever lookin' wif his new mustache—sich times ez dey was erbout dat house nobidy never seed befo'. All de frien's an' neighbours, 'scusin', o' co'se, de Jamiesons, was invited to a big dinner dat lasted fu' hours. Dey was speeches by de gent'men, an' evahbidy drinked de graderate's health an' wished him good luck. But all de time I could see dat Mas' Tho'nton was n't happy, dough he was smilin' an' mekin' merry wif evahbidy. It 'pressed me so dat I spoke erbout hit to Aunt Emmerline. Aunt Emmerline was Mas' Tho'nton's mammy, an' sence he 'd growed up, she did n't do much but he'p erroun' de house a little."

"'You don' mean to tell me dat you noticed dat too?' says she when I to? huh erbout it.

"'Yes, I did,' says I, 'an' I noticed hit strong.'

"'Dey's somep'n' ain't gwine right wif my po' chile,' she say, 'an' dey ain't no tellin' whut it is.'

"'Hain't you got no idee, Aunt Emmerline?' I say.

"'La! chile,' she say in a way dat mek me think she keepin' so'mep'n' back, 'la! chile, don' you know young mans don' come to dey mammys wif dey secuts lak dey do when dey's babies? How I gwine to know whut's pesterin' Mas' Tho'nton?'

"Den I knowed she was hidin' somep'n', an' jes' to let huh know dat I 'd been had my eyes open too, I say slow an' 'pressive lak, 'Aunt Emmerline, don' you reckon hit Miss Nellie Jamieson?' She jumped lak she was skeered, an' looked at me right ha'd; den she say, 'I ain' reck'nin' nuffin' 'bout de white folks' bus'ness.' An' she pinched huh mouf up right tight, an' I could n't git another word outen huh; but I knowed dat I 'd hit huh jes' erbout right.

"One mo'nin' erbout a week after de big dinner, jes' ez dey was eatin', Mas' Tho'nton say, 'Father, I 'd lak to see you in de liberry ez soon ez you has de time. I want to speak to you 'bout somep'n' ve'y impo'tant.' De ole man look up right quick an' sha'p, but he say ve'y quiet lak, 'Ve'y well, my son, ve'y well; I 's at yo' service at once.'

"Dey went into de liberry, an' Mas' Tho'nton shet de do' behin' him. I could hyeah dem talkin' kin' o' low while I was cl'arin' erway de dishes. After while dey 'menced to talk louder. I had to go out an' dus' de hall den near de liberry do', an' once I hyeahd ole Mas' say right sho't an' sha'p, 'Never!' Den young Mas' he say, 'But evah man has de right to choose fu' his own se'f.'

"'Man, man!' I hyeahd his pappy say in a way I had never hyeahd him use to his son befo', 'evah male bein' dat wahs men's clothes an' has a mustache ain't a man.'

"'Man er whut not,' po' young Mastah's voice was a-tremblin', 'I am at leas' my father's son an' I deserve better dan dis at his han's.' I hyeahd somebody a-walkin' de no', an' I was feared dey 'd come out an' think dat I was a-listenin', so I dus'es on furder down de hall, an' did n't hyeah no mo' ontwell Mas' Tho'nton come hurryin' out an' say, 'Ike, saddle my hoss.' He was ez pale ez he could be, an' when he spoke sho't an' rough lak dat, he was so much lak his father dat hit skeered me. Ez soon ez his hoss was ready, he jumped into de saddle an' went flyin' outen de ya'd lak mad, never eben lookin' back at de house. I did n't see Mas' Jack fu' de res' of de day, an' he did n't come in to suppah, But I seed Aunt Emmerline an' I knowed dat she had been somewhah an' knowed ez much ez I did erbout whut was gwine on, but I never broached a word erbout hit to huh. I seed she was oneasy, but I kep' still 'twell she say, 'Whut you reckon keepin' Mas' Tho'nton out so late?' Den I jes say, 'I ain't reck'nin' 'bout de white folks' bus'ness.' She looked a little bit cut at fus', den she jes' go on lak nuffin' had n't happened : 'I 's mighty 'sturbed 'bout young Mas'; he never stays erway f'om suppah 'dout sayin' somep'n'.'

"'Oh, I reckon he kin fin' suppah somewhah else.' I says dis don't keer lak jes' fu' to lead huh on.

"'I ain't so much pestered 'bout his suppah,' she say; 'I 's feared he gwine do somep'n' he had n't ought to do after dat qua'l 'twixt him an' his pappy.'

"'Did dey have a qua'l?' says I.

"'G' long! 'Aunt Emmerline say, 'you was n't dus'in' one place in de hall so long fu' nuffin'. You knows an' I knows eben ef we don't talk a heap. I 's troubled myse'f. Hit jes' in dat Venable blood to go right straight an' git Miss Nellie an' ma'y huh right erway, an' ef he do it, I p'intly know his pa 'll never fu'give him.' Den Aunt Emmerline 'mence to cry, an' I feel right sorry fu' huh, 'ca'se Mas' Tho'nton huh boy, an' she think a mighty heap o' him.

"Well, we had n't had time to say much mo' when we hyeahd a hoss gallopin' into de ya'd.

"Aunt Emmerline jes' say, 'Dat 's Gineral's lope! 'an' she bus' outen de do'. I waits, 'spectin' huh to come back an' say dat Mas' Tho'nton done come at las'. But after while she come in wif a mighty long face an' say, 'Hit's one o' Jamieson's darkies; he brung de hoss back an' a note Mas' gin him fu' his pappy. Mas' Tho'nton done gone to Lexin'ton wif Miss Nellie an' got ma'ied.' Den she jes' brek down an' 'mence a-cryin' ergin an' a-rockin' huhse'f back an fofe an' sayin', 'Oh, my po' chile, my po' boy, whut 's to 'come o' you!'

"I went upstairs an' lef huh—we bofe stayed at de big house—but I did n't sleep much, 'ca'se all thoo de night I could hyeah ole Mas' a-walkin' back an' fofe ercross his flo', an' when Aunt Emmerline come up to baid, she mou'ned all night, eben in huh sleep. I tell you, honey, dem was mou'nin' times."

Nex' mo'nin' when ole Mas' come down to brekfus', he looked lak he done had a long spell o' sickness. But he was n't no man to 'spose his feelin's. He never let on, never eben spoke erbout Mas' Tho'nton bein' erway f'om de table. He did n't eat much, an' fin'ly I see him look right long an' stiddy at de place whah Mas' Tho'nton used to set an' den git up an' go 'way f'om de table. I knowed dat he was done filled up. I went to de liberry do' an' I could hyeah him sobbin' lak a chile. I tol' Aunt Emmerline 'bout it, but she jes' shuck huh haid an' did n't say nuffin' a'-tall.

"Well, hit went dis erway fu' 'bout a week. Mas' Jack was gittin' paler an' paler evah day, an' hit jes' 'menced to come to my min' how ole he was. One day Aunt Emmerline say she gwine erway, an' she mek Jim hitch up de spring wagon an' she dribe on erway by huhse'f. Co'se, now, Aunt Emmerline she do putty much ez she please, so I don't think nuffin' 'bout hit. When she come back, 'long to'ds ebenin', I say, 'Aunt Emmerline, whah you been all day?'

"'Nemmine, honey, you see,' she say, an' laff. Well, I ain't seed nobidy laff fu' so long dat hit jes mek me feel right wa'm erroun' my hea't, an' I laff an' keep on laffin' jes' at nuffin'.

"Nex' mo'nin' Aunt Emmerline mighty on-easy, an' I don' know whut de matter ontwell I hyeah some un say, 'Tek dat hoss, Ike, an' feed him, but keep de saddle on.' Aunt Emmerline jes' fa'ly fall out de do' an' I lak to drap, 'ca'se hit's Mas' Thornton's voice. In a minute he come to me an' say, 'Doshy, go tell my father I 'd lak to speak to him.'

"I don' skeercely know how I foun' my way to de liberry, but I did. Ole Mas' was a-settin' dah wif a open book in his han', but his eyes was jes' a-starin' at de wall, an' I knowed he wasn't a-readin'. I say, 'Mas' Jack,' an' he sta't jes' lak he rousin' up, 'Mas' Jack, Mas' Tho'nton want to speak to you.' He jump up quick, an' de book fall on de flo', but he grab a cheer an' stiddy hisse'f. I done tol' you Mas' Jack was n't no man to 'spose his feelin's. He jes' say, slow lak he hol'in' hisse'f, 'Sen' him in hyeah.' I goes back an' 'livers de message, den I flies roun' to de po'ch whah de liberry winder opens out, 'ca'se, I ain't gwine lie erbout it, I was mighty tuk up wif all dis gwine on an' I wanted to see an' hyeah,—an' who you reckon 'roun' dah but Aunt Emmerline! She jes' say, 'S-sh!' ez I come 'roun', an' clas' huh han's. In a minute er so, de liberry do' open an' Mas' Tho'nton come in. He shet hit behin' him, an' den stood lookin' at his pa, dat ain't never tu'ned erroun' yit. Den he say sof', 'Father.' Mas' Jack tu'ned erroun' raal slow an' look at his son fu' a while. Den he say, 'Do you still honour me wif dat name?' Mas' Tho'nton got red in de face, but he answer, 'I don' know no other name to call you.'

"'Will you set down?' Mas' speak jes' lak he was a-talkin' to a stranger.

"'Ef you desiah me to.' I see Mas' Tho'nton was a-bridlin' up too. Mas' jes' th'owed back his haid an' say, 'Fa' be it f'om any Venable to fu'git cou'tesy to his gues'.' Young Mas' moved erway f'om de cheer whah he was a-gwine to set, an' his haid went up. He spoke up slow an' delibut, jes' lak his pa, 'I do not come, suh, in dat cha'acter, I is hyeah ez yo' son.'

"Well, ole Mas' eyes fa'ly snapped flah. He was white ez a sheet, but he still spoke slow an' quiet, hit made me creep, 'You air late in 'memberin' yo' relationship, suh.'

"'I hab never fu'got it.'

"'Den, suh, you have thought mo' of yo' rights dan of yo' duties.' Mas' Jack was mad an' so was Mas' Tho'nton; he say, 'I did n't come hyeah to 'scuss dat.' An' he tu'ned to'ds de do'. I hyeah Aunt Emmerline groan jes' ez Mas' say, 'Well, whut did you come fu'?'

"'To be insulted in my father's house by my father, an' I 's got all dat I come fu'!' Mas' Tho'nton was ez white ez his pa now, an' his han' was on de do'-knob. Den all of a sudden I hyeah de winder go up, an' I lak to fall over gittin' outen de way to keep Pom bein' seed. Aunt Emmerline done opened de winder an' gone in. Dey bofe tu'ned an' looked at huh s'prised lak, an' Mas' Jack sta'ted to say somep'n', but she th'owed up huh han' an' say 'Wait!' 'lak she owned de house. 'Mas' Jack,' she say, 'you an' Mas' Tho'nton ain't gwine pa't dis way. You mus' n't. You 's father an' son. You loves one another. I knows I ain't got no bus'ness meddlin' in yo' 'fairs, but I cain't see you all qua'l dis way. Mastah, you 's bofe stiffnecked. You 's bofe wrong. I know Mas' Tho'nton did n't min' you, but he did n't mean no ha'm—he could n't he'p it—it was in de Venable blood, an' you mus' n't 'spise him Fu' it.'

"'Emmerline'—ole Mas' tried to git in a word, but she would n't let him.

"'Yes, Mastah, yes, but I nussed dat boy an' tuk keer o' him when he was a little bit of a he'pless thing; an' when his po' mammy went to glory, I 'member how she look up at me wif dem blessed eyes o' hern an' lay him in my arms an' say, "Emmerline, tek keer o'my baby." I 's done it, Mastah, I 's done it de bes' I could. I 's nussed him thoo sickness when hit seemed lak his little soul mus' foller his mother anyhow, but I 's seen de look in yo' eyes, an' prayed to God to gin de chile back to you. He done it, he done it, an' you sha'n't th'ow erway de gif' of God! 'Aunt Emmerline was a-cryin' an' so was Mas' Tho'nton. Ole Mas' mighty red, but he clared his th'oat an' said wif his voice tremblin', 'Emmerline, leave de room.' De ole ooman come out a-cryin' lak huh hea't 'u'd brek, an' jes' ez de do' shet behin' huh, ole Mas' brek down an' hoi' out his arms, cryin', 'My son, my son.' An' in a minute he an' Mas' Tho'nton was a-hol'in' one another lak dey 'd never let go, an' his pa was a-pattin' de boy's haid lak he was a baby. All of a sudden ole Mas' hel' him off an' looked at him an' say, 'Dat ole fool talkin' to me erbout yo' mother's eyes, an' you stannin' hyeah a-lookin' at me wif 'em.' An' den he was a-cryin' ergin, an' dey was bofe huggin'.

"Well, after while dey got all settled down, an' Mas' Tho'nton tol' his pa how Aunt Emmerline drib to Lexin'ton an' foun' him an' made him come home. c I was wrong, father,' he say, 'but I reckon ef it had n't 'a' been fu' Aunt Emmerline, I would 'a' stuck it out.'

"'It was in de Venable blood,' his pa say, an' dey bofe laff. Den ole Mas' say, kin' o' lak it hu't him, 'An' whah 's yo' wife?' Young Mas' got mighty red ergin ez he answer, 'She ain't fu' erway.'

"'Go bring huh,' Mas' Jack say.

"Well, I reckon Mas' Tho'nton lak to flew, an' he had Miss Nellie dah in little er no time. When dey come, Mas' he say, 'Come hyeah,' den he pause awhile—'my daughter.' Den Miss Nellie run to him, an' dey was another cryin' time, an' I went on to my work an' lef' 'em talkin' an' laffin' an' cryin'.'

"Well, Aunt Emmerline was skeered to def. She jes' p'intly knowed dat she was gwine to eit a tono-ue-lashin'. I don' know whether she was mos' skeered er mos' happy. Mas' sont fu' huh after while, an' I listened when she went in. He was tryin' to talk an' look pow'ful stern, but I seed a twinkle in his eye. He say, 'I want you to know, Emmerline, dat hit ain't yo' place to dictate to yo' mastah whut he shell do—Shet up, shet up! I don' want a word outen you. You been on dis place so long, an' been bossin' de other darkies an' yo' Mas' Tho'nton erroun' so long, dat I 'low you think you own de place. Shet up, not a word outen you! Ef you an' yo' young Mas' 's a-gwine to run dis place, I reckon I 'd better step out. Humph! You was so sma't to go to Lexin'ton de other day, you kin go back dah ergin. You seem to think you 's white, an' hyeah 's de money to buy a new dress fu' de ole fool darky dat nussed yo' son an' made you fu'give his foo'ishness when you wanted to be a fool yo'se'f." His voice was sof ergin, an' he put de money in Aunt Emmerline's han' an' pushed huh out de do', huh a-cryin' an' him put' nigh it.

"After dis, Mas' Jack was jes' bent an' boun' dat de young people mus' go on a weddin' trip. So dey got ready, an' Miss Nellie went an' tol' huh pa goo'bye. Min' you, dey had n't been nuffin' said 'bout him an' Mas' not bein' frien's. He done fu'give Miss Nellie right erway fu' runnin' off. But de mo'nin' dey went erway, we all was out in de ya'd, an' Aunt

Emmerline settin' on de seat wif Jim, lookin' ez proud ez you please. Mastah was ez happy ez a boy. 'Emmerline,' he hollahs ez dey drib off, 'tek good keer o' dat Venable blood.' De ca'iage stopped ez it went out de gate, an' Mas' Tom Jamieson kissed his daughter. He had rid up de road to see de las' of huh. Mastah seed him, an' all of a sudden somep'n' seemed to tek holt o' him an' he hollahed, 'Come in, Tom.'

"'Don' keer ef I do,' Mas' Jamieson say, a-tu'nin' his hoss in de gate. 'You Venables has got de res' o' my fambly.' We all was mos' s'prised to def.

"Mas' Jamieson jumped offen his hoss, an' Mas' Venable come down de steps to meet him. Dey shuk han's, an' Mas' Jack say, 'Dey ain't no fool lak a ole fool.'

"'An' fu' unekaled foo'ishness,' Mas' Tom say, 'reckermen' me to two ole fools.' Dey went into de house a-laffin', an' I knowed hit was all right 'twixt 'em, fu' putty soon I seed Ike out in de ya'd a-getherin' mint."

THE FAITH CURE MAN

H ope is tenacious. It goes on living and working when science has dealt it what should be its deathblow.

In the close room at the top of the old tenement house little Lucy lay wasting away with a relentless disease. The doctor had said at the beginning of the winter that she could not live. Now he said that he could do no more for her except to ease the few days that remained for the child.

But Martha Benson would not believe him. She was confident that doctors were not infallible. Anyhow, this one wasn't, for she saw life and health ahead for her little one.

Did not the preacher at the Mission Home say: "Ask, and ye shall receive?" and had she not asked and asked again the life of her child, her last and only one, at the hands of Him whom she worshipped?

No, Lucy was not going to die. What she needed was country air and a place to run about in. She had been housed up too much; these long Northern winters were too severe for her, and that was what made her so pinched and thin and weak. She must have air, and she should have it.

"Po' little lammie," she said to the child, "Mammy's little gal boun' to git well. Mammy gwine sen' huh out in de country when the spring comes, whaih she kin roll in de grass an' pick flowers an' git good an' strong. Don' baby want to go to de country? Don' baby want to see de sun shine?" And the child had looked up at her with wide, bright eyes, tossed her thin arms and moaned for reply.

"Nemmine, we gwine fool dat doctah. Some day we'll th'ow all his nassy medicine 'way, an' he come in an' say: 'Whaih's all my medicine?' Den we answeh up sma't like: 'We done th'owed it out. We don' need no nassy medicine.' Den he look 'roun' an' say: 'Who dat I see runnin' roun' de flo' hyeah, a-lookin' so fat?' an' you up an' say: 'Hit's me, dat's who 'tis, mistah doctor man!' Den he go out an' slam de do' behin' him. Ain' dat fine?"

But the child had closed her eyes, too weak even to listen. So her mother kissed her little thin forehead and tiptoed out, sending in a child from across the hall to take care of Lucy while she was at work, for sick as the little one was she could not stay at home and nurse her.

Hope grasps at a straw, and it was quite in keeping with the condition of Martha's mind that she should open her ears and her heart when they told her of the wonderful works of the faith-cure man. People had gone to him on crutches, and he had touched or rubbed them and they had come away whole. He had gone to the homes of the bed-ridden, and they had risen up to bless him. It was so easy for her to believe it all. The only religion she had ever known, the wild, emotional religion of most of her race, put her credulity to stronger tests than that. Her only question was, would such a man come to her humble room. But she put away even this thought. He must come. She would make him. Already she saw Lucy strong, and running about like a mouse, the joy of her heart and the light of her eyes.

As soon as she could get time she went humbly to see the faith doctor, and laid her case before him, hoping, fearing, trembling.

Yes, he would come. Her heart leaped for joy.

"There is no place," said the faith curist, "too humble for the messenger of heaven to enter. I am following One who went among the humblest and the lowliest, and was not ashamed to be found among publicans and sinners. I will come to your child, madam, and put her again under the law. The law of life is health, and no one who will accept the law need be sick. I am not a physician. I do not claim to be. I only claim to teach people how not to be sick. My fee is five dollars, merely to defray my expenses, that's all. You know the servant is worthy of his hire. And in this little bottle here I have an elixir which has never been known to fail in any of the things claimed for it. Since the world has got used to taking medicine we must make some concessions to its prejudices. But this in reality is not a medicine at all. It is only a symbol. It is really liquefied prayer and faith."

Martha did not understand anything of what he was saying. She did not try to; she did not want to. She only felt a blind trust in him that filled her heart with unspeakable gladness.

Tremulous with excitement, she doled out her poor dollars to him, seized the precious elixir and hurried away home to Lucy, to whom she was carrying life and strength. The little one made a weak attempt to smile at her mother, but the light flickered away and died into greyness on her face.

"Now mammy's little gal gwine to git well fu' sho'. Mammy done bring huh somep'n' good." Awed and reverent, she tasted the wonderful elixir before giving it to the child. It tasted very like sweetened water to her, but she knew that it was not, and had no doubt of its virtues.

Lucy swallowed it as she swallowed everything her mother brought to her. Poor little one! She had nothing to buoy her up or to fight science with.

In the course of an hour her mother gave her the medicine again, and persuaded herself that there was a perceptible brightening in her daughter's face.

Mrs. Mason, Caroline's mother, called across the hall: "How Lucy dis evenin', Mis' Benson?"

"Oh, I think Lucy air right peart," Martha replied. "Come over an' look at huh."

Mrs. Mason came, and the mother told her about the new faith doctor and his wonderful powers.

"Why, Mis' Mason," she said, "'pears like I could see de change in de child de minute she swallowed dat medicine."

Her neighbor listened in silence, but when she went back to her own room it was to shake her head and murmur: "Po' Marfy, she jes' ez blind ez a bat. She jes' go 'long, holdin' on to dat chile wid all huh might, an' I see death in Lucy's face now. Dey ain't no faif nur prayer, nur Jack-leg doctors nuther gwine to save huh."

But Martha needed no pity then. She was happy in her self-delusion.

On the morrow the faith doctor came to see Lucy. She had not seemed so well that morning, even to her mother, who remained at home until the doctor arrived. He carried a conquering air, and a baggy umbrella, the latter of which he laid across the foot of the bed as he bent over the moaning child.

"Give me some brown paper," he commanded.

Martha hastened to obey, and the priestly practitioner dampened it in water and laid it on Lucy's head, all the time murmuring prayers—or were they incantations?—to himself. Then he placed pieces of the paper on the soles of the child's feet and on the palms of her hands, and bound them there.

When all this was done he knelt down and prayed aloud, ending with a peculiar version of the Lord's prayer, supposed to have mystic effect. Martha was greatly impressed, but through it all Lucy lay and moaned.

The faith curist rose to go. "Well, we can look to have her out in a few days. Remember, my good woman, much depends upon you. You must try to keep your mind in a state of belief. Are you saved?"

"Oh, yes, suh. I'm a puffessor," said Martha, and having completed his mission, the man of prayers went out, and Caroline again took Martha's place at Lucy's side.

In the next two days Martha saw, or thought she saw, a steady improvement in Lucy. According to instructions, the brown paper was moved everyday, moistened, and put back.

Martha had so far spurred her faith that when she went out on Saturday morning she promised to bring Lucy something good for her Christmas dinner, and a pair of shoes against the time of her going out, and also a little doll. She brought them home that night. Caroline had grown tired and, lighting the lamp, had gone home.

"I done brung my little lady bird huh somep'n nice," said Martha, "here's a lil' doll and de lil' shoes, honey. How's de baby feel?" Lucy did not answer.

"You sleep?" Martha went over to the bed. The little face was pinched and ashen. The hands were cold.

"Lucy! Lucy!" called the mother. "Lucy! Oh, Gawd! It ain't true! She ain't daid! My little one, my las' one!"

She rushed for the elixir and brought it to the bed. The thin dead face stared back at her, unresponsive.

She sank down beside the bed, moaning.

"Daid, daid, oh, my Gawd, gi' me back my chile! Oh, don't I believe you enough? Oh, Lucy, Lucy, my little lamb! I got you yo' gif'. Oh, Lucy!"

The next day was set apart for the funeral. The Mission preacher read: "The Lord giveth and the Lord taketh away, blessed be the name of the Lord," and someone said "Amen!" But Martha could not echo it in her heart. Lucy was her last, her one treasured lamb.

The Intervention of Peter

No one knows just what statement it was of Harrison Randolph's that Bob Lee doubted. The annals of these two Virginia families have not told us that. But these are the facts:—

It was at the home of the Fairfaxes that a few of the sons of the Old Dominion were giving a dinner,—not to celebrate anything in particular, but the joyousness of their own souls,—and a brave dinner it was. The courses had come and gone, and over their cigars they had waxed more than merry. In those days men drank deep, and these men were young, full of the warm blood of the South and the joy of living. What wonder then that the liquor that had been mellowing in the Fairfax cellars since the boyhood of their revolutionary ancestor should have its effect upon them?

It is true that it was only a slight thing which Bob Lee affected to disbelieve, and that his tone was jocosely bantering rather than impertinent.

But sometimes Virginia heads are not less hot than Virginia hearts. The two young men belonged to families that had intermarried. They rode together. They hunted together, and were friends as far as two men could be who had read the message of love in the dark eyes of the same woman. So perhaps there was some thought of the long-contested hand of Miss Sallie Ford in Harrison Randolph's mind when he chose to believe that his honour had been assailed.

His dignity was admirable. There was no scene to speak of. It was all very genteel.

"Mr. Lee," he said, "had chosen to doubt his word, which to a gentleman was the final insult. But he felt sure that Mr. Lee would not refuse to accord him a gentleman's satisfaction." And the other's face had waxed warm and red and his voice cold as he replied: "I shall be most happy to give you the satisfaction you demand."

Here friends interposed and attempted to pacify the two. But without avail. The wine of the Fairfaxes has a valiant quality in it, and these two who had drunken of it could not be peaceably reconciled.

Each of the young gentlemen nodded to a friend and rose to depart. The joyous dinner- party bade fair to end with much more serious business.

"You shall hear from me very shortly," said Randolph, as he strode to the door.

"I shall await your pleasure with impatience, sir, and give you such a reply as even you cannot disdain."

It was all rather high-flown, but youth is dramatic and plays to the gallery of its own eyes and ears. But to one pair of ears there was no ring of anything but tragedy in the grandiloquent sentences. Peter, the personal attendant of Harrison Randolph, stood at the door as his master passed out, and went on before him to hold his stirrup. The young master and his friend and cousin, Dale, started off briskly and in silence, while Pete, with wide eyes and disturbed face, followed on behind. Just as they were turning into the avenue of elms that led to their own house, Randolph wheeled his horse and came riding back to his servant.

"Pete," said he, sternly, "what do you know?"

"Nuffin', Mas' Ha'ison, nuffin' 't all. I do' know nuffin'."

"I don't believe you." The young master's eyes were shining through the dusk. "You're always slipping around spying on me."

"Now dah you goes, Mas' Randolph. I ain't done a t'ing, and you got to 'mence pickin' on me—"

"I just want you to remember that my business is mine."

"Well, I knows dat."

"And if you do know anything, it will be well for you to begin forgetting right now." They were at the door now and in the act of dismounting. "Take Bess around and see her attended to. Leave Dale's horse here, and—I won't want you anymore tonight."

"Now how does you an' Mas' Dale 'spect dat you gwine to wait on yo'se'ves tonight?"

"I shall not want you again tonight, I tell you."

Pete turned away with an injured expression on his dark face. "Bess," he said to the spirited black mare as he led her toward the stables, "you jes' bettah t'ank yo' Makah dat you ain't no human-bein', 'ca'se human-bein's is cur'ous articles. Now you's a hoss, ain't you? An' dey say you ain't got no soul, but you got sense, Bess, you got sense. You got blood an' fiah an' breedin' in you too, ain't you? Co'se you has. But you knows how to answah de rein. You's a high steppah, too: but you don' go to work an' try to brek yo' naik de fus' chanst you git. Bess, I 'spect you 'ca'se you got jedgment, an' you don' have to have a black man runnin' 'roun aftah you all de time plannin' his haid off jes' to keep you out o' trouble. Some folks dat's human-bein's does. Yet an' still, Bess, you ain't nuffin' but a dumb beas', so dey says. Now, what I gwine to do? Co'se

dey wants to fight. But whah an' when an' how I gwine to stop hit? Do'
want me to wait on him tonight, huh! No, dey want to mek dey plans
an' do' want me 'roun' to hyeah, dat's what's de mattah. Well, I lay I'll
hyeah somep'n' anyhow."

Peter hurried through his work and took himself up to the big house
and straight to his master's room. He heard voices within, but though he
took many liberties with his owner, eavesdropping was not one of them.
It proved too dangerous. So, though "he kinder lingered on the mat,
some doubtful of the sekle," it was not for long, and he unceremoniously
pushed the door open and walked in. With a great show of haste, he
made for his master's wardrobe and began busily searching among the
articles therein. Harrison Randolph and his cousin were in the room,
and their conversation, which had been animated, suddenly ceased
when Peter entered.

"I thought I told you I did n't want you anymore tonight."

"I's a-lookin' fu' dem striped pants o' yo'n. I want to tek 'em out an'
bresh 'em: dey's p'intly a livin' sight." "You get out o' here."

"But, Mas' Ha'ison, now—now—look—a—hyeah—"

"Get out, I tell you—"

Pete shuffled from the room, mumbling as he went: "Dah now,
dah now! driv' out lak a dog! How 's I gwine to fin' out anyt'ing dis
away? It do 'pear lak Mas' Ha'ison do try to gi'e me all de trouble he
know how. Now he plannin' an' projickin' wif dat cousin Dale, an' one
jes' ez scattah-brained ez de othah. Well, I 'low I got to beat dey time
somehow er ruther."

He was still lingering hopeless and worried about the house when
he saw young Dale Randolph come out, mount his horse and ride away.
After a while his young master also came out and walked up and down
in the soft evening air. The rest of the family were seated about on the
broad piazza.

"I wonder what is the matter with Harrison tonight," said the young
man's father, "he seems so preoccupied."

"Thinking of Sallie Ford, I reckon," someone replied; and the remark
passed with a laugh. Pete was near enough to catch this, but he did not
stop to set them right in their conjectures. He slipped into the house as
noiselessly as possible.

It was less than two hours after this when Dale Randolph returned
and went immediately to his cousin's room, where Harrison followed
him.

"Well?" said the latter, as soon as the door closed behind them.

"It's all arranged, and he's anxious to hurry it through for fear someone may interfere. Pistols, and tomorrow morning at day-break."

"And the place?"

"The little stretch of woods that borders Ford's Creek. I say, Harrison, it isn't too late to stop this thing yet. It's a shame for you two fellows to fight. You're both too decent to be killed for a while yet."

"He insulted me."

"Without intention, everyone believes."

"Then let him apologise."

"As well ask the devil to take Communion."

"We'll fight then."

"All right. If you must fight, you must. But you'd better get to bed; for you'll need a strong arm and a steady hand tomorrow."

If a momentary paleness struck into the young fellow's face, it was for a moment only, and he set his teeth hard before he spoke.

"I am going to write a couple of letters," he said, "then I shall lie down for an hour or so. Shall we go down and drink a steadier?"

"One won't hurt, of course."

"And, by the way, Dale, if I—if it happens to be me tomorrow, you take Pete—he's a good fellow."

The cousins clasped hands in silence and passed out. As the door closed behind them, a dusty form rolled out from under the bed, and the disreputable, eavesdropping, backsliding Pete stood up and rubbed a sleeve across his eyes.

"It ain't me dat 's gwine to be give to nobody else. I hates to do it, but dey ain't no othah way. Mas' Ha'ison cain't be spaihed." He glided out mysteriously, some plan of salvation working in his black head.

Just before daybreak next morning, three stealthy figures crept out and made their way toward Ford's Creek. One skulked behind the other two, dogging their steps and taking advantage of the darkness to keep very near to them. At the grim trysting-place they halted and were soon joined by other stealthy figures, and together they sat down to wait for the daylight. The seconds conferred for a few minutes. The ground was paced off, and a few low-pitched orders prepared the young men for business.

"I will count three, gentlemen," said Lieutenant Custis. "At three, you are to fire."

At last daylight came, gray and timid at first, and then red and bold as the sun came clearly up. The pistols were examined and the men placed face to face.

"Are you ready, gentlemen?"

But evidently Harrison Randolph was not. He was paying no attention to the seconds. His eyes were fixed on an object behind his opponent's back. His attitude relaxed and his mouth began twitching. Then he burst into a peal of laughter.

"Pete," he roared, "drop that and come out from there!" and away he went into another convulsion of mirth. The others turned just in time to see Pete cease his frantic grimaces of secrecy at his master, and sheepishly lower an ancient fowling-piece which he had had levelled at Bob Lee.

"What were you going to do with that gun levelled at me?" asked Lee, his own face twitching.

"I was gwine to fiah jes' befo' dey said free. I wa'n't gwine to kill you, Mas' Bob. I was on'y gwine to lame you."

Another peal of laughter from the whole crowd followed this condescending statement.

"You unconscionable scoundrel, you! If I was your master, I'd give you a hundred lashes."

"Pete," said his master, "don't you know that it is dishonourable to shoot a man from behind? You see you have n't in you the making of a gentleman."

"I do' know nuffin' 'bout mekin' a gent'man, but I does know how to save one dat 's already made."

The prime object of the meeting had been entirely forgotten. They gathered around Pete and examined the weapon.

"Gentlemen," said Randolph, "we have been saved by a miracle. This old gun, as well as I can remember and count, has been loaded for the past twenty-five years, and if Pete had tried to fire it, it would have torn up all of this part of the county." Then the eyes of the two combatants met. There was something irresistibly funny in the whole situation, and they found themselves roaring again. Then, with one impulse, they shook hands without a word.

And Pete led the way home, the willing butt of a volume of good-natured abuse.

JIMSELLA

No one could ever have accused Mandy Mason of being thrifty. For the first twenty years of her life conditions had not taught her the necessity for thrift. But that was before she had come North with Jim. Down there at home one either rented or owned a plot of ground with a shanty set in the middle of it, and lived off the products of one's own garden and coop. But here it was all very different: one room in a crowded tenement house, and the necessity of grinding day after day to keep the wolf—a very terrible and ravenous wolf—from the door. No wonder that Mandy was discouraged and finally gave up to more than her old shiftless ways.

Jim was no less disheartened. He had been so hopeful when he first came, and had really worked hard. But he could not go higher than his one stuffy room, and the food was not so good as it had been at home. In this state of mind, Mandy's shiftlessness irritated him. He grew to look on her as the source of all his disappointments. Then, as he walked Sixth or Seventh Avenue, he saw other coloured women who dressed gayer than Mandy, looked smarter, and did not wear such great shoes. These he contrasted with his wife, to her great disadvantage.

"Mandy," he said to her one day, "why don't you fix yo'sc'f up an' look like people? You go 'roun' hyeah lookin' like I dunno what."

"Why n't you git me somep'n' to fix myse'f up in?" came back the disconcerting answer.

"Ef you had any git up erbout you, you 'd git somep'n' fu' yo'se'f an' not wait on me to do evahthing."

"Well, ef I waits on you, you keeps me waitin', fu' I ain' had nothin' fit to eat ner waih since I been up hyeah."

"Nev' min'! You's mighty free wid yo' talk now, but some o' dese days you won't be so free. You's gwine to wake up some mo'nin' an' fin' dat I's lit out; dat's what you will."

"Well, I 'low nobody ain't got no string to you."

Mandy took Jim's threat as an idle one, so she could afford to be independent. But the next day had found him gone. The deserted wife wept for a time, for she had been fond of Jim, and then she set to work to struggle on by herself. It was a dismal effort, and the people about her were not kind to her. She was hardly of their class. She was only a simple, honest countrywoman, who did not go out with them to walk the avenue.

When a month or two afterward the sheepish Jim returned, ragged and dirty, she had forgiven him and taken him back. But immunity from punishment spoiled him, and hence of late his lapses had grown more frequent and of longer duration.

He walked in one morning, after one of his absences, with a more than usually forbidding face, for he had heard the news in the neighbourhood before he got in. During his absence a baby had come to share the poverty of his home. He thought with shame at himself, which turned into anger, that the child must be three months old and he had never seen it.

"Back ag'in, Jim?" was all Mandy said as he entered and seated himself sullenly.

"Yes, I's back, but I ain't back fu' long. I jes' come to git my clothes. I's a-gwine away fu' good."

"Gwine away ag'in! Why, you been gone fu' nigh on to fou' months a'ready. Ain't you nevah gwine to stay home no mo'?"

"I tol' you I was gwine away fu' good, did n't I? Well, dat 's what I mean."

"Ef you didn't want me, Jim, I wish to Gawd dat you 'd 'a' lef' me back home among my folks, whaih people knowed me an' would 'a' give me a helpin' han'. Dis hyeah No'f ain't no fittin' place fu' a lone colo'ed ooman less 'n she got money."

"It ain't no place fu' nobody dat 's jes' lazy an' no 'count."

"I ain't no' count. I ain't wuffless. I does de bes' I kin. I been wo'kin' like a dog to try an' keep up while you trapsein' 'roun', de Lawd knows whaih. When I was single I could git out an' mek my own livin'. I did n't ax nobody no odds; but you wa'n't satisfied ontwell I ma'ied you, an' now, when I's tied down wid a baby, dat 's de way you treats me."

The woman sat down and began to cry, and the sight of her tears angered her husband the more.

"Oh, cry!" he exclaimed. "Cry all you want to. I reckon you'll cry yo' fill befo' you gits me back. What do I keer about de baby! Dat 's jes' de trouble. It wa' n't enough fu' me to have to feed an' clothe you a-layin' 'roun' doin' nothin', a baby had to go an' come too."

"It's yo'n, an' you got a right to tek keer of it, dat 's what you have. I ain't a-gwine to waih my soul-case out a-tryin' to pinch along an' sta've to def at las'. I 'll kill myse'f an' de chile, too, fus."

The man looked up quickly. "Kill yo'se'f," he said. Then he laughed. "Who evah hyeahed tell of a niggah killin' hisse'f?"

"Nev' min', nev' min', you jes' go on yo' way rejoicin'. I 'spect you runnin' 'roun' aftah somebody else—dat 's de reason you cain't nevah stay at home no mo'."

"Who tol' you dat?" exclaimed the man, fiercely. "I ain't runnin' aftah nobody else—'t ain't none o' yo' business ef I is."

The denial and implied confession all came out in one breath.

"Ef hit ain't my bus'ness, I'd like to know whose it gwine to be. I's yo' lawful wife an' hit's me dat 's a-sta'vin' to tek keer of yo' chile."

"Doggone de chile; I's tiahed o' hyeahin' 'bout huh."

"You done got tiahed mighty quick when you ain't nevah even seed huh yit. You done got tiahed quick, sho."

"No, an' I do' want to see huh, neithah."

"You do' know nothin' 'bout de chile, you do' know whethah you wants to see huh er not."

"Look hyeah, ooman, don't you fool wid me. I ain't right, nohow!"

Just then, as if conscious of the hubbuh she had raised, and anxious to add to it, the baby awoke and began to wail. With quick mother instinct, the black woman went to the shabby bed, and, taking the child in her arms, began to croon softly to it: "Go s'eepy, baby; don' you be 'f'aid; mammy ain' gwine let nuffin' hu't you, even ef pappy don' wan' look at huh li'l face. Bye, bye, go s'eepy, mammy's li'l gal." Unconsciously she talked to the baby in a dialect that was even softer than usual. For a moment the child subsided, and the woman turned angrily on her husband: "I don' keer whethah you evah sees dis chile er not. She's a blessed li'l angel, dat 's what she is, an' I'll wo'k my fingahs off to raise huh, an' when she grows up, ef any nasty niggah comes erroun' mekin' eyes at huh, I'll tell huh 'bout huh pappy an' she'll stay wid me an' be my comfo't." "Keep yo' comfo't. Gawd knows I do' want huh."

"De time 'll come, though, an' I kin wait fu' it. Hush-a-bye, Jimsella."

The man turned his head slightly. "What you call huh?"

"I calls huh Jimsella, dat 's what I calls huh, 'ca'se she de ve'y spittin' image of you. I gwine to jes' lun to huh dat she had a pappy, so she know she's a hones' chile an' kin hoi' up huh haid."

"Oomph!"

They were both silent for a while, and then Jim said, "Huh name ought to be Jamsella—don't you know Jim's sho't fu' James?"

"I don't keer what it's sho't fu'." The woman was holding the baby close to her breast and sobbing now. "It was n't no James dat come a-cou'tin' me down home. It was jes' plain Jim. Dat 's what de mattah, I reckon you done got to be James." Jim did n't answer, and there was another space of silence, only interrupted by two or three contented gurgles from the baby.

"I bet two bits she don't look like me," he said finally, in a dogged tone that was a little tinged with curiosity.

"I know she do. Look at huh yo'se'f."

"I ain' gwine look at huh."

"Yes, you's 'fraid—dat 's de reason."

"I ain' 'fraid nuttin' de kin'. What I got to be 'fraid fu'? I reckon a man kin look at his own darter. I will look jes' to spite you." He could n't see much but a bundle of rags, from which sparkled a pair of beady black eyes. But he put his finger down among the rags. The baby seized it and gurgled. The sweat broke out on Jim's brow.

"Cain't you let me hold de baby a minute?" he said angrily. "You must be 'fraid I'll run off wid huh." He took the child awkwardly in his arms.

The boiling over of Mandy's clothes took her to the other part of the room, where she was busy for a few minutes. When she turned to look for Jim, he had slipped out, and Jimsella was lying on the bed trying to kick free of the coils which swaddled her.

At supper-time that evening Jim came in with a piece of "shoulder-meat" and a head of cabbage.

"You'll have to git my dinnah ready fu' me to ca'y tomorrer. I's wo' kin' on de street, an' I cain't come home twell night."

"Wha', what!" exclaimed Mandy, "den you ain' gwine leave, aftah all."

"Don't bothah me, ooman," said Jim. "Is Jimsella' sleep?"

The Lynching of Jube Benson

Gordon Fairfax's library held but three men, but the air was dense with clouds of smoke. The talk had drifted from one topic to another much as the smoke wreaths had puffed, floated, and thinned away. Then Handon Gay, who was an ambitious young reporter, spoke of a lynching story in a recent magazine, and the matter of punishment without trial put new life into the conversation.

"I should like to see a real lynching," said Gay rather callously.

"Well, I should hardly express it that way," said Fairfax, "but if a real, live lynching were to come my way, I should not avoid it."

"I should," spoke the other from the depths of his chair, where he had been puffing in moody silence. Judged by his hair, which was freely sprinkled with gray, the speaker might have been a man of forty-five or fifty, but his face, though lined and serious, was youthful, the face of a man hardly past thirty.

"What, you, Dr. Melville? Why, I thought that you physicians wouldn't weaken at anything."

"I have seen one such affair," said the doctor gravely, "in fact, I took a prominent part in it."

"Tell us about it," said the reporter, feeling for his pencil and notebook, which he was, nevertheless, careful to hide from the speaker.

The men drew their chairs eagerly up to the doctor's, but for a minute he did not seem to see them, but sat gazing abstractedly into the fire, then he took a long draw upon his cigar and began:

"I can see it all very vividly now. It was in the summer time and about seven years ago. I was practising at the time down in the little town of Bradford. It was a small and primitive place, just the location for an impecunious medical man, recently out of college.

"In lieu of a regular office, I attended to business in the first of two rooms which I rented from Hiram Daly, one of the more prosperous of the townsmen. Here I boarded and here also came my patients—white and black—whites from every section, and blacks from 'nigger town,' as the west portion of the place was called.

"The people about me were most of them coarse and rough, but they were simple and generous, and as time passed on I had about abandoned my intention of seeking distinction in wider fields and determined to settle into the place of a modest country doctor. This was rather a strange conclusion for a young man to arrive at, and I will not deny that the presence in the house of my host's beautiful young daughter, Annie, had something to do with my decision. She was a beautiful young girl of seventeen or eighteen, and very far superior to her surroundings. She had a native grace and a pleasing way about her that made everybody that came under her spell her abject slave. White and black who knew her loved her, and none, I thought, more deeply and respectfully than Jube Benson, the black man of all work about the place.

"He was a fellow whom everybody trusted; an apparently steady-going, grinning sort, as we used to call him. Well, he was completely under Miss Annie's thumb, and would fetch and carry for her like a faithful dog. As soon as he saw that I began to care for Annie, and anybody could see that, he transferred some of his allegiance to me and became my faithful servitor also. Never did a man have a more devoted adherent in his wooing than did I, and many a one of Annie's tasks which he volunteered to do gave her an extra hour with me. You can imagine that I liked the boy and you need not wonder anymore that as both wooing and my practice waxed apace, I was content to give up my great ambitions and stay just where I was.

"It wasn't a very pleasant thing, then, to have an epidemic of typhoid break out in the town that kept me going so that I hardly had time for the courting that a fellow wants to carry on with his sweetheart while he is still young enough to call her his girl. I fumed, but duty was duty, and I kept to my work night and day. It was now that Jube proved how invaluable he was as a coadjutor. He not only took messages to Annie, but brought sometimes little ones from her to me, and he would tell me little secret things that he had overheard her say that made me throb with joy and swear at him for repeating his mistress' conversation. But best of all, Jube was a perfect Cerberus, and no one on earth could have been more effective in keeping away or deluding the other young fellows who visited the Dalys. He would tell me of it afterwards, chuckling softly to himself. 'An,' Doctah, I say to Mistah Hemp Stevens, "'Scuse us, Mistah Stevens, but Miss Annie, she des gone out,' an' den he go outer de gate lookin' moughty lonesome. When Sam Elkins come, I say, 'Sh, Mistah Elkins, Miss Annie, she done tuk down,' an' he say, 'What, Jube, you don' reckon hit de—' Den he stop an' look skeert, an' I say, 'I feared hit is, Mistah Elkins,' an' sheks my haid ez solemn. He goes outer de gate lookin' lak his bes' frien' done daid, an' all de time Miss Annie behine de cu'tain ovah de po'ch des' a laffin' fit to kill."

"Jube was a most admirable liar, but what could I do? He knew that I was a young fool of a hypocrite, and when I would rebuke him for these deceptions, he would give way and roll on the floor in an excess of delighted laughter until from very contagion I had to join him— and, well, there was no need of my preaching when there had been no beginning to his repentance and when there must ensue a continuance of his wrong-doing.

"This thing went on for over three months, and then, pouf! I was down like a shot. My patients were nearly all up, but the reaction from overwork made me an easy victim of the lurking germs. Then Jube loomed up as a nurse. He put everyone else aside, and with the doctor, a friend of mine from a neighbouring town, took entire charge of me. Even Annie herself was put aside, and I was cared for as tenderly as a baby. Tom, that was my physician and friend, told me all about it afterward with tears in his eyes. Only he was a big, blunt man and his expressions did not convey all that he meant. He told me how my nigger had nursed me as if I were a sick kitten and he my mother. Of how fiercely he guarded his right to be the sole one to 'do' for me, as he called it, and how, when the crisis came, he hovered, weeping, but hopeful, at my bedside, until it was safely passed, when they drove him, weak and exhausted, from the room. As for me, I knew little about it at the time, and cared less. I was too busy in my fight with death. To my chimerical vision there was only a black but gentle demon that came and went, alternating with a white fairy, who would insist on coming in on her head, growing larger and larger and then dissolving. But the pathos and devotion in the story lost nothing in my blunt friend's telling.

"It was during the period of a long convalescence, however, that I came to know my humble ally as he really was, devoted to the point of abjectness. There were times when for very shame at his goodness to me, I would beg him to go away, to do something else. He would go, but before I had time to realise that I was not being ministered to, he would be back at my side, grinning and pottering just the same. He manufactured duties for the joy of performing them. He pretended to see desires in me that I never had, because he liked to pander to them, and when I became entirely exasperated, and ripped out a good round oath, he chuckled with the remark, 'Dah, now, you sholy is gittin' well. Nevah did hyeah a man anywhaih nigh Jo'dan's sho' cuss lak dat.'

"Why, I grew to love him, love him, oh, yes, I loved him as well— oh, what am I saying? All human love and gratitude are damned poor things; excuse me, gentlemen, this isn't a pleasant story. The truth is usually a nasty thing to stand.

"It was not six months after that that my friendship to Jube, which he had been at such great pains to win, was put to too severe a test.

"It was in the summer time again, and as business was slack, I had ridden over to see my friend, Dr. Tom. I had spent a good part of the day there, and it was past four o'clock when I rode leisurely into Bradford. I was in a particularly joyous mood and no premonition of the impending catastrophe oppressed me. No sense of sorrow, present or to come, forced itself upon me, even when I saw men hurrying through the almost deserted streets. When I got within sight of my home and saw a crowd surrounding it, I was only interested sufficiently to spur my horse into a jog trot, which brought me up to the throng, when something in the sullen, settled horror in the men's faces gave me a sudden, sick thrill. They whispered a word to me, and without a thought, save for Annie, the girl who had been so surely growing into my heart, I leaped from the saddle and tore my way through the people to the house.

"It was Annie, poor girl, bruised and bleeding, her face and dress torn from struggling. They were gathered round her with white faces, and, oh, with what terrible patience they were trying to gain from her fluttering lips the name of her murderer. They made way for me and I knelt at her side. She was beyond my skill, and my will merged with theirs. One thought was in our minds.

"'Who?' I asked.

"Her eyes half opened, 'That black—' She fell back into my arms dead.

"We turned and looked at each other. The mother had broken down and was weeping, but the face of the father was like iron.

"'It is enough,' he said; 'Jube has disappeared.' He went to the door and said to the expectant crowd, 'She is dead.'

"I heard the angry roar without swelling up like the noise of a flood, and then I heard the sudden movement of many feet as the men separated into searching parties, and laying the dead girl back upon her couch, I took my rifle and went out to join them.

"As if by intuition the knowledge had passed among the men that Jube Benson had disappeared, and he, by common consent, was to be the object of our search. Fully a dozen of the citizens had seen him hastening toward the woods and noted his skulking air, but as he had grinned in his old good-natured way they had, at the time, thought nothing of it. Now, however, the diabolical reason of his slyness was apparent. He had been shrewd enough to disarm suspicion, and by now was far away. Even Mrs. Daly, who was visiting with a neighbour, had seen him stepping out by a back way, and had said with a laugh, 'I reckon that black rascal's a-running off somewhere.' Oh, if she had only known.

"'To the woods! To the woods!' that was the cry, and away we went, each with the determination not to shoot, but to bring the culprit alive into town, and then to deal with him as his crime deserved.

"I cannot describe the feelings I experienced as I went out that night to beat the woods for this human tiger. My heart smouldered within me like a coal, and I went forward under the impulse of a will that was half my own, half some more malignant power's. My throat throbbed drily, but water nor whiskey would not have quenched my thirst. The thought has come to me since that now I could interpret the panther's desire for blood and sympathise with it, but then I thought nothing. I simply went forward, and watched, watched with burning eyes for a familiar form that I had looked for as often before with such different emotions.

"Luck or ill-luck, which you will, was with our party, and just as dawn was graying the sky, we came upon our quarry crouched in the corner of a fence. It was only half light, and we might have passed, but my eyes had caught sight of him, and I raised the cry. We levelled our guns and he rose and came toward us.

"'I t'ought you wa'n't gwine see me,' he said sullenly, 'I didn't mean no harm.'

"'Harm!'

"Some of the men took the word up with oaths, others were ominously silent.

"We gathered around him like hungry beasts, and I began to see terror dawning in his eyes. He turned to me, 'I's moughty glad you's hyeah, doc,' he said, 'you ain't gwine let 'em whup me.'

"'Whip you, you hound,' I said, 'I'm going to see you hanged,' and in the excess of my passion I struck him full on the mouth. He made a motion as if to resent the blow against even such great odds, but controlled himself.

"'W'y, doctah,' he exclaimed in the saddest voice I have ever heard, 'w'y, doctah! I ain't stole nuffin' o' yo'n, an' I was comin' back. I only run off to see my gal, Lucy, ovah to de Centah.'

"'You lie!' I said, and my hands were busy helping the others bind him upon a horse. Why did I do it? I don't know. A false education, I reckon, one false from the beginning. I saw his black face glooming there in the half light, and I could only think of him as a monster. It's tradition. At first I was told that the black man would catch me, and when I got over that, they taught me that the devil was black, and when I had recovered from the sickness of that belief, here were Jube and his fellows with faces of menacing blackness. There was only one conclusion: This black man stood for all the powers of evil, the result of whose machinations had been gathering in my mind from childhood up. But this has nothing to do with what happened.

"After firing a few shots to announce our capture, we rode back into town with Jube. The ingathering parties from all directions met us as we made our way up to the house. All was very quiet and orderly. There was no doubt that it was as the papers would have said, a gathering of the best citizens. It was a gathering of stern, determined men, bent on a terrible vengeance.

"We took Jube into the house, into the room where the corpse lay. At sight of it, he gave a scream like an animal's and his face went the colour of storm-blown water. This was enough to condemn him. We divined, rather than heard, his cry of 'Miss Ann, Miss Ann, oh, my God, doc, you don't t'ink I done it?'

"Hungry hands were ready. We hurried him out into the yard. A rope was ready. A tree was at hand. Well, that part was the least of it, save that Hiram Daly stepped aside to let me be the first to pull upon the rope. It was lax at first. Then it tightened, and I felt the quivering soft weight resist my muscles. Other hands joined, and Jube swung off his feet.

"No one was masked. We knew each other. Not even the Culprit's face was covered, and the last I remember of him as he went into the air was a look of sad reproach that will remain with me until I meet him face to face again.

"We were tying the end of the rope to a tree, where the dead man might hang as a warning to his fellows, when a terrible cry chilled us to the marrow.

"'Cut 'im down, cut 'im down, he ain't guilty. We got de one. Cut him down, fu' Gawd's sake. Here's de man, we foun' him hidin' in de barn!'

"Jube's brother, Ben, and another Negro, came rushing toward us, half dragging, half carrying a miserable-looking wretch between them. Someone cut the rope and Jube dropped lifeless to the ground.

"'Oh, my Gawd, he's daid, he's daid!' wailed the brother, but with blazing eyes he brought his captive into the centre of the group, and we saw in the full light the scratched face of Tom Skinner—the worst white ruffian in the town—but the face we saw was not as we were accustomed to see it, merely smeared with dirt. It was blackened to imitate a Negro's.

"God forgive me; I could not wait to try to resuscitate Jube. I knew he was already past help, so I rushed into the house and to the dead girl's side. In the excitement they had not yet washed or laid her out. Carefully, carefully, I searched underneath her broken finger nails. There was skin there. I took it out, the little curled pieces, and went with it to my office.

"There, determinedly, I examined it under a powerful glass, and read my own doom. It was the skin of a white man, and in it were embedded strands of short, brown hair or beard.

"How I went out to tell the waiting crowd I do not know, for something kept crying in my ears, 'Blood guilty! Blood guilty!'

"The men went away stricken into silence and awe. The new prisoner attempted neither denial nor plea. When they were gone I would have helped Ben carry his brother in, but he waved me away fiercely, 'You he'ped murder my brothah, you dat was *his* frien', go 'way, go 'way! I'll tek him home myse'f' I could only respect his wish, and he and his comrade took up the dead man and between them bore him up the street on which the sun was now shining full.

"I saw the few men who had not skulked indoors uncover as they passed, and I—I—stood there between the two murdered ones, while all the while something in my ears kept crying, 'Blood guilty! Blood guilty!'"

The doctor's head dropped into his hands and he sat for sometime in silence, which was broken by neither of the men, then he rose, saying, "Gentlemen, that was my last lynching."

Scene—Race track. *Enter old coloured man, seating himself.*

"Oomph, oomph. De work of de devil sho' do p'ospah. How 'do, suh? Des tol'able, thankee, suh. How you come on? Oh, I was des a-sayin' how de wo'k of de ol' boy do p'ospah. Doesn't I frequent the racetrack? No, suh; no, suh. I's Baptis' myse'f, an' I 'low hit's all devil's doin's. Wouldn't 'a' be'n hyeah today, but I got a boy named Jim dat's long gone in sin an' he gwine ride one dem hosses. Oomph, dat boy! I sut'ny has talked to him and labohed wid him night an' day, but it was allers in vain, an' I's feahed dat de day of his reckonin' is at han'.

"Ain't I nevah been intrusted in racin'? Humph, you don't s'pose I been dead all my life, does you? What you laffin' at? Oh, scuse me, scuse me, you unnerstan' what I means. You don' give a ol' man time to splain hisse'f. What I means is dat dey has been days when I walked in de counsels of de on-gawdly and set in de seats of sinnahs; and long erbout dem times I did tek most ovahly strong to racin'.

"How long dat been? Oh, dat's way long back, 'fo' I got religion, mo'n thuty years ago, dough I got to own I has fell from grace several times sense.

"Yes, suh, I ust to ride. Ki-yi! I nevah furgit de day dat my ol' Mas' Jack put me on 'June Boy,' his black geldin', an' say to me, 'Si,' says he, 'if you don' ride de tail offen Cunnel Scott's mare, "No Quit," I's gwine to larrup you twell you cain't set in de saddle no mo'.' Hyah, hyah. My ol' Mas' was a mighty han' fu' a joke. I knowed he wan't gwine to do nuffin' to me.

"Did I win? Why, whut you spec' I's doin' hyeah ef I hadn' winned? W'y, ef I'd 'a' let dat Scott maih beat my 'June Boy' I'd 'a' drowned myse'f in Bull Skin Crick.

"Yes, suh, I winned; w'y, at de finish I come down dat track lak hit was de Jedgment Day an' I was de las' one up! Ef I didn't race dat maih's tail clean off, I 'low I made hit do a lot o' switchin'. An' aftah dat my wife Mandy she ma'ed me. Hyah, hyah, I ain't bin much on hol'in' de reins sence.

"Sh! dey comin' in to wa'm up. Dat Jim, dat Jim, dat my boy; you nasty putrid little rascal. Des a hundred an' eight, suh, des a hundred an' eight. Yas, suh, dat's my Jim; I don't know whaih he gits his dev'ment at.

"What's de mattah wid dat boy? Whyn't he hunch hisse'f up on dat saddle right? Jim, Jim, whyn't you limber up, boy; hunch yo'se'f up on dat hoss lak you belonged to him and knowed you was dah. What I done showed you? De black raskil, goin' out dah tryin' to disgrace his own daddy. Hyeah he come back. Dat 's bettah, you scoun'ril.

"Dat 's a right smaht-lookin' hoss he's a-ridin', but I ain't a-trustin' dat bay wid de white feet—dat is, not altogethah. She's a favourwright too; but dey's sumpin' else in dis worl' sides playin' favourwrights. Jim bettah had win dis race. His hoss ain't a five to one shot, but I spec's to go way fum hyeah wid money ernuff to mek a donation on de pa'sonage.

"Does I bet? Well, I don' des call hit bettin'; but I resks a little w'en I t'inks I kin he'p de cause. 'Tain't gamblin', o' co'se; I wouldn't gamble fu nothin', dough my ol' Mastah did ust to say dat a honest gamblah was ez good ez a hones' preachah an' mos' nigh ez skace.

"Look out dah, man, dey's off, dat nasty bay maih wid de white feet leadin' right fu'm 'de pos'. I knowed it! I knowed it! I had my eye on huh all de time. Oh, Jim, Jim, why didn't you git in bettah, way back dah fouf? Dah go de gong! I knowed dat wasn't no staht. Troop back dah, you raskils, hyah, hyah.

"I wush dat boy wouldn't do so much jummying erroun' wid dat hoss. Fust t'ing he know he ain't gwine to know whaih he's at.

"Dah, dah dey go ag'in. Hit's a sho' t'ing dis time. Bettah, Jim, bettah. Dey didn't leave you dis time. Hug dat bay mare, hug her close, boy. Don't press dat hoss yit. He holdin' back a lot o' t'ings.

"He's gainin'! doggone my cats, he's gainin'! an' dat hoss o' his'n gwine des ez stiddy ez a rockin'-chair. Jim allus was a good boy.

"Confound these spec's, I cain't see 'em skacely; huh, you say dey's neck an' neck; now I see 'em! now I see 'em! and Jimmy's a-ridin' like——Huh, huh, I laik to said sumpin'.

"De bay maih's done huh bes', she's done huh bes'! Dey's turned into the stretch an' still see-sawin'. Let him out, Jimmy, let him out! Dat boy done th'owed de reins away. Come on, Jimmy, come on! He's leadin' by a nose. Come on, I tell you, you black rapscallion, come on! Give 'em hell, Jimmy! give 'em hell! Under de wire an' a len'th ahead. Doggone my cats! wake me up w'en dat othah hoss comes in.

"No, suh, I ain't gwine stay no longah, I don't app'ove o' racin', I's gwine 'roun' an' see dis hyeah bookmakah an' den I's gwine dreckly home, suh, dreckly home. I's Baptis' myse'f, an' I don't app'ove o' no sich doin's!"

The Strength of Gideon

Old Mam' Henry, and her word may be taken, said that it was "De powerfulles' sehmont she ever had hyeahd in all huh bo'n days." That was saying a good deal, for the old woman had lived many years on the Stone place and had heard many sermons from preachers, white and black. She was a judge, too.

It really must have been a powerful sermon that Brother Lucius preached, for Aunt Doshy Scott had fallen in a trance in the middle of the aisle, while "Merlatter Mag," who was famed all over the place for having white folk's religion and never "waking up," had broken through her reserve and shouted all over the camp ground.

Several times Cassie had shown signs of giving way, but because she was frail some of the solicitous sisters held her with self-congratulatory care, relieving each other now and then, that each might have a turn in the rejoicings. But as the preacher waded out deeper and deeper into the spiritual stream, Cassie's efforts to make her feelings known became more and more decided. He told them how the spears of the Midianites had "clashed upon de shiels of de Gideonites, an' aftah while, wid de powah of de Lawd behin' him, de man Gideon triumphed mightily," and swaying then and wailing in the dark woods, with grim branches waving in the breath of their own excitement, they could hear above the tumult the clamor of the fight, the clashing of the spears, and the ringing of the shields. They could see the conqueror coming home in triumph. Then when he cried, "A-who, I say, a-who is in Gideon's ahmy today?" and the wailing chorus took up the note, "A-who!" it was too much even for frail Cassie, and, deserted by the solicitous sisters, in the words of Mam' Henry, "she broke a-loose, and faihly tuk de place."

Gideon had certainly triumphed, and when a little boy baby came to Cassie two or three days later, she named him Gideon in honor of the great Hebrew warrior whose story had so wrought upon her. All the plantation knew the spiritual significance of the name, and from the day of his birth the child was as one set apart to a holy mission on earth.

Say what you will of the influences which the circumstances surrounding birth have upon a child, upon this one at least the effect was unmistakable. Even as a baby he seemed to realize the weight of responsibility which had been laid upon his little black shoulders, and there was a complacent dignity in the very way in which he drew upon the sweets of his dirty sugar-teat when the maternal breast was far off bending over the sheaves of the field.

He was a child early destined to sacrifice and self-effacement, and as he grew older and other youngsters came to fill Cassie's cabin, he took up his lot with the meekness of an infantile Moses. Like a Moses he was, too, leading his little flock to the promised land, when he grew to the age at which, barefooted and one-shifted, he led or carried his little brothers and sisters about the quarters. But the "promised land" never took him into the direction of the stables, where the other pickaninnies worried the horses, or into the region of the hen-coops, where egg-sucking was a common crime.

No boy ever rolled or tumbled in the dirt with a heartier glee than did Gideon, but no warrior, not even his illustrious prototype himself, ever kept sterner discipline in his ranks when his followers seemed prone to overstep the bounds of right. At a very early age his shrill voice could be heard calling in admonitory tones, caught from his mother's very lips, "You 'Nelius, don' you let me ketch you th'owin' at ol' mis' guinea-hens no mo'; you hyeah me?" or "Hi'am, you come offen de top er dat shed 'fo' you fall an' brek yo' naik all to pieces."

It was a common sight in the evening to see him sitting upon the low rail fence which ran before the quarters, his shift blowing in the wind, and his black legs lean and bony against the whitewashed rails, as he swayed to and fro, rocking and singing one of his numerous brothers to sleep, and always his song was of war and victory, albeit crooned in a low, soothing voice. Sometimes it was "Turn Back Pharaoh's Army," at others "Jinin' Gideon's Band." The latter was a favorite, for he seemed to have a proprietary interest in it, although, despite the martial inspiration of his name, "Gideon's band" to him meant an aggregation of people with horns and fiddles.

Steve, who was Cassie's man, declared that he had never seen such a child, and, being quite as religious as Cassie herself, early began to talk Scripture and religion to the boy. He was aided in this when his master, Dudley Stone, a man of the faith, began a little Sunday class for the religiously inclined of the quarters, where the old familiar stories were told in simple language to the slaves and explained. At these meetings Gideon became a shining light. No one listened more eagerly to the teacher's words, or more readily answered his questions at review. No one was wider-mouthed or whiter-eyed. His admonitions to his family now took on a different complexion, and he could be heard calling across a lot to a mischievous sister, "Bettah tek keer daih, Lucy Jane, Gawd's a-watchin' you; bettah tek keer."

The appointed man is always marked, and so Gideon was by always receiving his full name. No one ever shortened his scriptural appellation into Gid. He was always Gideon from the time he bore the name out of the heat of camp-meeting fervor until his master discovered his worthiness and filled Cassie's breast with pride by taking him into the house to learn "mannahs and 'po'tment."

As a house servant he was beyond reproach, and next to his religion his Mas' Dudley and Miss Ellen claimed his devotion and fidelity. The young mistress and young master learned to depend fearlessly upon his faithfulness.

It was good to hear old Dudley Stone going through the house in a mock fury, crying, "Well, I never saw such a house; it seems as if there isn't a soul in it that can do without Gideon. Here I've got him up here to wait on me, and it's Gideon here and Gideon there, and everytime I turn around some of you have sneaked him off. Gideon, come here!" And the black boy smiled and came.

But all his days were not days devoted to men's service, for there came a time when love claimed him for her own, when the clouds took on a new color, when the sough of the wind was music in his ears, and he saw heaven in Martha's eyes. It all came about in this way.

Gideon was young when he got religion and joined the church, and he grew up strong in the faith. Almost by the time he had become a valuable house servant he had grown to be an invaluable servant of the Lord. He had a good, clear voice that could lead a hymn out of all the labyrinthian wanderings of an ignorant congregation, even when he had to improvise both words and music; and he was a mighty man of prayer. It was thus he met Martha. Martha was brown and buxom and comely, and her rich contralto voice was loud and high on the sisters' side in meeting time. It was the voices that did it at first. There was no hymn or "spiritual" that Gideon could start to which Martha could not sing an easy blending second, and never did she open a tune that Gideon did not swing into it with a wonderfully sweet, flowing, natural bass. Often he did not know the piece, but that did not matter, he sang anyway. Perhaps when they were out he would go to her and ask, "Sis' Martha, what was that hymn you stahrted today?" and she would probably answer, "Oh, dat was jes' one o' my mammy's ol' songs."

"Well, it sholy was mighty pretty. Indeed it was."

"Oh, thanky, Brothah Gidjon, thanky."

Then a little later they began to walk back to the master's house together, for Martha, too, was one of the favored ones, and served, not in the field, but in the big house.

The old women looked on and conversed in whispers about the pair, for they were wise, and what their old eyes saw, they saw.

"Oomph," said Mam' Henry, for she commented on everything, "dem too is jes' natchelly singin' demse'ves togeddah."

"Dey's lak de mo'nin' stahs," interjected Aunt Sophy.

"How 'bout dat?" sniffed the older woman, for she objected to anyone's alluding to subjects she did not understand.

"Why, Mam' Henry, ain' you nevah hyeahd tell o' de mo'nin' stahs whut sung deyse'ves togeddah?"

"No, I ain't, an' I been livin' a mighty sight longah'n you, too. I knows all 'bout when de stahs fell, but dey ain' nevah done no singin' dat I knows 'bout."

"Do heish, Mam' Henry, you sho' su'prises me. W'y, dat ain' happenin's, dat 's Scripter."

"Look hyeah, gal, don't you tell me dat 's Scripter, an' me been a-settin' undah de Scripter fu' nigh onto sixty yeah."

"Well, Mam' Henry, I may 'a' been mistook, but sho' I took hit fu' Scripter. Mebbe de preachah I hyeahd was jes' inlinin'."

"Well, wheddah hit's Scripter er not, dey's one t'ing su'tain, I tell you,—dem two is singin' deyse'ves togeddah."

"Hit's a fac', an' I believe it."

"An' it's a mighty good thing, too. Brothah Gidjon is de nicest house dahky dat I ever hyeahd tell on. Dey jes' de same diffunce 'twixt him an' de othah house-boys as dey is 'tween real quality an' strainers—he got mannahs, but he ain't got aihs."

"Heish, ain't you right!"

"An' while de res' of dem ain' thinkin' 'bout nothin' but dancin' an' ca'in' on, he makin' his peace, callin', an' 'lection sho'."

"I tell you, Mam' Henry, dey ain' nothin' like a spichul named chile."

"Humph! g'long, gal; 'tain't in de name; de biggest devil I evah knowed was named Moses Aaron. 'Tain't in de name, hit's all in de man hisse'f."

But notwithstanding what the gossips said of him, Gideon went on his way, and knew not that the one great power of earth had taken hold of him until they gave the great party down in the quarters, and he saw Martha in all her glory. Then love spoke to him with no uncertain sound.

It was a dancing-party, and because neither he nor Martha dared countenance dancing, they had strolled away together under the pines that lined the white road, whiter now in the soft moonlight. He had never known the pine-cones smell so sweet before in all his life. She had never known just how the moonlight flecked the road before. This was lovers' lane to them. He didn't understand why his heart kept throbbing so furiously, for they were walking slowly, and when a shadow thrown across the road from a by-standing bush frightened her into pressing close up to him, he could not have told why his arm stole round her waist and drew her slim form up to him, or why his lips found hers, as eye looked into eye. For their simple hearts love's mystery was too deep, as it is for wiser ones.

Some few stammering words came to his lips, and she answered the best she could. Then why did the moonlight flood them so, and why were the heavens so full of stars? Out yonder in the black hedge a mocking-bird was singing, and he was translating—oh, so poorly— the song of their hearts. They forgot the dance, they forgot all but their love.

"An' you won't ma'y nobody else but me, Martha?"

"You know I won't, Gidjon."

"But I mus' wait de yeah out?"

"Yes, an' den don't you think Mas' Stone'll let us have a little cabin of ouah own jest outside de quahtahs?"

"Won't it be blessid? Won't it be blessid?" he cried, and then the kindly moon went under a cloud for a moment and came out smiling, for he had peeped through and had seen what passed. Then they walked back hand in hand to the dance along the transfigured road, and they found that the first part of the festivities were over, and all the people had sat down to supper. Everyone laughed when they went in. Martha held back and perspired with embarrassment. But even though he saw some of the older heads whispering in a corner, Gideon was not ashamed. A new light was in his eyes, and a new boldness had come to him. He led Martha up to the grinning group, and said in his best singing voice, "Whut you laughin' at? Yes, I's popped de question, an' she says 'Yes,' an' long 'bout a yeah f'om now you kin all'spec' a' invitation." This was a formal announcement. A shout arose from the happy-go-lucky people, who sorrowed alike in each other's sorrows, and joyed in each other's joys. They sat down at a table, and their health was drunk in cups of cider and persimmon beer.

Over in the corner Mam' Henry mumbled over her pipe, "Wha'd I tell you? wha'd I tell you?" and Aunt Sophy replied, "Hit's de pa'able of de mo'nin' stahs."

"Don't talk to me 'bout no mo'nin' stahs," the mammy snorted; "Gawd jes' fitted dey voices togeddah, an' den j'ined dey hea'ts. De mo'nin' stahs ain't got nothin' to do wid it."

"Mam' Henry," said Aunt Sophy, impressively, "you's a' oldah ooman den I is, an' I ain' sputin' hit; but I say dey done 'filled Scripter 'bout de mo'nin' stahs; dey's done sung deyse'ves togeddah."

The old woman sniffed.

The next Sunday at meeting someone got the start of Gideon, and began a new hymn. It ran:

> *"At de ma'ige of de Lamb, oh Lawd,*
> *God done gin His 'sent.*
> *Dey dressed de Lamb all up in white,*
> *God done gin His 'sent.*
> *Oh, wasn't dat a happy day,*
> *Oh, wasn't dat a happy day, Good Lawd,*
> *Oh, wasn't dat a happy day,*
> *De ma'ige of de Lamb!"*

The wailing minor of the beginning broke into a joyous chorus at the end, and Gideon wept and laughed in turn, for it was his wedding-song.

The young man had a confidential chat with his master the next morning, and the happy secret was revealed.

"What, you scamp!" said Dudley Stone. "Why, you've got even more sense than I gave you credit for; you've picked out the finest girl on the plantation, and the one best suited to you. You couldn't have done better if the match had been made for you. I reckon this must be one of the marriages that are made in heaven. Marry her, yes, and with a preacher. I don't see why you want to wait a year."

Gideon told him his hopes of a near cabin.

"Better still," his master went on; "with you two joined and up near the big house, I'll feel as safe for the folks as if an army was camped around, and, Gideon, my boy,"—he put his arms on the black man's shoulders,—"if I should slip away some day—"

The slave looked up, startled.

"I mean if I should die—I'm not going to run off, don't be alarmed—I want you to help your young Mas' Dud look after his mother and Miss Ellen; you hear? Now that's the one promise I ask of you,—come what may, look after the women folks." And the man promised and went away smiling.

His year of engagement, the happiest time of a young man's life, began on golden wings. There came rumors of war, and the wings of the glad-hued year drooped sadly. Sadly they drooped, and seemed to fold, when one day, between the rumors and predictions of strife, Dudley Stone, the old master, slipped quietly away out into the unknown.

There were wife, daughter, son, and faithful slaves about his bed, and they wept for him sincere tears, for he had been a good husband and father and a kind master. But he smiled, and, conscious to the last, whispered to them a cheery goodbye. Then, turning to Gideon, who stood there bowed with grief, he raised one weak finger, and his lips made the word, "Remember!"

They laid him where they had laid one generation after another of the Stones and it seemed as if a pall of sorrow had fallen upon the whole place. Then, still grieving, they turned their long-distracted attention to the things that had been going on around, and lo! the ominous mutterings were loud, and the cloud of war was black above them.

It was on an April morning when the storm broke, and the plantation, master and man, stood dumb with consternation, for they had hoped, they had believed, it would pass. And now there was the buzz of men who talked in secret corners. There were hurried saddlings and feverish rides to town. Somewhere in the quarters was whispered the forbidden word "freedom," and it was taken up and dropped breathlessly from the ends of a hundred tongues. Some of the older ones scouted it, but from some who held young children to their breasts there were deep-souled prayers in the dead of night. Over the meetings in the woods or in the log church a strange reserve brooded, and even the prayers took on a guarded tone. Even from the fulness of their hearts, which longed for liberty, no open word that could offend the mistress or the young master went up to the Almighty. He might know their hearts, but no tongue in meeting gave vent to what was in them, and even Gideon sang no more of the gospel army. He was sad because of this new trouble coming hard upon the heels of the old, and Martha was grieved because he was.

Finally the trips into town budded into something, and on a memorable evening when the sun looked peacefully through the pines, young Dudley Stone rode into the yard dressed in a suit of gray, and on his shoulders were the straps of office. The servants gathered around him with a sort of awe and followed him until he alighted at the porch. Only Mam' Henry, who had been nurse to both him and his sister, dared follow him in. It was a sad scene within, but such a one as any Southern home where there were sons might have shown that awful year. The mother tried to be brave, but her old hands shook, and her tears fell upon her son's brown head, tears of grief at parting, but through which shone the fire of a noble pride. The young Ellen hung about his neck with sobs and caresses.

"Would you have me stay?" he asked her.

"No! no! I know where your place is, but oh, my brother!"

"Ellen," said the mother in a trembling voice, "you are the sister of a soldier now."

The girl dried her tears and drew herself up. "We won't burden your heart, Dudley, with our tears, but we will weight you down with our love and prayers."

It was not so easy with Mam' Henry. Without protest, she took him to her bosom and rocked to and fro, wailing "My baby! my baby!" and the tears that fell from the young man's eyes upon her grey old head cost his manhood nothing.

Gideon was behind the door when his master called him. His sleeve was traveling down from his eyes as he emerged.

"Gideon," said his master, pointing to his uniform, "you know what this means?"

"Yes, suh."

"I wish I could take you along with me. But—"

"Mas' Dud," Gideon threw out his arms in supplication.

"You remember father's charge to you, take care of the women-folks." He took the servant's hand, and, black man and white, they looked into each other's eyes, and the compact was made. Then Gideon gulped and said "Yes, suh" again.

Another boy held the master's horse and rode away behind him when he vaulted into the saddle, and the man of battle-song and warrior name went back to mind the women-folks.

Then began the disintegration of the plantation's population. First Yellow Bob slipped away, and no one pursued him. A few blamed him, but they soon followed as the year rolled away. More were missing everytime a Union camp lay near, and great tales were told of the chances for young negroes who would go as body-servants to the Yankee officers. Gideon heard all and was silent.

Then as the time of his marriage drew near he felt a greater strength, for there was one who would be with him to help him keep his promise and his faith.

The spirit of freedom had grown strong in Martha as the days passed, and when her lover went to see her she had strange things to say. Was he going to stay? Was he going to be a slave when freedom and a livelihood lay right within his grasp? Would he keep her a slave? Yes, he would do it all—all.

She asked him to wait.

Another year began, and one day they brought Dudley Stone home to lay beside his father. Then most of the remaining negroes went. There was no master now. The two bereaved women wept, and Gideon forgot that he wore the garb of manhood and wept with them.

Martha came to him.

"Gidjon," she said, "I's waited a long while now. Mos' eve'ybody else is gone. Ain't you goin'?"

"No."

"But, Gidjon, I wants to be free. I know how good dey've been to us; but, oh, I wants to own myse'f. They're talkin' 'bout settin' us free every hour."

"I can wait."

"They's a camp right near here."

"I promised."

"The of'cers wants body-servants, Gidjon—"

"Go, Martha, if you want to, but I stay."

She went away from him, but she or someone else got word to young Captain Jack Griswold of the near camp that there was an excellent servant on the plantation who only needed a little persuading, and he came up to see him.

"Look here," he said, "I want a body-servant. I'll give you ten dollars a month."

"I've got to stay here."

"But, you fool, what have you to gain by staying here?"

"I'm goin' to stay."

"Why, you'll be free in a little while, anyway."

"All right."

"Of all fools," said the Captain. "I'll give you fifteen dollars."

"I do' want it."

"Well, your girl's going, anyway. I don't blame her for leaving such a fool as you are."

Gideon turned and looked at him.

"The camp is going to be moved up on this plantation, and there will be a requisition for this house for officers' quarters, so I'll see you again," and Captain Griswold went his way.

Martha going! Martha going! Gideon could not believe it. He would not. He saw her, and she confirmed it. She was going as an aid to the nurses. He gasped, and went back to mind the women-folks.

They did move the camp up nearer, and Captain Griswold came to see Gideon again, but he could get no word from him, save "I'm goin' to stay," and he went away in disgust, entirely unable to understand such obstinacy, as he called it.

But the slave had his moments alone, when the agony tore at his breast and rended him. Should he stay? The others were going. He would soon be free. Everyone had said so, even his mistress one day. Then Martha was going. "Martha! Martha!" his heart called.

The day came when the soldiers were to leave, and he went out sadly to watch them go. All the plantation, that had been white with tents, was dark again, and everywhere were moving, blue-coated figures.

Once more his tempter came to him. "I'll make it twenty dollars," he said, but Gideon shook his head. Then they started. The drums tapped. Away they went, the flag kissing the breeze. Martha stole up to say goodbye to him. Her eyes were overflowing, and she clung to him.

"Come, Gidjon," she plead, "fu' my sake. Oh, my God, won't you come with us—it's freedom." He kissed her, but shook his head.

"Hunt me up when you do come," she said, crying bitterly, "fu' I do love you, Gidjon, but I must go. Out yonder is freedom," and she was gone with them.

He drew out a pace after the troops, and then, turning, looked back at the house. He went a step farther, and then a woman's gentle voice called him, "Gideon!" He stopped. He crushed his cap in his hands, and the tears came into his eyes. Then he answered, "Yes, Mis' Ellen, I's a-comin'."

He stood and watched the dusty column until the last blue leg swung out of sight and over the grey hills the last drum-tap died away, and then turned and retraced his steps toward the house.

Gideon had triumphed mightily.

PAUL LAURENCE DUNBAR AND ALICE DUNBAR NELSON

The Trial Sermons on Bull-Skin

The congregation on Bull-Skin Creek was without a pastor. You will probably say that this was a deficiency easily remedied among a people who possess so much theological material. But you will instantly perceive how different a matter it was, when you learn that the last shepherd who had guided the flock at Bull-skin had left that community under a cloud. There were, of course, those who held with the departed minister, as well as those who were against him; and so two parties arose in the church, each contending for supremacy. Each party refused to endorse any measure or support any candidate suggested by the other; and as neither was strong enough to run the church alone, they were in a state of inactive equipoise very gratifying to that individual who is supposed to take delight in the discomfort of the righteous.

It was in this complicated state of affairs that Brother Hezekiah Sneedon, who was the representative of one of the candidates for the vacant pastorate, conceived and proposed a way out of the difficulty. Brother Sneedon's proposition was favourably acted upon by the whole congregation, because it held out the promise of victory to each party. It was, in effect, as follows:

Each faction—it had come to be openly recognised that there were two factions—should name its candidate, and then they should be invited to preach, on successive Sundays, trial sermons before the whole congregation, the preacher making the better impression to be called as pastor.

"And," added Brother Sneedon, pacifically, "in ordah dat dis little diffunce between de embahs may be settled in ha'mony, I do hope an' pray dat de pahty dat fin's itse'f outpreached will give up to de othah in Christun submission, an' th'ow in all deir might to hoi' up de ban's of whatever pastor de Lawd may please to sen'."

Sister Hannah Williams, the leader of the opposing faction, expressed herself as well pleased with the plan, and counselled a like submission to the will of the majority. And thus the difficulty at Bull-skin seemed in a fair way to settlement. But could anyone have read that lady's thoughts as she wended her homeward way after the meeting, he would have had some misgivings concerning the success of the proposition which she so willingly endorsed. For she was saying to herself,—

"Uh huh! ol' Kiah Sneedon thinks he's mighty sma't, puttin' up dat plan. Reckon he thinks ol' Abe Ma'tin kin outpreach anything near an' fur, but ef Brothah 'Lias Smith don't fool him, I ain't talkin'."

And Brother Sneedon himself was not entirely guiltless of some selfish thought as he hobbled away from the church door.

"Ann," said he to his wife, "I wunner ef Hannah Williams ca'culates dat 'Lias Smith kin beat Brother Abe Ma'tin preachin', ki yi! but won't she be riley when she fin's out how mistaken she is? Why, dey ain't nobody 'twixt hyeah an' Louisville kin beat Brothah Abe Ma'tin preachin'. I's hyeahed dat man preach 'twell de winders rattled an' it seemed lak de skies mus' come down anyhow, an' sinnahs was a-fallin' befo' de Wo'd lak leaves in a Novembah bias'; an' she 'lows to beat him, oomph!" The "coomph" meant disgust, incredulity, and, above all, resistance.

The first of the momentous Sundays had been postponed two weeks, in order, it was said, to allow the members to get the spiritual and temporal elements of the church into order that would be pleasing to the eyes of a new pastor. In reality, Brother Sneedon and Sister Williams used the interval of time to lay their plans and to marshal their forces. And during the two weeks previous to the Sunday on which, by common consent, it had been agreed to invite the Reverend Elias Smith to preach, there was an ominous quiet on the banks of Bull-Skin,—the calm that precedes a great upheaval, when clouds hang heavy with portents and forebodings, but silent withal.

But there were events taking place in which the student of diplomacy might have found food for research and reflection. Such an event was the taffy-pulling which Sister Williams' daughters, Dora and Caroline, gave to the younger members of the congregation on Thursday evening. Such were the frequent incursions of Sister Williams herself upon the domains of the neighbours, with generous offerings of "a taste o' my ketchup" or "a sample o' my jelly." She did not stop with rewarding her own allies, but went farther, gift-bearing, even into the camp of the enemy himself.

It was on Friday morning that she called on Sister Sneedon. She found the door ajar and pushed it open, saying, "You see, Sis' Sneedon, I's jes' walkin' right in."

"Oh, it's you, Sis' Williams; dat 's right, come in. I was jes' settin' hyeah sawtin' my cyahpet rags, de mof do seem to pestah 'em so. Tek dis cheer"—industriously dusting one with her apron. "How you be'n sence I seen you las'?"

"Oh, jes' sawt o' so."

"How's Do' an' Ca'line?"

"Oh, Ca'line's peart enough, but Do's feelin' kind o' peekid."

"Don't you reckon she grow too fas'?"

"'Spec' dat's about hit; dat gal do sutny seem to run up lak a weed."

"It don't nevah do 'em no good to grow so fas', hit seem to tek away all deir strengf."

"Yes, 'm, it sholy do; gals ain't whut dey used to be in yo' an' my day, nohow." "Lawd, no; dey's ez puny ez white folks now."

"Well, dem sholy is lovely cyahpet rags—put' nigh all wool, ain't dey?"

"Yes, ma'am, dey is wool, evah speck an' stitch; dey ain't a bit o' cotton among 'em. I ain't lak some folks; I don't b'lieve in mixin' my rags evah-which-way. Den when you gits 'em wove have de cyahpet wah in holes, 'cause some 'll stan' a good deal o' strain an' some won't; yes, 'm, dese is evah one wool."

"An' you sholy have be'n mighty indust'ous in gittin' 'em togethah."

"I's wo'ked ha'd an' done my level bes', dat's sho."

"Dat's de mos' any of us kin do. But I must n't be settin' hyeah talkin' all day an' keepin' you f'om yo' wo'k. Why, la! I'd mos' nigh fu'got what I come fu'—I jes' brung you ovah a tas'e o' my late greens. I knows how you laks greens, so I thought mebbe you'd enjoy dese."

"Why, sho enough; now ain't dat good o' you, Sis' Williams? Dey's right wa'm, too, an' tu'nip tops—bless me! Why, dese mus' be de ve'y las' greens o' de season."

"Well, I reely don't think you 'll fin' none much latah. De fros' had done teched dese, but I kin' o' kivered 'em up wif leaves ontwell dey growed up wuf cuttin'."

"Well, I knows I sholy shell relish dem." Mrs. Sneedon beamed as she emptied the dish and insisted upon washing it for her visitor to take home with her. "Fu'," she said, by way of humour, "I's a mighty po' han' to retu'n nice dishes when I gits 'em in my cu'boa'd once."

Sister Williams rose to go. "Well, you'll be out to chu'ch Sunday to hyeah Broth' 'Lias Smith; he's a powahful man, sho."

"Dey do tell me so. I'll be thah. You kin 'pend on me to be out whenevah thah's to be any good preachin'."

"Well, we kin have dat kin' o' preachin' all de time ef we gits Broth' 'Lias Smith."

"Yes, 'm."

"Dey ain't no'sputin' he'll be a movin' powah at Bull-Skin."

"Yes, 'm."

"We sistahs 'll have to ban' togethah an' try to do whut is bes' fu' de chu'ch."

"Yes, 'm."

"Co'se, Sistah Sneedon, ef you's pleased wif his sermon, I suppose you'll be in favoh o' callin' Broth' 'Lias Smith."

"Well, Sis' Williams, I do' know; you see Hezekier's got his hea't sot on Broth' Abe Ma'tin fum Dokesville; he's mighty sot on him, an' when he's sot he's sot, an' you know how it is wif us women when de men folks says dis er dat."

Sister Williams saw that she had overshot her mark. "Oh, hit's all right, Sis' Sneedon, hit's all right. I jes' spoke of it a-wunnerin'. What we women folks wants to do is to ban' togethah to hoi' up de han' of de pastah dat comes, whoms'ever he may be."

"Dat 's hit, dat 's hit," assented her companion; "an' you kin 'pend on me thah, fu' I's a powahful han' to uphol' de ministah whoms'ever he is."

"An' you right too, fu' dey's de shepuds of de flock. Well, I mus' be goin'—come ovah."

"I's a-comin'—come ag'in yo'se'f, goodbye."

As soon as her visitor was gone, Sister Sneedon warmed over the greens and sat down to the enjoyment of them. She had just finished the last mouthful when her better half entered. He saw the empty plate and the green liquor. Evidently he was not pleased, for be it said that Brother Sneedon had himself a great tenderness for turnip greens.

"Wha'd you git dem greens?" he asked.

"Sistah Hannah Williams brung 'em ovah to me."

"Sistah Hannah—who?" exclaimed he.

"Sis' Williams, Sis' Williams, you know Hannah Williams."

"What! dat wolf in sheep's clothin' dat 's a-gwine erroun' a-seekin' who she may devowah, an' you hyeah a-projickin' wif huh, eatin' de greens she gives you! How you know whut's in dem greens?"

"Oh, g'long, 'Kiah, you so funny! Sis' Williams ain't gwine conju' nobidy."

"You hyeah me, you hyeah me now. Keep on foolin' wif dat ooman, she'll have you crawlin' on yo' knees an' ba'kin, lak a dog. She kin do it, she kin do it, fu' she's long-haided, I tell you."

"Well, ef she wants to hu't me it's done, fu' I's eat de greens now."

"Yes," exclaimed Brother Sneedon, "you eat 'em up lak a hongry hog an' never saved me a smudgeon."

"Oomph! I thought you's so afeard o' gittin' conju'ed."

"Heish up! you's alius tryin' to raise some kin'er contentions in de fambly. I nevah seed a ooman lak you." And old Hezekiah strode out of the cabin in high dudgeon.

And so, smooth on the surface, but turbulent beneath, the stream of days flowed on until the Sunday on which Reverend Elias Smith was to preach his trial sermon. His fame as a preacher, together with the circumstances surrounding this particular sermon, had brought together such a crowd as the little church on Bull-Skin had never seen before even in the heat of the most successful revivals. Outsiders had come from as far away as Cbristiansburg, which was twelve, and Fox Run, which was fifteen miles distant, and the church was crowded to the doors.

Sister Williams with her daughters Dora and Caroline were early in their seats. Their ribbons were fluttering to the breeze like the banners of an aggressive host. There were smiles of anticipated triumph upon their faces. Brother and Sister Sneedon arrived a little later. They took their seat far up in the "amen corner," directly behind the Williams family. Sister Sneedon sat very erect and looked about her, but her spouse leaned his chin upon his cane and gazed at the floor, nor did he raise his head, when, preceded by a buzz of expectancy, the Reverend Elias Smith, accompanied by Brother Abner Williams, who was a local preacher, entered and ascended to the pulpit, where he knelt in silent prayer.

At the entrance of their candidate, the female portion of the Williams family became instantly alert.

They were all attention when the husband and father arose and gave out the hymn: "Am I a Soldier of the Cross?" They joined lustily in the singing, and at the lines, "Sure I must fight if I would reign," their voices rose in a victorious swell far above the voices of the rest of the congregation. Prayer followed, and then Brother Williams rose and said,—

"Brothahs an' sistahs, I teks gret pleasuah in interducin' to you Eldah Smith, of Dokeville, who will preach fu' us at dis howah. I want to speak fu' him yo' pra'ful attention." Sister Williams nodded her head in approval, even this much was good; but Brother Sneedon sighed aloud.

The Reverend Elias Smith arose and glanced over the congregation. He was young, well-appearing, and looked as though he might have been unmarried. He announced his text in a clear, resonant voice: "By deir fruits shell you know dem."

The great change that gave to the blacks fairly trained ministers from the schools had not at this time succeeded their recently accomplished emancipation. And the sermon of Elder Smith was full of all the fervour, common-sense, and rude eloquence of the old plantation exhorter. He spoke to his hearers in the language that they understood, because he himself knew no other. He drew his symbols and illustrations from the things which he saw most commonly about him,—things which he and his congregation understood equally well. He spent no time in dallying about the edge of his subject, but plunged immediately into the middle of things, and soon had about him a shouting, hallooing throng of frantic people. Of course it was the Williams faction who shouted. The spiritual impulse did not seem to reach those who favoured Brother Sneedon's candidate. They sat silent and undemonstrative. That earnest disciple himself still sat with his head bent upon his cane, and still at intervals sighed audibly. He had only raised his head once, and that was when some especially powerful period in the sermon had drawn from the partner of his joys and sorrows an appreciative "Oomph!" Then the look that he shot forth from his eyes, so full of injury, reproach, and menace, repressed her noble rage and settled her back into a quietude more consonant with her husband's ideas.

Meanwhile, Sister Hannah Williams and her sylph-like daughters "Do" and "Ca'line" were in an excess of religious frenzy. Whenever any of the other women in the congregation seemed to be working their way too far forward, those enthusiastic sisters shouted their way directly across the approach to the pulpit, and held place there with such impressive and menacing demonstrativeness that all comers were warned back. There had been times when, actuated by great religious fervour, women had ascended the rostrum and embraced the minister. Rest assured, nothing of that kind happened in this case, though the preacher waxed more and more eloquent as he proceeded,—an eloquence more of tone, look, and gesture than of words. Fie played upon the emotions of his willing hearers, except those who had steeled themselves against his power, as a skilful musician upon the strings of his harp. At one time they were boisterously exultant, at another they were weeping and moaning, as if in the realisation of many sins. The minister himself lowered his voice to a soft rhythmical moan, almost a chant, as he said,—

"You go 'long by de road an' you see an ol' shabby tree a-standin' in de o'chud. It ain't ha'dly got a apple on it. Its leaves are put' nigh all gone. You look at de branches, dey's all rough an' crookid. De tree's all full of sticks an' stones an' wiah an' ole tin cans. Hit's all bruised up an' hit's a ha'd thing to look at altogether. You look at de tree an' whut do you say in yo' hea't? You say de tree ain't no 'count, fu' 'by deir fruits shell you know dem.' But you wrong, my frien's, you wrong. Dat tree did ba' good fruit, an' by hits fruit was hit knowed. John tol' Gawge an' Gawge toF Sam, an' evah one dat passed erlong de road had to have a shy at dat fruit. Dey be'n th'owin' at dat tree evah sence hit begun to ba' fruit, an' dey's 'bused hit so dat hit could n't grow straight to save hits life. Is dat whut's de mattah wif you, brothah, all bent ovah yo' staff an' a-groanin' wif yo' burdens? Is dat whut's de mattah wif you, brothah, dat yo' steps are a-weary an' you's longin' fu' yo' home? Have dey be'n th'owin' stones an' cans at you? Have dey be'n beatin' you wif sticks? Have dey tangled you up in ol' wiah twell you could n't move han' ner foot? Have de way be'n all trouble? Have de sky be'n all cloud? Have de sun refused to shine an' de day be'n all da'kness? Don't git werry, be consoled. Whut de mattah! Why, I tell you ba'in' good fruit, an' de debbil cain't stan' It— 'By deir fruits shell you know dem.'

"You go 'long de road a little furder an' you see a tree standin' right by de fence. Standin' right straight up in de air, evah limb straight out in hits place, all de leaves green an' shinin' an' lovely. Not a stick ner a stone ner a can in sight. You look 'way up in de branches, an' dey hangin' full o' fruit, big an' roun' an' solid. You look at dis tree an' whut now do you say in yo' hea't? You say dis is a good tree, fu' 'by deir fruits shell you know dem.' But you wrong, you wrong ag'in, my frien's. De apples on dat tree are so sowah dat dey'd puckah up yo' mouf wuss 'n a green pu'simmon, an' evahbidy knows hit, by hits fruit is hit knowed. Dey don't want none o' dat fruit, an' dey pass hit by an' don't bothah dey haids about it.

"Look out, brothah, you gwine erlong thoo dis work sailin' on flowery beds of ease. Look out, my sistah, you's a-walkin' in de sof' pafs an' a-dressin' fine. Ain't nobidy a-troublin' you, nobidy ain't-a-backbitin' you, nobidy ain't-a-castin' yo' name out as evil. You all right an' movin' smoov. But I want you to stop an' 'zamine yo'se'ves. I want you to settle whut kin' o' fruit you ba'in,' whut kin' o' light you showin' fo'f to de worl'. An' I want you to stop an' tu'n erroun' when you fin' out dat you ba'in' bad fruit, an' de debbil ain't bothahed erbout you 'ca'se he knows you his'n anyhow. By deir fruits shell you know dem.'"

The minister ended his sermon, and the spell broke. Collection was called for and taken, and the meeting dismissed.

"Wha' 'd you think o' dat sermon?" asked Sister Williams of one of her good friends; and the good friend answered,—

"Tsch, pshaw! dat man jes' tuk his tex' at de fust an' nevah lef' it."

Brother Sneedon remarked to a friend: "Well, he did try to use a good deal o' high langgidge, but whut we want is grace an' speritual feelin'." The Williams faction went home with colours flying. They took the preacher to dinner. They were exultant. The friends of Brother Sneedon were silent but thoughtful.

It was true, beyond the shadow of a doubt, that the Reverend Elias Smith had made a wonderful impression upon his hearers,— an impression that might not entirely fade away before the night on which the new pastor was to be voted for. Comments on the sermon did not end with the closing of that Sabbath day. The discussion of its excellences was prolonged into the next week, and continued with a persistency dangerous to the aspirations of any rival candidate. No one was more fully conscious of this menacing condition of affairs than Hezekiah Sneedon himself. He knew that for the minds of the people to rest long upon the exploits of Elder Smith would be fatal to the chances of his own candidate; so he set about inventing some way to turn the current of public thought into another channel. And nothingbut a powerful agency could turn it. But in fertility of resources Hezekiah Sneedon was Napoleonic. Though his diplomacy was greatly taxed in this case, he came out victorious and with colours flying when he hit upon the happy idea of a "'possum supper." That would give the people something else to talk about beside the Reverend Elias Smith and his wonderful sermon. But think not, O reader, that the intellect that conceived this new idea was so lacking in the essential qualities of diplomacy as to rush in his substitute, have done with it, and leave the public's attention to revert to its former object. Brother Sneedon was too wary for this. Indeed, he did send his invitations out early to the congregation; but this only aroused discussion and created anticipation which was allowed to grow and gather strength until the very Saturday evening on which the event occurred.

Sister Hannah Williams saw through the plot immediately, but she could not play counter, so she contented herself with saying: "Dat Hezikiah Sneedon is sholy de bigges' scamp dat evah trod shoe-leathah." But nevertheless, she did not refuse an invitation to be present at the supper. She would go, she said, for the purpose of seeing "how things went on." But she added, as a sort of implied apology to her conscience, w and den I's powahful fond o' 'possum, anyhow."

In inviting Sister Williams, Brother Sneedon had taken advantage of the excellent example which that good woman had set him, and was carrying the war right into the enemy's country; but he had gone farther in one direction, and by the time the eventful evening arrived had prepared for his guests a *coup d'etat* which was unanticipated even by his own wife.

He had been engaged in a secret correspondence, the result of which was seen when, just after the assembling of the guests in the long, low room which was parlour, sitting, and dining room in the Sneedon household, the wily host ushered in and introduced to the astonished people the Reverend Abram Martin. They were not allowed to recover from their surprise before they were seated at the table, grace said by the reverend brother, and the supper commenced. And such a supper as it was,—one that could not but soften the feelings and touch the heart of any Negro. It was a supper that disarmed opposition. Sister Hannah was seated at the left of Reverend Abram Martin, who was a fluent and impressive talker; and what with his affability and the delight of the repast, she grew mollified and found herself laughing and chatting. The other members of her faction looked on, and, seeing her pleased with the minister, grew pleased themselves. The Reverend Abram Martin's magnetic influence ran round the board like an electric current.

He could tell a story with a dignified humour that was irresistible,— and your real Negro is a lover of stories and a teller of them. Soon, next to the 'possum, he was the centre of attraction around the table, and he held forth while the diners listened respectfully to his profound observations or laughed uproariously at his genial jokes. All the while Brother Sneedon sat delightedly by, watchful, but silent, save for the occasional injunction to his guests to help themselves. And they did so with a gusto that argued well for their enjoyment of the food set before them. As the name by which the supper was designated would imply, 'possum was the principal feature, but, even after including the sweet potatoes and brown gravy, that was not all. There was hog jole and cold cabbage, ham and Kentucky oysters, more widely known as chittlings. What more there was it boots not to tell. Suffice it to say that there was little enough of anything left to do credit to the people's dual powers of listening and eating, for in all this time the Reverend Abram Martin had not abated his conversational efforts nor they their unflagging attention.

Just before the supper was finished, the preacher was called upon, at the instigation of Hezekiah Sneedon, of course, to make a few remarks, which he proceeded to do in a very happy and taking vein. Then the affair broke up, and the people went home with myriad comments on their tongues. But one idea possessed the minds of all, and that was that the Reverend Abram Martin was a very able man, and charming withal.

It was at this hour, when opportunity for sober reflection returned, that Sister Williams first awakened to the fact that her own conduct had compromised her cause. She did not sleep that night—she lay awake and planned, and the result of her planning was a great fumbling the next morning in the little bag where she kept her earnings, and the despatching of her husband on an early and mysterious errand.

The day of meeting came, and the church presented a scene precisely similar to that of the previous Sunday. If there was any difference, it was only apparent in the entirely alert and cheerful attitude of Brother Sneedon and the reversed expressions of the two factions. But even the latter phase was not so marked, for the shrewd Sister Williams saw with alarm that her forces were demoralised. Some of them were sitting near the pulpit with expressions of pleasant anticipation on their faces, and as she looked at them she groaned in spirit. But her lips were compressed in a way that to a close observer would have seemed ominous, and ever and anon she cast anxious and expectant glances toward the door. Her husband sat upon her left, an abashed, shamefaced expression dominating his features. He continual'y followed her glances toward the door with a furtive, half-frightened look; and when Sneedon looked his way, he avoided his eye.

That arch schemer was serene and unruffled. He had perpetrated a stroke of excellent policy by denying himself the pleasure of introducing the new minister, and had placed that matter in the hands of Isaac Jordan, a member of the opposing faction and one of Sister Williams' stanchest supporters. Brother Jordan was pleased and flattered by the distinction, and converted.

The service began. The hymn was sung, the prayer said, and the minister, having been introduced, was already leading out from his text, when, with a rattle and bang that instantly drew every eye rearward, the door opened and a man entered. Apparently oblivious to the fact that he was the centre of universal attention, he came slowly down the aisle and took a seat far to the front of the church. A gleam of satisfaction shot from the eye of Sister Williams, and with a sigh she settled herself in her seat and turned her attention to the sermon. Brother Sneedon glanced at the new-comer and grew visibly disturbed. One sister leaned over and whispered to another,—

"I wunner whut Bud Lewis is a-doin' hyeah?"

"I do' know," answered the other, "but I do hope an' pray dat he won't git into none o' his shoutin' tantrums today."

"Well, ef he do, I's a-leavin' hyeah, you hyeah me," rejoined the first speaker.

The sermon had progressed about one-third its length, and the congregation had begun to show frequent signs of awakening life, when on an instant, with startling suddenness, Bud Lewis sprang from his seat and started on a promenade down the aisle, swinging his arms in sweeping semi-circles, and uttering a sound like the incipient bellow of a steamboat. "Whough! Whough!" he puffed, swinging from side to side down the narrow passageway.

At the first demonstration from the newcomer, people began falling to right and left out of his way. The fame of Bud Lewis' "shoutin' tantrums" was widespread, and they who knew feared them. This unregenerate mulatto was without doubt the fighting man of Bull-Skin.

While, as a general thing, he shunned the church, there were times when a perverse spirit took hold of him, and he would seek the meeting-house, and promptly, noisily, and violently "get religion." At these times he made it a point to knock people helter-skelter, trample on tender toes, and do other mischief, until in many cases the meeting broke up in confusion. The saying finally grew to be proverbial among the people in the Bull-Skin district that they would rather see a thunderstorm than Bud Lewis get religion.

On this occasion he made straight for the space in front of the pulpit, where his vociferous hallelujahs entirely drowned the minister's voice; while the thud, thud, thud of his feet upon the floor, as he jumped up and down, effectually filled up any gap of stillness which his hallelujahs might have left.

Hezekiah Sneedon knew that the Reverend Mr. Martin's sermon would be ruined, and he saw all his cherished hopes destroyed in a moment. He was a man of action, and one glance at Sister Williams' complacent countenance decided him. He rose, touched Isaac Jordan, and said, "Come on, let's hold him." Jordan hesitated a minute; but his leader was going on, and there was nothing to do but to follow him. They approached Lewis, and each seized an arm. The man began to struggle. Several other men joined them and laid hold on him.

"Quiet, brother, quiet," said Hezekiah Sneedon; "dis is de house o' de Lawd."

"You lemme go," shrieked Bud Lewis. "Lemme go, I say."

"But you mus' be quiet, so de res' o' de congregation kin hyeah."

"I don't keer whethah dey hyeahs er not. I reckon I kin shout ef I want to." The minister had paused in his sermon, and the congregation was alert.

"Brother, you mus' not distu'b de meetin'. Praise de Lawd all you want to, but give somebidy else a chance too."

"I won't, I won't; lemme go. I's paid fu' shoutin', an' I's gwine to shout." Hezekiah Sneedon caught the words, and he followed up his advantage.

"You's paid fu' shoutin'! Who paid you?"

"Hannah Williams, dat 's who! Now you lemme go; I's gwine to shout."

The effect of this declaration was magical. The brothers, by their combined efforts, lifted the struggling mulatto from his feet and carried him out of the chapel, while Sister Williams' face grew ashen in hue.

The congregation settled down, and the sermon was resumed. Disturbance and opposition only seemed to have heightened the minister's power, and he preached a sermon that is remembered to this day on Bull-Skin. Before it was over, Bud Lewis' guards filed back into church and listened with enjoyment to the remainder of the discourse.

The service closed, and under cover of the crowd that thronged about the altar to shake the minister's hand Hannah Williams escaped.

As the first item of business at the church meeting on the following Wednesday evening, she was formally "churched" and expelled from fellowship with the flock at Bull-Skin for planning to interrupt divine service. The next business was the unanimous choice of Reverend Abram Martin for the pastorate of the church.

The Trustfulness of Polly

Polly Jackson was a model woman. She was practical and hard-working. She knew the value of a dollar, could make one and keep one, sometimes—fate permitting. Fate was usually Sam and Sam was Polly's husband. Any morning at six o'clock she might be seen, basket on arm, wending her way to the homes of her wealthy patrons for the purpose of bringing in their washing, for by this means did she gain her livelihood. She had been a person of hard common sense, which suffered its greatest lapse when she allied herself with the man whose name she bore. After that the lapses were more frequent.

How she could ever have done so no one on earth could tell. Sam was her exact opposite. He was an easy-going, happy-go-lucky individual, who worked only when occasion demanded and inclination and the weather permitted. The weather was usually more acquiescent than inclination. He was sanguine of temperament, highly imaginative and a dreamer of dreams. Indeed, he just missed being a poet. A man who dreams takes either to poetry or policy. Not being able quite to reach the former, Sam had declined upon the latter, and, instead of meter, feet and rhyme, his mind was taken up with "hosses," "gigs" and "straddles."

He was always "jes' behin' dem policy sha'ks, an' I'll be boun', Polly, but I gwine to ketch 'em dis time."

Polly heard this and saw the same result so often that even her stalwart faith began to turn into doubt. But Sam continued to reassure her and promise that some day luck would change. "An' when hit do change," he would add, impressively, "it's gwine change fu' sho', an' we'll have one wakenin' up time. Den I bet you'll git dat silk dress you been wantin' so long."

Polly did have ambitions in the direction of some such finery, and this plea always melted her. Trust was restored again, and Hope resumed her accustomed place.

It was, however, not through the successful culmination of any of Sam's policy manipulations that the opportunity at last came to Polly to realize her ambitions. A lady for whom she worked had a second-hand silk dress, which she was willing to sell cheap. Another woman had spoken for it, but if Polly could get the money in three weeks she would let her have it for seven dollars.

To say that the companion of Sam Jackson jumped at the offer hardly indicates the attitude of eagerness with which she received the proposition.

"Yas'm, I kin sholy git dat much money together in th'ee weeks de way I's a-wo'kin'."

"Well, now, Polly, be sure; for if you are not prompt I shall have to dispose of it where it was first promised," was the admonition.

"Oh, you kin 'pend on me, Mis' Mo'ton; fu' when I sets out to save money I kin save, I tell you." Polly was not usually so sanguine, but what changes will not the notion of the possession of a brown silk dress trimmed with passementrie make in the disposition of a woman?

Polly let Sam into the secret, and, be it said to his credit, he entered into the plan with an enthusiasm no less intense than her own. He had always wanted to see her in a silk dress, he told her, and then in a quizzically injured tone of voice, "but you ought to waited tell I ketched dem policy sha'ks an' I'd 'a' got you a new one." He even went so far as to go to work for a week and bring Polly his earnings, of course, after certain "little debts" which he mentioned but did not specify, had been deducted.

But in spite of all this, when washing isn't bringing an especially good price; when one must eat and food is high; when a grasping landlord comes around once every week and exacts tribute for the privilege of breathing foul air from an alley in a room up four flights; when, I say, all this is true, and it generally is true in the New York tenderloin, seven whole dollars are not easily saved. There was much raking and scraping and pinching during each day that at night Polly might add a few nickels or pennies to the store that jingled in a blue jug in one corner of her closet. She called it her bank, and Sam had laughed at the conceit, telling her that that was one bank anyhow that couldn't "bust."

As the days went on how she counted her savings and exulted in their growth! She already saw herself decked out in her new gown, the envy and admiration of every woman in the neighborhood. She even began to wish that she had a full-length glass in order that she might get the complete effect of her own magnificence. So saving, hoping, dreaming, the time went on until a few days before the limit, and there was only about a dollar to be added to make the required amount. This she could do easily in the remaining time. So Polly was jubilant.

Now everything would have been all right and matters would have ended happily if Sam had only kept on at work. But, no. He must needs stop, and give his mind the chance to be employed with other things. And that is just what happened. For about this time, having nothing else to do, like that old king of Bible renown, he dreamed a dream. But unlike the royal dreamer, he asked no seer or prophet to interpret his dream to him. He merely drove his hand down into his inside pocket, and fished up an ancient dream-book, greasy and tattered with use. Over this he pored until his eyes bulged and his hands shook with excitement.

"Got 'em at last!" he exclaimed. "Dey ain't no way fu' dem to git away f'om me. I's behind 'em. I's behind 'em I tell you," and then his face fell and he sat for a long time with his chin in his hand thinking, thinking.

"Polly," said he when his wife came in, "d'you know what I dremp 'bout las' night?"

"La! Sam Jackson, you ain't gone to dreamin' agin. I thought you done quit all dat foolishness."

"Now jes' listen at you runnin' on. You ain't never axed me what I dremp 'bout yit."

"Hit don' make much diffunce to me, less 'n you kin dream 'bout a dollah mo' into my pocket."

"Dey has been sich things did," said Sam sententiously. He got up and went out. If there is one thing above another that your professional dreamer does demand, it is appreciation. Sam had failed to get it from Polly, but he found a balm for all his hurts when he met Bob Davis.

"What!" exclaimed Bob. "Dreamed of a nakid black man. Fu' de Lawd sake, Sam, don' let de chance pass. You got 'em dis time sho'. I'll put somep'n' on it myse'f. Wha'd you think ef we'd win de 'capital'?"

That was enough. The two parted and Sam hurried home. He crept into the house. Polly was busy hanging clothes on the roof. Where now are the guardian spirits that look after the welfare of trusting women? Where now are the enchanted belongings that even in the hands of the thief cry out to their unsuspecting owners? Gone. All gone with the ages of faith that gave them birth. Without an outcry, without even so much as a warning jingle, the contents of the blue jug and the embodied hope of a woman's heart were transferred to the gaping pocket of Sam Jackson. Polly went on hanging up clothes on the roof.

Sam chuckled to himself: "She won't never have a chanst to scol' me. I'll git de drawin's early dis evenin', an' go ma'chin' home wif a new silk fu' huh, an' money besides. I do' want my wife waihin' no white folks' secon'-han' clothes nohow. My, but won't she be su'prised an' tickled. I kin jes' see huh now. Oh, mistah policy-sha'k, I got you now. I been layin' fu' you fu' a long time, but you's my meat at las'."

He marched into the policy shop like a conqueror. To the amazement of the clerk, he turned out a pocketful of small coin on the table and played it all in "gigs," "straddles and combinations."

"I'll call on you about ha' pas' fou', Mr. McFadden," he announced exultantly as he went out.

"Faith, sor," said McFadden to his colleague, "if that nagur does ketch it he'll break us, sure."

Sam could hardly wait for half-past four. A minute before the time he burst in upon McFadden and demanded the drawings. They were handed to him. He held his breath as his eye went down the column of figures. Then he gasped and staggered weakly out of the room. The policy sharks had triumphed again.

Sam walked the streets until nine o'clock that night. He was afraid to go home to Polly. He knew that she had been to the jug and found—. He groaned, but at last his very helplessness drove him in. Polly, with swollen eyes, was sitting by the table, the empty jug lying on its side before her.

"Sam," she exclaimed, "whaih's my money? Whaih's my money I been wo'kin' fu' all dis time?"

"Why—Why, Polly—"

"Don' go beatin' 'roun' de bush. I want 'o know whaih my money is; you tuck it."

"Polly, I dremp—"

"I do' keer what you dremp, I want my money fu' my dress."

His face was miserable.

"I thought sho' dem numbers 'u'd come out, an'—"

The woman flung herself upon the floor and burst into a storm of tears. Sam bent over her. "Nemmine, Polly," he said. "Nemmine. I thought I'd su'prise you. Dey beat me dis time." His teeth clenched. "But when I ketch dem policy sha'ks—"

Uncle Simon's Sundays Out

Mr. Marston sat upon his wide veranda in the cool of the summer Sabbath morning. His hat was off, the soft breeze was playing with his brown hair, and a fragrant cigar was rolled lazily between his lips. He was taking his ease after the fashion of a true gentleman. But his eyes roamed widely, and his glance rested now on the blue-green sweep of the great lawn, again on the bright blades of the growing corn, and anon on the waving fields of tobacco, and he sighed a sigh of ineffable content. The breath had hardly died on his lips when the figure of an old man appeared before him, and, hat in hand, shuffled up the wide steps of the porch.

It was a funny old figure, stooped and so one-sided that the tail of the long and shabby coat he wore dragged on the ground. The face was black and shrewd, and little patches of snow-white hair fringed the shiny pate.

"Good-morning, Uncle Simon," said Mr. Marston, heartily.

"Mornin' Mas' Gawge. How you come on?"

"I'm first-rate. How are you? How are your rheumatics coming on?"

"Oh, my, dey's mos' nigh well. Dey don' trouble me no mo'!"

"Most nigh well, don't trouble you anymore?"

"Dat is none to speak of."

"Why, Uncle Simon, who ever heard tell of a man being cured of his aches and pains at your age?"

"I ain' so powahful ol', Mas', I ain' so powahful ol'."

"You're not so powerful old! Why, Uncle Simon, what's taken hold of you? You're eighty if a day."

"Sh—sh, talk dat kin' o' low, Mastah, don' 'spress yo'se'f so loud!" and the old man looked fearfully around as if he feared someone might hear the words.

The master fell back in his seat in utter surprise.

"And, why, I should like to know, may I not speak of your age aloud?"

Uncle Simon showed his two or three remaining teeth in a broad grin as he answered:

"Well, Mastah, I 's 'fraid ol' man Time mought hyeah you an' t'ink he done let me run too long." He chuckled, and his master joined him with a merry peal of laughter.

"All right, then, Simon," he said, "I'll try not to give away any of your secrets to old man Time. But isn't your age written down somewhere?"

"I reckon it's in dat ol' Bible yo' pa gin me."

"Oh, let it alone then, even Time won't find it there."

The old man shifted the weight of his body from one leg to the other and stood embarrassedly twirling his ancient hat in his hands. There was evidently something more that he wanted to say. He had not come to exchange commonplaces with his master about age or its ailments.

"Well, what is it now, Uncle Simon?" the master asked, heeding the servant's embarrassment, "I know you've come up to ask or tell me something. Have any of your converts been backsliding, or has Buck been misbehaving again?"

"No, suh, de converts all seem to be stan'in' strong in de faif, and Buck, he actin' right good now."

"Doesn't Lize bring your meals regular, and cook them good?"

"Oh, yes, suh, Lize ain' done nuffin'. Dey ain' nuffin' de mattah at de quahtahs, nuffin' 't'al."

"Well, what on earth then—"

"Hol' on, Mas', hol' on! I done tol' you dey ain' nuffin' de mattah 'mong de people, an' I ain' come to 'plain 'bout nuffin'; but—but—I wants to speak to you 'bout somefin' mighty partic'ler."

"Well, go on, because it will soon be time for you to be getting down to the meeting-house to exhort the hands."

"Dat 's jes' what I want to speak 'bout, dat 'zortin'."

"Well, you've been doing it for a good many years now."

"Dat 's de very idee, dat 's in my haid now. Mas' Gawge, huccume you read me so nigh right?"

"Oh, that's not reading anything, that's just truth. But what do you mean, Uncle Simon, you don't mean to say that you want to resign. Why what would your old wife think if she was living?"

"No, no, Mas' Gawge, I don't ezzactly want to 'sign, but I'd jes' lak to have a few Sundays off."

"A few Sundays off! Well, now, I do believe that you are crazy. What on earth put that into your head?"

"Nuffin', Mas' Gawge, I wants to be away f'om my Sabbaf labohs fu' a little while, dat 's all."

"Why, what are the hands going to do for someone to exhort them on Sunday. You know they've got to shout or burst, and it used to be your delight to get them stirred up until all the back field was ringing."

"I do' say dat I ain' gwine try an' do dat some mo', Mastah, min' I do' say dat. But in de mean time I's got somebody else to tek my place, one dat I trained up in de wo'k right undah my own han'. Mebbe he ain' endowed wif de sperrit as I is, all men cain't be gifted de same way, but dey ain't no sputin' he is powahful. Why, he can handle de Scriptures wif bof han's, an' you kin hyeah him prayin' fu' two miles."

"And you want to put this wonder in your place?"

"Yes, suh, fu' a while, anyhow."

"Uncle Simon, aren't you losing your religion?"

"Losin' my u'ligion? Who, me losin' my u'ligion! No, suh."

"Well, aren't you afraid you'll lose it on the Sundays that you spend out of your meeting-house?"

"Now, Mas' Gawge, you a white man, an' you my mastah, an' you got larnin'. But what kin' o' argyment is dat? Is dat good jedgment?"

"Well, now if it isn't, you show me why, you're a logician." There was a twinkle in the eye of George Marston as he spoke.

"No, I ain' no 'gician, Mastah," the old man contended. "But what kin' o' u'ligion you spec' I got anyhow? Hyeah me been sto'in' it up fu' lo, desc many yeahs an' ain' got enough to las' ovah a few Sundays. What kin' o' u'ligion is dat?"

The master laughed, "I believe you've got me there, Uncle Simon; well go along, but see that your flock is well tended."

"Thanky, Mas' Gawge, thanky. I'll put a shepherd in my place dat'll put de food down so low dat de littles' lambs kin enjoy it, but'll mek it strong enough fu' de oldes' ewes." And with a profound bow the old man went down the steps and hobbled away.

As soon as Uncle Simon was out of sight, George Marston threw back his head and gave a long shout of laughter.

"I wonder," he mused, "what crotchet that old darkey has got into his head now. He comes with all the air of a white divine to ask for a vacation. Well, I reckon he deserves it. He had me on the religious argument, too. He's got his grace stored." And another peal of her husband's laughter brought Mrs. Marston from the house.

"George, George, what is the matter. What amuses you so that you forget that this is the Sabbath day?"

"Oh, don't talk to me about Sunday anymore, when it comes to the pass that the Reverend Simon Marston wants a vacation. It seems that the cares of his parish have been too pressing upon him and he wishes to be away for sometime. He does not say whether he will visit Europe or the Holy Land, however, we shall expect him to come back with much new and interesting material for the edification of his numerous congregation."

"I wish you would tell me what you mean by all this."

Thus adjured, George Marston curbed his amusement long enough to recount to his wife the particulars of his interview with Uncle Simon.

"Well, well, and you carry on so, only because one of the servants wishes his Sundays to himself for awhile? Shame on you!"

"Mrs. Marston," said her husband, solemnly, "you are hopeless—positively, undeniably, hopeless. I do not object to your failing to see the humor in the situation, for you are a woman; but that you should not be curious as to the motives which actuate Uncle Simon, that you should be unmoved by a burning desire to know why this staunch old servant who has for so many years pictured hell each Sunday to his fellow-servants should wish a vacation—that I can neither understand nor forgive."

"Oh, I can see why easily enough, and so could you, if you were not so intent on laughing at everything. The poor old man is tired and wants rest, that's all." And Mrs. Marston turned into the house with a stately step, for she was a proud and dignified lady.

"And that reason satisfies you? Ah, Mrs. Marston, Mrs. Marston, you discredit your sex!" her husband sighed, mockingly after her.

There was perhaps some ground for George Marston's perplexity as to Uncle Simon's intentions. His request for "Sundays off," was so entirely out of the usual order of things. The old man, with the other servants on the plantation had been bequeathed to Marston by his father. Even then, Uncle Simon was an old man, and for many years in the elder Marston's time had been the plantation exhorter. In this position he continued, and as his age increased, did little of anything else. He had a little log house built in a stretch of woods convenient to the quarters, where Sunday after Sunday he held forth to as many of the hands as could be encouraged to attend.

With time, the importance of his situation grew upon him. He would have thought as soon of giving up his life as his pulpit to anyone else. He was never absent a single meeting day in all that time. Sunday after Sunday he was in his place expounding his doctrine. He had grown officious, too, and if any of his congregation were away from service, Monday morning found him early at their cabins to find out the reason why.

After a life, then, of such punctilious rigidity, it is no wonder that his master could not accept Mrs. Marston's simple excuse for Uncle Simon's dereliction, "that the old man needed rest." For the time being, the good lady might have her way, as all good ladies should, but as for him, he chose to watch and wait and speculate.

Mrs. Marston, however, as well as her husband, was destined to hear more that day of Uncle Simon's strange move, for there was one other person on the place who was not satisfied with Uncle Simon's explanation of his conduct, and yet could not as easily as the mistress formulate an opinion of her own. This was Lize, who did about the quarters and cooked the meals of the older servants who were no longer in active service.

It was just at the dinner hour that she came hurrying up to the "big house," and with the freedom of an old and privileged retainer went directly to the dining room.

"Look hyeah, Mis' M'ree," she exclaimed, without the formality of prefacing her remarks, "I wants to know whut's de mattah wif Brothah Simon—what mek him ac' de way he do?"

"Why, I do not know, Eliza, what has Uncle Simon been doing?"

"Why, some o' you all mus' know, lessn' he couldn' 'a' done hit. Ain' he ax you nuffin', Marse Gawge?"

"Yes, he did have some talk with me."

"Some talk! I reckon he did have some talk wif somebody!"

"Tell us, Lize," Mr. Marston said, "what has Uncle Simon done?"

"He done brung somebody else, dat young Merrit darky, to oc'py his pu'pit. He in'juce him, an' 'en he say dat he gwine be absent a few Sundays, an' 'en he tek hissef off, outen de chu'ch, widout even waitin' fu' de sehmont."

"Well, didn't you have a good sermon?"

"It mought 'a' been a good sehmont, but dat ain' whut I ax you. I want to know whut de mattah wif Brothah Simon."

"Why, he told me that the man he put over you was one of the most powerful kind, warranted to make you shout until the last bench was turned over."

"Oh, some o' dem, dey shouted enough, dey shouted dey fill. But dat ain' whut I's drivin' at yit. Whut I wan' 'o know, whut mek Brothah Simon do dat?"

"Well, I'll tell you, Lize," Marston began, but his wife cut him off.

"Now, George," she said, "you shall not trifle with Eliza in that manner." Then turning to the old servant, she said: "Eliza, it means nothing. Do not trouble yourself about it. You know Uncle Simon is old; he has been exhorting for you now for many years, and he needs a little rest these Sundays. It is getting toward midsummer, and it is warm and wearing work to preach as Uncle Simon does."

Lize stood still, with an incredulous and unsatisfied look on her face. After a while she said, dubiously shaking her head:

"Huh uh! Miss M'ree, dat may 'splain t'ings to you, but hit ain' mek 'em light to me yit."

"Now, Mrs. Marston"—began her husband, chuckling.

"Hush, I tell you, George. It's really just as I tell you, Eliza, the old man is tired and needs rest!"

Again the old woman shook her head, "Huh uh," she said, "ef you'd' a' seen him gwine lickety split outen de meetin'-house you wouldn' a' thought he was so tiahed."

Marston laughed loud and long at this. "Well, Mrs. Marston," he bantered, "even Lize is showing a keener perception of the fitness of things than you."

"There are some things I can afford to be excelled in by my husband and my servants. For my part, I have no suspicion of Uncle Simon, and no concern about him either one way or the other."

"'Scuse me, Miss M'ree," said Lize, "I didn' mean no ha'm to you, but I ain' a trustin' ol' Brothah Simon, I tell you."

"I'm not blaming you, Eliza; you are sensible as far as you know."

"Ahem," said Mr. Marston.

Eliza went out mumbling to herself, and Mr. Marston confined his attentions to his dinner; he chuckled just once, but Mrs. Marston met his levity with something like a sniff.

On the first two Sundays that Uncle Simon was away from his congregation nothing was known about his whereabouts. On the third Sunday he was reported to have been seen making his way toward the west plantation. Now what did this old man want there? The west plantation, so called, was a part of the Marston domain, but the land there was worked by a number of slaves which Mrs. Marston had brought with her from Louisiana, where she had given up her father's gorgeous home on the Bayou Lafourche, together with her proud name of Marie St. Pierre for George Marston's love. There had been so many bickerings between the Marston servants and the contingent from Louisiana that the two sets had been separated, the old remaining on the east side and the new ones going to the west. So, to those who had been born on the soil the name of the west plantation became a reproach. It was a synonym for all that was worldly, wicked and unregenerate. The east plantation did not visit with the west. The east gave a dance, the west did not attend. The Marstons and St. Pierres in black did not intermarry. If a Marston died, a St. Pierre did not sit up with him. And so the division had kept up for years.

It was hardly to be believed then that Uncle Simon Marston, the very patriarch of the Marston flock, was visiting over the border. But on another Sunday he was seen to go straight to the west plantation.

At her first opportunity Lize accosted him:—

"Look a-hyeah, Brothah Simon, whut's dis I been hyeahin' 'bout you, huh?"

"Well, sis' Lize, I reckon you'll have to tell me dat yo' se'f, 'case I do' know. Whut you been hyeahin'?"

"Brothah Simon, you's a ol' man, you's ol'."

"Well, sis' Lize, dah was Methusalem."

"I ain' jokin', Brothah Simon, I ain' jokin', I's a talkin' right straightfo'wa'd. Yo' conduc' don' look right. Hit ain' becomin' to you as de shepherd of a flock."

"But whut I been doin', sistah, whut I been doin'?"

"You know."

"I reckon I do, but I wan' see whethah you does er not."

"You been gwine ovah to de wes' plantation, dat 's whut you been doin'. You can' 'ny dat, you's been seed!"

"I do' wan' 'ny it. Is dat all?"

"Is dat all!" Lize stood aghast. Then she said slowly and wonderingly, "Brothah Simon, is you losin' yo' senses er yo' grace?"

"I ain' losin' one ner 'tothah, but I do' see no ha'm in gwine ovah to de wes' plantation."

"You do' see no ha'm in gwine ovah to de wes' plantation! You stan' hyeah in sight o' Gawd an' say dat?"

"Don't git so 'cited, sis' Lize, you mus' membah dat dey's souls on de wes' plantation, jes' same as dey is on de eas'."

"Yes, an' dey's souls in hell, too," the old woman fired back.

"Cose dey is, but dey's already damned; but dey's souls on de wes' plantation to be saved."

"Oomph, uh, uh, uh!" grunted Lize.

"You done called me de shepherd, ain't you, sistah? Well, sayin' I is, when dey's little lambs out in de col' an' dey ain' got sense 'nough to come in, er dey do' know de way, whut do de shepherd do? Why, he go out, an' he hunt up de po' shiverin', bleatin' lambs and brings 'em into de fol'. Don't you bothah 'bout de wes' plantation, sis' Lize." And Uncle Simon hobbled off down the road with surprising alacrity, leaving his interlocutor standing with mouth and eyes wide open.

"Well, I nevah!" she exclaimed when she could get her lips together, "I do believe de day of jedgmen' is at han'."

Of course this conversation was duly reported to the master and mistress, and called forth some strictures from Mrs. Marston on Lize's attempted interference with the old man's good work.

"You ought to be ashamed of yourself, Eliza, that you ought. After the estrangement of all this time if Uncle Simon can effect a reconciliation between the west and the east plantations, you ought not to lay a straw in his way. I am sure there is more of a real Christian spirit in that than in shouting and singing for hours, and then coming out with your heart full of malice. You need not laugh, Mr. Marston, you need not laugh at all. I am very much in earnest, and I do hope that Uncle Simon will continue his ministrations on the other side. If he wants to, he can have a room built in which to lead their worship."

"But you do' want him to leave us altogethah?"

"If you do not care to share your meeting-house with them, they can have one of their own."

"But, look hyeah, Missy, dem Lousiany people, dey bad—an' dey hoodoo folks, an' dey Cath'lics—"

"Eliza!"

"'Scuse me, Missy, chile, bless yo' hea't, you know I do' mean no ha'm to you. But somehow I do' feel right in my hea't 'bout Brothah Simon."

"Never mind, Eliza, it is only evil that needs to be watched, the good will take care of itself."

It was not one, nor two, nor three Sundays that Brother Simon was away from his congregation, but six passed before he was there again. He was seen to be very busy tinkering around during the week, and then one Sunday he appeared suddenly in his pulpit. The church nodded and smiled a welcome to him. There was no change in him. If anything he was more fiery than ever. But, there was a change. Lize, who was news-gatherer and carrier extraordinary, bore the tidings to her owners. She burst into the big house with the cry of "Whut I tell you! Whut I tell you!"

"Well, what now," exclaimed both Mr. and Mrs. Marston.

"Didn' I tell you ol' Simon was up to some'p'n'?"

"Out with it," exclaimed her master, "out with it, I knew he was up to something, too."

"George, try to remember who you are."

"Brothah Simon come in chu'ch dis mo'nin' an' he 'scended up de pulpit—"

"Well, what of that, are you not glad he is back?"

"Hol' on, lemme tell you—he 'scended up de pu'pit, an' 'menced his disco'se. Well, he hadn't no sooner got sta'ted when in walked one o' dem brazen Lousiany wenches—"

"Eliza!"

"Hol' on, Miss M'ree, she walked in lak she owned de place, an' flopped huhse'f down on de front seat."

"Well, what if she did," burst in Mrs. Marston, "she had a right. I want you to understand, you and the rest of your kind, that that meeting-house is for any of the hands that care to attend it. The woman did right. I hope she'll come again."

"I hadn' got done yit, Missy. Jes' ez soon ez de sehmont was ovah, whut mus' Brothah Simon, de 'zortah, min' you, whut mus' he do but come hoppin' down f'om de pu'pit, an' beau dat wench home! 'Scorted huh clah 'crost de plantation befo' evahbody's face. Now whut you call dat?"

"I call it politeness, that is what I call it. What are you laughing at, Mr. Marston? I have no doubt that the old man was merely trying to set an example of courtesy to some of the younger men, or to protect the woman from the insults that the other members of the congregation would heap upon her. Mr. Marston, I do wish you would keep your face serious. There is nothing to laugh at in this matter. A worthy old man tries to do a worthy work, his fellow-servants cavil at him, and his master, who should encourage him, laughs at him for his pains."

"I assure you, my dear, I'm not laughing at Uncle Simon."

"Then at me, perhaps; that is infinitely better."

"And not at you, either; I'm amused at the situation."

"Well, Manette ca'ied him off dis mo'nin'," resumed Eliza.

"Manette!" exclaimed Mrs. Marston.

"It was Manette he was a beauin'. Evahbody say he likin' huh moughty well, an' dat he look at huh all th'oo preachin'."

"Oh my! Manette's one of the nicest girls I brought from St. Pierre. I hope—oh, but then she is a young woman, she would not think of being foolish over an old man."

"I do' know, Miss M'ree. De ol' men is de wuss kin'. De young oomans knows how to tek de young mans, 'case dey de same age, an' dey been lu'nin' dey tricks right along wif dem'; but de ol' men, dey got sich a long sta't ahaid, dey been lu'nin' so long. Ef I had a darter, I wouldn' be afeard to let huh tek keer o' huhse'f wif a young man, but ef a ol' man come a cou'tin' huh, I'd keep my own two eyes open."

"Eliza, you're a philosopher," said Mr. Marston. "You're one of the few reasoners of your sex."

"It is all nonsense," said his wife. "Why Uncle Simon is old enough to be Manette's grandfather."

"Love laughs at years."

"And you laugh at everything."

"That's the difference between love and me, my dear Mrs. Marston."

"Do not pay any attention to your master, Eliza, and do not be so suspicious of everyone. It is all right. Uncle Simon had Manette over, because he thought the service would do her good."

"Yes'm, I 'low she's one o' de young lambs dat he gone out in de col' to fotch in. Well, he tek'n' moughty good keer o' dat lamb."

Mrs. Marston was compelled to laugh in spite of herself. But when Eliza was gone, she turned to her husband, and said:

"George, dear, do you really think there is anything in it?"

"I thoroughly agree with you, Mrs. Marston, in the opinion that Uncle Simon needed rest, and I may add on my own behalf, recreation."

"Pshaw! I do not believe it."

All doubts, however, were soon dispelled. The afternoon sun drove Mr. Marston to the back veranda where he was sitting when Uncle Simon again approached and greeted him.

"Well, Uncle Simon, I hear that you're back in your pulpit again?"

"Yes, suh, I's done 'sumed my labohs in de Mastah's vineya'd."

"Have you had a good rest of it?"

"Well, I ain' ezzackly been restin'," said the aged man, scratching his head. "I's been pu'su'in' othah 'ployments."

"Oh, yes, but change of work is rest. And how's the rheumatism, now, any better?"

"Bettah? Why, Mawse Gawge, I ain' got a smidgeon of hit. I's jes' limpin' a leetle bit on 'count o' habit."

"Well, it's good if one can get well, even if his days are nearly spent."

"Heish, Mas' Gawge. I ain' t'inkin' 'bout dyin'."

"Aren't you ready yet, in all these years?"

"I hope I's ready, but I hope to be spaihed a good many yeahs yit."

"To do good, I suppose?"

"Yes, suh; yes, suh. Fac' is, Mawse Gawge, I jes' hop up to ax you some'p'n."

"Well, here I am."

"I want to ax you—I want to ax you—er—er—I want—"

"Oh, speak out. I haven't time to be bothering here all day."

"Well, you know, Mawse Gawge, some o' us ain' nigh ez ol' ez dey looks."

"That's true. A person, now, would take you for ninety, and to my positive knowledge, you're not more than eighty-five."

"Oh, Lawd. Mastah, do heish."

"I'm not flattering you, that's the truth."

"Well, now, Mawse Gawge, couldn' you mek me' look lak eighty-fo', an' be a little youngah?"

"Why, what do you want to be younger for?"

"You see, hit's jes' lak dis, Mawse Gawge. I come up hyeah to ax you—I want—dat is—me an' Manette, we wants to git ma'ied."

"Get married!" thundered Marston. "What you, you old scarecrow, with one foot in the grave!"

"Heish, Mastah, 'buse me kin' o' low. Don't th'ow yo' words 'roun' so keerless."

"This is what you wanted your Sundays off for, to go sparking around—you an exhorter, too."

"But I's been missin' my po' ol' wife so much hyeah lately."

"You've been missing her, oh, yes, and so you want to get a woman young enough to be your granddaughter to fill her place."

"Well, Mas' Gawge, you know, ef I is ol' an' feeble, ez you say, I need a strong young han' to he'p me down de hill, an' ef Manette don' min' spa'in' a few mont's er yeahs—"

"That'll do, I'll see what your mistress says. Come back in an hour."

A little touched, and a good deal amused, Marston went to see his wife. He kept his face straight as he addressed her. "Mrs. Marston, Manette's hand has been proposed for."

"George!"

"The Rev. Simon Marston has this moment come and solemnly laid his heart at my feet as proxy for Manette."

"He shall not have her, he shall not have her!" exclaimed the lady, rising angrily.

"But remember, Mrs. Marston, it will keep her coming to meeting."

"I do not care; he is an old hypocrite, that is what he is."

"Think, too, of what a noble work he is doing. It brings about a reconciliation between the east and west plantations, for which we have been hoping for years. You really oughtn't to lay a straw in his way."

"He's a sneaking, insidious, old scoundrel."

"Such poor encouragement from his mistress for a worthy old man, who only needs rest!"

"George!" cried Mrs. Marston, and she sank down in tears, which turned to convulsive laughter as her husband put his arm about her and whispered, "He is showing the true Christian spirit. Don't you think we'd better call Manette and see if she consents? She is one of his lambs, you know."

"Oh, George, George, do as you please. If the horrid girl consents, I wash my hands of the whole affair."

"You know these old men have been learning such a long while."

By this time Mrs. Marston was as much amused as her husband. Manette was accordingly called and questioned. The information was elicited from her that she loved "Brothah Simon" and wished to marry him.

"'Love laughs at age,'" quoted Mr. Marston again when the girl had been dismissed. Mrs. Marston was laughingly angry, but speechless for a moment. Finally she said: "Well, Manette seems willing, so there is nothing for us to do but to consent, although, mind you, I do not approve of this foolish marriage, do you hear?"

After a while the old man returned for his verdict. He took it calmly. He had expected it. The disparity in the years of him and his betrothed did not seem to strike his consciousness at all. He only grinned.

"Now look here, Uncle Simon," said his master, "I want you to tell me how you, an old, bad-looking, half-dead darky won that likely young girl."

The old man closed one eye and smiled.

"Mastah, I don' b'lieve you looks erroun' you," he said. "Now, 'mongst white folks, you knows a preachah 'mongst de ladies is mos' nigh i'sistible, but 'mongst col'ed dey ain't no pos'ble way to git erroun' de gospel man w'en he go ahuntin' fu' anything."

Viney's Free Papers

Part I

THERE WAS JOY IN THE bosom of Ben Raymond. He sang as he hoed in the field. He cheerfully worked overtime and his labors did not make him tired. When the quitting horn blew he executed a double shuffle as he shouldered his hoe and started for his cabin. While the other men dragged wearily over the ground he sprang along as if all day long he had not been bending over the hoe in the hot sun, with the sweat streaming from his face in rivulets.

And this had been going on for two months now—two happy months—ever since Viney had laid her hand in his, had answered with a coquettish "Yes," and the master had given his consent, his blessing and a five-dollar bill.

It had been a long and trying courtship—that is, it had been trying for Ben, because Viney loved pleasure and hungered for attention and the field was full of rivals. She was a merry girl and a pretty one. No one could dance better; no girl on the place was better able to dress her dark charms to advantage or to show them off more temptingly. The toss of her head was an invitation and a challenge in one, and the way she smiled back at them over her shoulder, set the young men's heads dancing and their hearts throbbing. So her suitors were many. But through it all Ben was patient, unflinching and faithful, and finally, after leading him a life full of doubt and suspense, the coquette surrendered and gave herself into his keeping.

She was maid to her mistress, but she had time, nevertheless, to take care of the newly whitewashed cabin in the quarters to which Ben took her. And it was very pleasant to lean over and watch him at work making things for the little house—a chair from a barrel and a wonderful box of shelves to stand in the corner. And she knew how to say merry things, and later outside his door Ben would pick his banjo and sing low and sweetly in the musical voice of his race. Altogether such another honeymoon there had never been.

For once the old women hushed up their prophecies of evil, although in the beginning they had shaken their wise old turbaned heads and predicted that marriage with such a flighty creature as Viney could come to no good. They had said among themselves that

Ben would better marry some good, solid-minded, strong-armed girl who would think more about work than about pleasures and coquetting.

"I 'low, honey," an old woman had said, "she'll mek his heart ache many a time. She'll comb his haid wid a three-legged stool an' bresh it wid de broom. Uh, huh—putty, is she? You ma'y huh 'cause she putty. Ki-yi! She fix you! Putty women fu' putty tricks."

And the old hag smacked her lips over the spice of malevolence in her words. Some women—and they are not all black and ugly—never forgive the world for letting them grow old.

But, in spite of all prophecies to the contrary, two months of unalloyed joy had passed for Ben and Viney, and tonight the climax seemed to have been reached. Ben hurried along, talking to himself as his hoe swung over his shoulder.

"Kin I do it?" he was saying. "Kin I do it?" Then he would stop his walk and his cogitations would bloom into a mirthful chuckle. Something very pleasant was passing through his mind.

As he approached, Viney was standing in the door of the little cabin, whose white sides with green Madeira clambering over them made a pretty frame for the dark girl in her print dress. The husband bent double at sight of her, stopped, took off his hat, slapped his knee, and relieved his feelings by a sounding "Who-ee!"

"What's de mattah wid you, Ben? You ac' lak you mighty happy. Bettah come on in hyeah an' git yo' suppah fo' hit gits col'."

For answer, the big fellow dropped the hoe and, seizing the slight form in his arms, swung her around until she gasped for breath.

"Oh, Ben," she shrieked, "you done tuk all my win'!"

"Dah, now," he said, letting her down; "dat 's what you gits fu' talkin' sassy to me!"

"Nev' min'; I'm goin' to fix you fu' dat fus' time I gits de chanst—see ef I don't."

"Whut you gwine do? Gwine to pizen me?"

"Worse'n dat!"

"Wuss'n dat? Whut you gwine fin' any wuss'n pizenin' me, less'n you conjuh me?"

"Huh uh—still worse'n dat. I'm goin' to leave you."

"Huh uh—no you ain', 'cause any place you'd go you wouldn' no more'n git dah twell you'd tu'n erroun' all of er sudden an' say, 'Why, dah's Ben!' an' dah I'd be."

They chattered on like children while she was putting the supper on the table and he was laving his hot face in the basin beside the door.

"I got great news fu' you," he said, as they sat down.

"I bet you ain' got nothin' of de kin'."

"All right. Den dey ain' no use in me a tryin' to 'vince you. I jes' be wastin' my bref."

"Go on—tell me, Ben."

"Huh uh—you bet I ain', an' ef I tell you you lose de bet."

"I don' keer. Ef you don' tell me, den I know you ain' got no news worth tellin'."

"Ain' go no news wuff tellin'! Who-ee!"

He came near choking on a gulp of coffee, and again his knee suffered from the pounding of his great hands.

"Huccume you so full of laugh tonight?" she asked, laughing with him.

"How you 'spec' I gwine tell you dat less'n I tell you my sec'ut?"

"Well, den, go on—tell me yo' sec'ut."

"Huh uh. You done bet it ain' wuff tellin'."

"I don't keer what I bet. I wan' to hyeah it now. Please, Ben, please!"

"Listen how she baig! Well, I gwine tell you now. I ain' gwine tease you no mo'."

She bent her head forward expectantly.

"I had a talk wid Mas' Raymond today," resumed Ben.

"Yes?"

"An' he say he pay me all my back money fu' ovahtime."

"Oh!"

"An' all I gits right along he gwine he'p me save, an' when I git fo' hund'ed dollahs he gwine gin me de free papahs fu' you, my little gal."

"Oh, Ben, Ben! Hit ain' so, is it?"

"Yes, hit is. Den you'll be you own ooman—leas'ways less'n you wants to be mine."

She went and put her arms around his neck. Her eyes were sparkling and her lips quivering.

"You don' mean, Ben, dat I'll be free?"

"Yes, you'll be free, Viney. Den I's gwine to set to wo'k an' buy my free papahs."

"Oh, kin you do it—kin you do it—kin you do it?"

"Kin I do it?" he repeated. He stretched out his arm, with the sleeve rolled to the shoulder, and curved it upward till the muscles stood out like great knots of oak. Then he opened and shut his fingers, squeezing them together until the joints cracked. "Kin I do it?" He looked down on her calmly and smiled simply, happily.

She threw her arms around his waist and sank on her knees at his feet sobbing.

"Ben, Ben! My Ben! I nevah even thought of it. Hit seemed so far away, but now we're goin' to be free—free, free!"

He lifted her up gently.

"It's gwine to tek a pow'ful long time," he said.

"I don' keer," she cried gaily. "We know it's comin' an' we kin wait."

The woman's serious mood had passed as quickly as it had come, and she spun around the cabin, executing a series of steps that set her husband a-grin with admiration and joy.

And so Ben began to work with renewed vigor. He had found a purpose in life and there was something for him to look for beyond dinner, a dance and the end of the day. He had always been a good hand, but now he became a model—no shirking, no shiftlessness—and because he was so earnest his master did what he could to help him. Numerous little plans were formulated whereby the slave could make or save a precious dollar.

Viney, too, seemed inspired by a new hope, and if this little house had been pleasant to Ben, nothing now was wanting to make it a palace in his eyes. Only one sorrow he had, and that one wrung hard at his great heart—no baby came to them—but instead he made a great baby of his wife, and went on his way hiding his disappointment the best he could. The banjo was often silent now, for when he came home his fingers were too stiff to play; but sometimes, when his heart ached for the laughter of a child, he would take down his old friend and play low, soothing melodies until he found rest and comfort.

Viney had once tried to console him by saying that had she had a child it would have taken her away from her work, but he had only answered, "We could a' stood that."

But Ben's patient work and frugality had their reward, and it was only a little over three years after he had set out to do it that he put in his master's hand the price of Viney's freedom, and there was sound of rejoicing in the land. A fat shoat, honestly come by—for it was the master's gift—was killed and baked, great jugs of biting persimmon beer were brought forth, and the quarters held high carnival to celebrate Viney's new-found liberty.

After the merrymakers had gone, and when the cabin was clear again, Ben held out the paper that had been on exhibition all evening to Viney.

"Hyeah, hyeah 's de docyment dat meks you yo' own ooman. Tek it."

During all the time that it had been out for show that night the people had looked upon it with a sort of awe, as if it was possessed of some sort of miraculous power. Even now Viney did not take hold of it, but shrunk away with a sort of gasp.

"No, Ben, you keep it. I can't tek keer o' no sich precious thing ez dat. Put hit in yo' chist."

"Tek hit and feel of hit, anyhow, so 's you'll know dat you's free."

She took it gingerly between her thumb and forefinger. Ben suddenly let go.

"Dah, now," he said; "you keep dat docyment. It's yo's. Keep hit undah yo' own 'sponsibility."

"No, no, Ben!" she cried. "I jes' can't!"

"You mus'. Dat 's de way to git used to bein' free. Whenevah you looks at yo'se'f an' feels lak you ain' no diff'ent f'om whut you been you tek dat papah out an' look at hit, an' say to yo'se'f, 'Dat means freedom.'"

Carefully, reverently, silently Viney put the paper into her bosom.

"Now, de nex' t'ing fu' me to do is to set out to git one dem papahs fu' myse'f. Hit'll be a long try, 'cause I can't buy mine so cheap as I got yo's, dough de Lawd knows why a great big ol' hunk lak me should cos' mo'n a precious mossell lak you."

"Hit's because dey's so much of you, Ben, an' evah bit of you's wo'th its weight in gol'."

"Heish, chile! Don' put my valy so high, er I'll be twell jedgment day a-payin' hit off."

Part II

So BEN WENT FORTH TO battle for his own freedom, undaunted by the task before him, while Viney took care of the cabin, doing what she could outside. Armed with her new dignity, she insisted upon her friends' recognizing the change in her condition.

Thus, when Mandy so far forgot herself as to address her as Viney Raymond, the new free woman's head went up and she said with withering emphasis:

"Mis' Viney Allen, if you please!"

"Viney Allen!" exclaimed her visitor. "Huccum you's Viney Allen now?"

"'Cause I don' belong to de Raymonds no mo', an' I kin tek my own name now."

"Ben 'longs to de Raymonds, an' his name Ben Raymond an' you his wife. How you git aroun' dat, Mis' Viney Allen?"

"Ben's name goin' to be Mistah Allen soon's he gits his free papahs."

"Oomph! You done gone now! Yo' naik so stiff you can't ha'dly ben' it. I don' see how dat papah mek sich a change in anybody's actions. Yo' face ain' got no whitah."

"No, but I's free, an' I kin do as I please."

Mandy went forth and spread the news that Viney had changed her name from Raymond to Allen. "She's Mis' Viney Allen, if you please!" was her comment. Great was the indignation among the older heads whose fathers and mothers and grandfathers before them had been Raymonds. The younger element was greatly amused and took no end of pleasure in repeating the new name or addressing each other by fantastic cognomens. Viney's popularity did not increase.

Some rumors of this state of things drifted to Ben's ears and he questioned his wife about them. She admitted what she had done.

"But, Viney," said Ben, "Raymond's good enough name fu' me."

"Don' you see, Ben," she answered, "dat I don' belong to de Raymonds no mo', so I ain' Viney Raymond. Ain' you goin' change w'en you git free?"

"I don' know. I talk about dat when I's free, and freedom's a mighty long, weary way off yet."

"Evahbody dat 's free has dey own name, an' I ain' nevah goin' feel free's long ez I's a-totin' aroun' de Raymonds' name."

"Well, change den," said Ben; "but wait ontwell I kin change wid you."

Viney tossed her head, and that night she took out her free papers and studied them long and carefully.

She was incensed at her friends that they would not pay her the homage that she felt was due her. She was incensed at Ben because he would not enter into her feelings about the matter. She brooded upon her fancied injuries, and when a chance for revenge came she seized upon it eagerly.

There were two or three free negro families in the vicinity of the Raymond place, but there had been no intercourse between them and the neighboring slaves. It was to these people that Viney now turned in anger against her own friends. It first amounted to a few visits back and forth, and then, either because the association became more intimate or because she was instigated to it by her new companions, she refused to have anything more to do with the Raymond servants. Boldly and without concealment she shut the door in Mandy's face, and, hearing this, few of the others gave her a similar chance.

Ben remonstrated with her, and she answered him:

"No, suh! I ain' goin' 'sociate wid slaves! I's free!"

"But you cuttin' out yo' own husban'."

"Dat's diff'ent. I's jined to my husban'." And then petulantly: "I do wish you'd hu'y up an' git yo' free papahs, Ben."

"Dey'll be a long time a-comin'," he said; "yeahs f'om now. Mebbe I'd abettah got mine fust."

She looked up at him with a quick, suspicious glance. When she was alone again she took her papers and carefully hid them.

"I's free," she whispered to herself, "an' I don' expec' to nevah be a slave no mo'."

She was further excited by the moving North of one of the free families with which she had been associated. The emigrants had painted glowing pictures of the Eldorado to which they were going, and now Viney's only talk in the evening was of the glories of the North. Ben would listen to her unmoved, until one night she said:

"You ought to go North when you gits yo' papahs."

Then he had answered her, with kindling eyes:

"No, I won't go Nawth! I was bo'n an' raised in de Souf, an' in de Souf I stay ontwell I die. Ef I have to go Nawth to injoy my freedom I won't have it. I'll quit wo'kin fu' it."

Ben was positive, but he felt uneasy, and the next day he told his master of the whole matter, and Mr. Raymond went down to talk to Viney.

She met him with a determination that surprised and angered him. To everything he said to her she made but one answer: "I's got my free papahs an' I's a-goin' Nawth."

Finally her former master left her with the remark:

"Well, I don't care where you go, but I'm sorry for Ben. He was a fool for working for you. You don't half deserve such a man."

"I won' have him long," she flung after him, with a laugh.

The opposition with which she had met seemed to have made her more obstinate, and in spite of all Ben could do, she began to make preparations to leave him. The money for the chickens and eggs had been growing and was to have gone toward her husband's ransom, but she finally sold all her laying hens to increase the amount. Then she calmly announced to her husband:

"I's got money enough an' I's a-goin' Nawth next week. You kin stay down hyeah an' be a slave ef you want to, but I's a-goin' Nawth."

"Even ef I wanted to go Nawth you know I ain' half paid out yit."

"Well, I can't he'p it. I can't spen' all de bes' pa't o' my life down hyeah where dey ain' no 'vantages."

"I reckon dey's 'vantages everywhah fu' anybody dat wants to wu'k."

"Yes, but what kin' o' wages does yo' git? Why, de Johnsons say dey had a lettah f'om Miss Smiff an' dey's gettin' 'long fine in de Nawth."

"De Johnsons ain' gwine?"

"Si Johnson is—"

Then the woman stopped suddenly.

"Oh, hit's Si Johnson? Huh!"

"He ain' goin' wid me. He's jes' goin' to see dat I git sta'ted right aftah I git thaih."

"Hit's Si Johnson?" he repeated.

"'Tain't," said the woman. "Hit's freedom."

Ben got up and went out of the cabin.

"Men's so 'spicious," she said. "I ain' goin' Nawth 'cause Si 's a-goin'—I ain't."

When Mr. Raymond found out how matters were really going he went to Ben where he was at work in the field.

"Now, look here, Ben," he said. "You're one of the best hands on my place and I'd be sorry to lose you. I never did believe in this buying business from the first, but you were so bent on it that I gave in. But before I'll see her cheat you out of your money I'll give you your free papers now. You can go North with her and you can pay me back when you find work."

"No," replied Ben doggedly. "Ef she cain't wait fu' me she don' want me, an' I won't roller her erroun' an' be in de way."

"You're a fool!" said his master.

"I loves huh," said the slave. And so this plan came to naught.

Then came the night on which Viney was getting together her belongings. Ben sat in a corner of the cabin silent, his head bowed in his hands. Every once in a while the woman cast a half-frightened glance at him. He had never once tried to oppose her with force, though she saw that grief had worn lines into his face.

The door opened and Si Johnson came in. He had just dropped in to see if everything was all right. He was not to go for a week.

"Let me look at yo' free papahs," he said, for Si could read and liked to show off his accomplishment at every opportunity. He stumbled through the formal document to the end, reading at the last: "This is a present from Ben to his beloved wife, Viney."

She held out her hand for the paper. When Si was gone she sat gazing at it, trying in her ignorance to pick from the, to her, senseless scrawl those last words. Ben had not raised his head.

Still she sat there, thinking, and without looking her mind began to take in the details of the cabin. That box of shelves there in the corner Ben had made in the first days they were together. Yes, and this chair on which she was sitting—she remembered how they had laughed over its funny shape before he had padded it with cotton and covered it with the piece of linsey "old Mis'" had given him. The very chest in which her things were packed he had made, and when the last nail was driven he had called it her trunk, and said she should put her finery in it when she went traveling like the white folks. She was going traveling now, and Ben—Ben? There he sat across from her in his chair, bowed and broken, his great shoulders heaving with suppressed grief.

Then, before she knew it, Viney was sobbing, and had crept close to him and put her arms around his neck. He threw out his arms with a convulsive gesture and gathered her up to his breast, and the tears gushed from his eyes.

When the first storm of weeping had passed Viney rose and went to the fireplace. She raked forward the coals.

"Ben," she said, "hit's been dese pleggoned free papahs. I want you to see em bu'n."

"No, no!" he said. But the papers were already curling, and in a moment they were in a blaze.

"Thaih," she said, "thaih, now, Viney Raymond!"

Ben gave a great gasp, then sprang forward and took her in his arms and kicked the packed chest into the corner.

And that night singing was heard from Ben's cabin and the sound of the banjo.

The Wisdom of Silence

Jeremiah Anderson was free. He had been free for ten years, and he was proud of it. He had been proud of it from the beginning, and that was the reason that he was one of the first to cast off the bonds of his old relations, and move from the plantation and take up land for himself. He was anxious to cut himself off from all that bound him to his former life. So strong was this feeling in him that he would not consent to stay on and work for his one-time owner even for a full wage.

To the proposition of the planter and the gibes of some of his more dependent fellows he answered, "No, suh, I's free, an' I sholy is able to tek keer o' myse'f. I done been fattenin' frogs fu' othah people's snakes too long now."

"But, Jerry," said Samuel Brabant, "I don't mean you any harm. The thing's done. You don't belong to me anymore, but naturally, I take an interest in you, and want to do what I can to give you a start. It's more than the Northern government has done for you, although such wise men ought to know that you have had no training in caring for yourselves."

There was a slight sneer in the Southerner's voice. Jerry perceived it and thought it directed against him. Instantly his pride rose and his neck stiffened.

"Nemmine me," he answered, "nemmine me. I's free, an' w'en a man's free, he's free."

"All right, go your own way. You may have to come back to me sometime. If you have to come, come. I don't blame you now. It must be a great thing to you, this dream—this nightmare." Jerry looked at him. "Oh, it isn't a nightmare now, but some day, maybe, it will be, then come to me."

The master turned away from the newly made freeman, and Jerry went forth into the world which was henceforth to be his. He took with him his few belongings; these largely represented by his wife and four lusty-eating children. Besides, he owned a little money, which he had got working for others when his master's task was done. Thus, bur'dened and equipped, he set out to tempt Fortune.

He might do one of two things—farm land upon shares for one of his short-handed neighbours, or buy a farm, mortgage it, and pay for it as he could. As was natural for Jerry, and not uncommendable, he chose at once the latter course, bargained for his twenty acres—for land was cheap then, bought his mule, built his cabin, and set up his household goods.

Now, slavery may give a man the habit of work, but it cannot imbue him with the natural thrift that long years of self-dependence brings. There were times when Jerry's freedom tugged too strongly at his easy inclination, drawing him away to idle when he should have toiled. What was the use of freedom, asked an inward voice, if one might not rest when one would? If he might not stop midway the furrow to listen and laugh at a droll story or tell one? If he might not go a-fishing when all the forces of nature invited and the jay-bird called from the tree and gave forth saucy banter like the fiery, blue shrew that she was?

There were times when his compunction held Jerry to his task, but more often he turned an end furrow and laid his misgivings snugly under it and was away to the woods or the creek. There was joy and a loaf for the present. What more could he ask?

The first year Fortune laughed at him, and her laugh is very different from her smile. She sent the swift rains to wash up the new planted seed, and the hungry birds to devour them. She sent the fierce sun to scorch the young crops, and the clinging weeds to hug the fresh greenness of his hope to death. She sent—cruellest jest of all—another baby to be fed, and so weakened Cindy Ann that for many days she could not work beside her husband in the fields.

Poverty began to teach the unlessoned delver in the soil the thrift which he needed; but he ended his first twelve months with barely enough to eat, and nothing paid on his land or his mule. Broken and discouraged, the words of his old master came to him. But he was proud with an obstinate pride and he shut his lips together so that he might not groan. He would not go to his master. Anything rather than that.

In that place sat certain beasts of prey, dealers, and lenders of money, who had their lairs somewhere within the boundaries of that wide and mysterious domain called The Law. They had their risks to run, but so must all beasts that eat flesh or drink blood. To them went Jerry, and they were kind to him. They gave him of their store. They gave him food and seed, but they were to own all that they gave him from what he raised, and they were to take their toll first from the new crops.

Now, the black had been warned against these same beasts, for others had fallen a prey to them even in so short a time as their emancipation measured, and they saw themselves the re-manacled slaves of a hopeless and ever-growing debt, but Jerry would not be warned. He chewed the warnings like husks between his teeth, and got no substance from them.

Then, Fortune, who deals in surprises, played him another trick. She smiled upon him. His second year was better than his first, and the brokers swore over his paid up note. Cindy Ann was strong again and the oldest boy was big enough to help with the work.

Samuel Brabant was displeased, not because he felt any malice toward his former servant, but for the reason that any man with the natural amount of human vanity must feel himself agrieved just as his cherished prophecy is about to come true. Isaiah himself could not have been above it. How much less, then, the uninspired Mr. Brabant, who had his "I told you so," all ready. He had been ready to help Jerry after giving him admonitions, but here it was not needed. An unused "I told you so," however kindly, is an acid that turns the milk of human kindness sour.

Jerry went on gaining in prosperity. The third year treated him better than the second, and the fourth better than the third. During the fifth he enlarged his farm and his house and took pride in the fact that his oldest boy, Matthew, was away at school. By the tenth year of his freedom he was arrogantly out of debt. Then his pride was too much for him. During all these years of his struggle the words of his master had been as gall in his mouth. Now he spat them out with a boast. He talked much in the market-place, and where many people gathered, he was much there, giving himself as a bright and shining example.

"Huh," he would chuckle to any listeners he could find, "Ol' Mas' Brabant, he say, 'Stay hyeah, stay hyeah, you do' know how to tek keer o' yo'se'f yit.' But I des' look at my two han's an' I say to myse'f, whut I been doin' wid dese all dese yeahs—tekin' keer o' myse'f an' him, too. I wo'k in de fiel', he set in de big house an' smoke. I wo'k in de fiel', his son go away to college an' come back a graduate. Das hit. Well, w'en freedom come, I des' bent an' boun' I ain' gwine do it no mo' an' I didn't. Now look at me. I sets down w'en I wants to. I does my own wo'kin' an' my own smokin'. I don't owe a cent, an' dis yeah my boy gwine graduate f'om de school. Dat 's me, an' I ain' called on ol' Mas' yit."

Now, an example is always an odious thing, because, first of all, it is always insolent even when it is bad, and there were those who listened to Jerry who had not been so successful as he, some even who had stayed on the plantation and as yet did not even own the mule they ploughed with. The hearts of those were filled with rage and their mouths with envy. Some of the sting of the latter got into their retelling of Jerry's talk and made it worse than it was.

Old Samuel Brabant laughed and said, "Well, Jerry's not dead yet, and although I don't wish him any harm, my prophecy might come true yet."

There were others who, hearing, did not laugh, or if they did, it was with a mere strained thinning of the lips that had no element of mirth in it. Temper and tolerance were short ten years after sixty-three.

The foolish farmer's boastings bore fruit, and one night when he and his family had gone to church he returned to find his house and barn in ashes, his mules burned and his crop ruined. It had been very quietly done and quickly. The glare against the sky had attracted few from the nearby town, and them too late to be of service.

Jerry camped that night across the road from what remained of his former dwelling. Cindy Ann and the children, worn out and worried, went to sleep in spite of themselves, but he sat there all night long, his chin between his knees, gazing at what had been his pride.

Well, the beasts lay in wait for him again, and when he came to them they showed their fangs in greeting. And the velvet was over their claws. He had escaped them before. He had impugned their skill in the hunt, and they were ravenous for him. Now he was fatter, too. He went away from them with hard terms, and a sickness at his heart. But he had not said "Yes" to the terms. He was going home to consider the almost hopeless conditions under which they would let him build again.

They were staying with a neighbour in town pending his negotiations and thither he went to ponder on his circumstances. Then it was that Cindy Ann came into the equation. She demanded to know what was to be done and how it was to be gone about.

"But Cindy Ann, honey, you do' know nuffin' 'bout bus'ness."

"T'ain't whut I knows, but whut I got a right to know," was her response.

"I do' see huccome you got any right to be a-pryin' into dese hyeah things."

"I's got de same right I had to w'ok an' struggle erlong an' he'p you get whut we's done los'."

Jerry winced and ended by telling her all.

"Dat ain't nuffin' but owdacious robbery," said Cindy Ann. "Dem people sees dat you got a little some'p'n, an' dey ain't gwine stop ontwell dey's bu'nt an' stoled evah blessed cent f'om you. Je'miah, don't you have nuffin' mo' to do wid 'em."

"I got to, Cindy Ann."

"Whut fu' you got to?"

"How I gwine buil' a cabin an' a ba'n an' buy a mule less'n I deal wid 'em?"

"Dah's Mas' Sam Brabant. He'd he'p you out."

Jerry rose up, his eyes flashing fire. "Cindy Ann," he said, "you a fool, you ain't got no mo' pride den a guinea hen, an' you got a heap less sense. W'y, befo' I go to ol' Mas' Sam Brabant fu' a cent, I'd sta've out in de road."

"Huh!" said Cindy Ann, shutting her mouth on her impatience.

One gets tired of thinking and saying how much more sense a woman has than a man when she comes in where his sense stops and his pride begins.

With the recklessness of despair Jerry slept late that next morning, but he might have awakened early without spoiling his wife's plans. She was up betimes, had gone on her mission and returned before her spouse awoke.

It was about ten o'clock when Brabant came to see him. Jerry grew sullen at once as his master approached, but his pride stiffened. This white man should see that misfortune could not weaken him.

"Well, Jerry," said his former master, "you would not come to me, eh, so I must come to you. You let a little remark of mine keep you from your best friend, and put you in the way of losing the labour of years."

Jerry made no answer.

"You've proved yourself able to work well, but Jerry," pausing, "you haven't yet shown that you're able to take care of yourself, you don't know how to keep your mouth shut."

The ex-slave tried to prove this a lie by negative pantomime.

"I'm going to lend you the money to start again."

"I won't—"

"Yes, you will, if you don't, I'll lend it to Cindy Ann, and let her build in her own name. She's got more sense than you, and she knows how to keep still when things go well."

"Mas' Sam," cried Jerry, rising quickly, "don' len' dat money to Cindy Ann. W'y ef a ooman's got anything she nevah lets you hyeah de las' of it."

"Will you take it, then?"

"Yes, suh; yes, suh, an' thank 'e, Mas' Sam." There were sobs some place back in his throat. "An' nex' time ef I evah gets a sta't agin, I'll keep my mouf shet. Fac' is, I'll come to you, Mas' Sam, an' borry fu' de sake o' hidin'."

Alice: My Darling,

Someday, when I can hold you in my arms and punctuate every sentence with a kiss and an embrace I may be able to tell you how happy your letter has made me. Happy and yet unhappy from the very strength of my longing to be with you, a longing not to be satisfied it seems to so distant a day.

You love me, Alice, you say; ah yes but could you know the intensity with which I worship you, you would realize that your strongest feelings are weak beside. You gave me no time to think or to resist had I willed to do so! You took my heart captive at once I yielded bravely, weak coward that I am, without a struggle. And how glad I am of my full surrender. I would rather be your captive than another woman's king. you have made life a new thing to me—a precious and sacred trust.

Will I love you tenderly and faithfully? Darling, darling, can you ask! You who are my heart, my all, my life I will love you as no man has ever loved before. Already I am living for you and working for you and through the gray days and the long nights I am longing and yearning for you;—for the sound of your voice, the touch of your hand, the magic of your presence, the thrill of your kiss.

You did wrong to kiss me? Oh sweet heart of mine, does the flower that turns its golden face up to the amorous kisses of the sun do wrong? Does the crystal wave that wrinkles at the touch of the moving wind do wrong? does the cloud that clasps the mountain close to its dewy breast do wrong? Do any of the ternal forces of nature do wrong? If so then you have done a wrong. But darling you could not have helped it. This love of ours was predestined. I had thought that I loved you before, and I had. I loved Alice Ruth Moore the writer of "Violets," but how I love Alice Ruth Moore, the woman,—and my queen. "All the current of my being runs to thee."

I am writing wildly my dear I know, but I am not stopping to think. My head has retired and it is my heart and my pen for it.

For your sake I will be true and pure. You will help me to be this for you are always in my thoughts. Last night I started out upon a rather new undertaking or rather phase of action, I took your letter with me and read it as I drove down town. "It will give me heart," I said. It did and I have never had before such a brilliant success. It was at a dinner of the Savage Club, artists, literateurs, scientist and actors, where every man could do something. I was an honored guest and held a unique position as the representative of a whole race. I took my turn with the rest, and,—dear is this egotism?—was received with wonderful enthusiasm.

You were with me all the time! You do not leave my thoughts. Alice, Alice, how I love you! Tell me over and over again that you love me. It will hearten me for the larger task that I have set myself here. I am so afraid that you may grow to care less for me. May God forbid! But if you do, let me know at once. I love you so that I am mindful only of your happiness. This is why I shall not complain about your being in New York although I do not like it. It is a *dangerous* place. But I know, darling that you will do me no injustice, and yourself no dishonor, so I am content. Go often to Miss Brown's but do not entirely usurp my place in the heart of that queen of women. Love me, dear, and tell me so. Write to me often and believe me ever.

Your Devoted Lover,
Paul

A Note About the Authors

Paul Laurence Dunbar (1872–1906) was an African American poet, novelist, and playwright. Born in Dayton, Ohio, Dunbar was the son of parents who were emancipated from slavery in Kentucky during the American Civil War. He began writing stories and poems as a young boy, eventually publishing some in a local newspaper at the age of sixteen. In 1890, Dunbar worked as a writer and editor for *The Tattler*, Dayton's first weekly newspaper for African Americans, which was a joint project undertaken with the help of Dunbar's friends Wilbur and Orville Wright. The following year, after completing school, he struggled to make ends meet with a job as an elevator operator and envisioned for himself a career as a professional writer. In 1893, he published *Oak and Ivy*, a debut collection of poetry blending traditional verse and poems written in dialect. In 1896, a positive review of his collection *Majors and Minors* from noted critic William Dean Howells established Dunbar's reputation as a rising star in American literature. Over the next decade, Dunbar wrote ten more books of poetry, four collections of short stories, four novels, a musical, and a play. In his brief career, Dunbar became a respected advocate for civil rights, participating in meetings and helping to found the American Negro Academy. His lyrics for *In Dahomey* (1903) formed the centerpiece to the first musical written and performed by African Americans on Broadway, and many of his essays and poems appeared in the nation's leading publications, including *Harper's Weekly* and the *Saturday Evening Post*. Diagnosed with tuberculosis in 1900, however, Dunbar's health steadily declined in his final years, leading to his death at the age of thirty-three while at the height of his career.

Alice Dunbar Nelson (1875–1935) was an African American poet, journalist, and political activist. Born in New Orleans to a formerly enslaved seamstress and a white seaman, Dunbar Nelson was raised in the city's traditional Creole community. In 1892, she graduated from Straight University and began working as a teacher in the New Orleans public school system. In 1895, having published her debut collection of poems and short stories, she moved to New York City, where she cofounded the White Rose Mission in Manhattan. Dunbar Nelson married poet Paul Laurence Dunbar in 1898 after several years of courtship, but their union soon proved abusive. She separated from Dunbar—whose violence and alcoholism had become intolerable—in 1902, after which Nelson taught at Howard High School in Wilmington, Delaware for around a decade. She continued to write and earned a reputation as a passionate activist for equality and the end of racial violence. Her one-act play *Mine Eyes Have Seen* (1918) was published in *The Crisis*, the journal of the NAACP. Dunbar Nelson settled in Philadelphia in 1932 with her third husband Robert J. Nelson and remained in the city until her death. Her career is exemplified by a mastery of literary forms—in her journalism, stories, plays, and poems, she made a place for herself in the male-dominated world of the Harlem Renaissance while remaining true to her vision of political change and social uplift for all African Americans.

A Note from the Publisher

Spanning many genres, from non-fiction essays to literature classics to children's books and lyric poetry, Mint Edition books showcase the master works of our time in a modern new package. The text is freshly typeset, is clean and easy to read, and features a new note about the author in each volume. Many books also include exclusive new introductory material. Every book boasts a striking new cover, which makes it as appropriate for collecting as it is for gift giving. Mint Edition books are only printed when a reader orders them, so natural resources are not wasted. We're proud that our books are never manufactured in excess and exist only in the exact quantity they need to be read and enjoyed.

Discover more of your favorite classics with Bookfinity™.

- Track your reading with custom book lists.
- Get great book recommendations for your personalized Reader Type.
- Add reviews for your favorite books.
- AND MUCH MORE!

Visit **bookfinity.com** and take the fun Reader Type quiz to get started.

Enjoy our classic and modern companion pairings!